# GETTING REAL ABOUT RUNNING

▶▶▶▶▶▶▶▶▶▶▶▶▶▶▶▶▶▶▶▶▶▶▶▶▶▶▶▶▶▶

# GETTING REAL
# ABOUT RUNNING

## GORDON BAKOULIS

▶▶▶▶▶▶▶▶▶▶▶▶▶▶▶▶▶▶▶▶▶▶▶▶▶▶▶▶▶▶▶

*BALLANTINE BOOKS*
*NEW YORK*

A Ballantine Book
Published by The Ballantine Publishing Group

Copyright © 2002 by Gordon Bakoulis

All rights reserved under International and Pan-American Copyright
Conventions. Published in the United States by The Ballantine Publishing Group,
a division of Random House, Inc., New York, and simultaneously in Canada
by Random House of Canada Limited, Toronto.


Ballantine and colophon are
registered trademarks of Random House, Inc.

www.ballantinebooks.com

*Library of Congress Cataloging-in-Publication Data is available upon request.*
ISBN 0-345-44727-1

Text design by Mary A. Wirth

Manufactured in the United States of America
First Edition: March 2002

10 9 8 7 6 5 4 3 2 1

*TO ALAN, OF COURSE*

# CONTENTS

# GETTING REAL ABOUT RUNNING

▶▶▶▶▶▶▶▶▶▶▶▶▶▶▶▶▶▶▶▶▶▶▶▶▶▶▶▶▶▶▶▶▶

# *Being a Runner*

*H*ello, my name is Gordon, and I'm a runner.

I rarely introduce myself that way, actually. Usually I'm a writer for such-and-such or the editor of so-and-so, or I'm Alan's wife or Joey and Sammy's mom. Or I'm a daughter or cousin or aunt, or a member of some organization or other, or the upstairs neighbor. Like you, I wear many different hats, answer to many different names, and sometimes feel confused about who, at my core being, I really am.

But I know I'm a runner. I can say that with absolute certainty, and I hope to be able to say it for as long as I live. I've been a runner all my adult life, though I spent many years running before I consistently thought of myself and referred to myself as a runner. Yeah, I run, I'd say when people asked. But I didn't want the activity to define who I was. I didn't want the "runner" part of my identity to be that big a deal.

It wasn't until a bizarre set of circumstances befell me in my early thirties that I embraced my "runner" identity. Following the 1992 New York City Marathon, I tested positive for a banned substance, a medication called probenecid. I had taken this drug to treat Lyme disease, and neglected to check it against the U.S. Olympic Committee's list of substances banned in international competition (a list used by all major races). Probenicid, though not itself a performance-enhancing drug, is prohibited because it can block the excretion of other drugs in the urine, thereby masking their presence. (In my case it simply strengthened the antibiotics I was taking by limiting their excretion.)

My oversight had devastating consequences: I was told I could not compete in any running event—from the Olympics to a local fun run—for four years. I fought the ruling through legal channels, and was granted permission to return to competition seven months later. Though the whole experience was one of the worst things that ever happened to me, it had a silver lining. During my ban, I could no longer run in the way that had become most meaningful to me—that is, as a world-class competitive athlete. For several months I barely ran at all. But even in my darkest moments, I realized something: I was still a runner. The ban could dictate, temporarily, what I *did*. But it couldn't tell me who I *was*. Once that truth came home to me, I ran—even though I could not compete—with a joy and commitment I had never felt before. I returned to competition and promised myself to never again take my running for granted, nor to deny, to myself or others, that *runner* is a fundamental part of who I am.

These days, my life is centered on running to a degree I find almost embarrassing. ("Doesn't she have any other interests?" I imagine people thinking.) I run almost every day, and compete as one of the top masters (40+) runners in the country. Most of my friends are runners. My husband is a runner, and we met through running. I coach runners. This is my third running book. I'm the editorial director of New York Road Runners, have been editor-in-chief of *Running Times* magazine, and have written for half a dozen running publications. As much as I try to pursue other interests and activities, I've seen all the running movies, read all the running novels, and checked out almost all the running Web sites. I hold out against a complete obsession with running in small ways, such as refusing to incorporate the word "run" into my e-mail address or sport an "I Love Running" bumper sticker.

I wanted to write a book that would share with other runners all that makes running the wonderfully enriching center of my life. I envisioned it as a book for people who, like me, call themselves runners. I know you're out there by the hundreds of thousands. I hope it didn't take an experience as traumatic as mine to make you realize the importance of running to who you are. More than that, I hope you don't imagine that when I say "runner" I mean only "serious (read: fast, sleek) competitor." I've been running, coaching, and writing about running for a long time, and as far as I'm concerned, too much is made of the fast runner/slow runner distinction. In the first place, no runner, from Khalid Khannouchi on down, is as fast as he or she wants to be, and we *all* can learn and do things to improve our running. Second, some of the most serious, committed runners I know will never be considered "fast," and some of the fastest—defined as covering ground quickly—have a surprisingly laid-back approach. I hope runners of all talent and fitness levels will read this book, and learn something from it.

This book is also for people like the runner I used to be, people who run but, for whatever reason, don't include "runner" as part of their identity. Perhaps running is just one of several sports and fitness activities that compete for your time and energy. Perhaps you've had a taste of running by doing a 5k fun run, a "charity" race to raise money and awareness for a cause, or a corporate team event. Perhaps you ran in high school or college, have been inactive—or busy with other activities—for years, and would like to return to running. Perhaps you've met some new friends who run, or have seen runners in your local park or noticed a flyer promoting a road race, a running club, or running classes. I've written this book to offer information, inspiration, and guidance to assist you in a running lifestyle that works for you.

Chapter 1 offers insights into the differences between running and being a runner, and helps runners move forward from the "now what?" stage they may find themselves in after doing their first race or completing a beginner running program. Chapter 2 explains the science behind running, in nonscientific language. Chapter 3 explains training in cycles and offers detailed weekly, monthly, 6-month, and 12-month training programs. Chapter 4 covers gear—shoes, clothing, and gizmos—that runners need to maximize their running enjoyment and performance.

Chapters 5 through 7 focus on health: avoiding and dealing

with injury and illness (5); maximizing running's mental health benefits (6); and advice on eating and drinking before, during, and after running (7). Chapter 8 explores the rich and varied world of racing—on the roads, track, trails, and elsewhere—that awaits runners at all levels. In Chapter 9 you'll read about cross-training, supplemental training, and active rest, three areas that will enhance any running program.

Chapters 10 through 13 discuss running as a part of life and throughout the life cycle: balancing running and other life issues and concerns in Chapter 10; women's running in Chapter 11; running for children and youth in Chapter 12; and running after age 50 in Chapter 13. I've also included a Resources section with contact information for dozens of sources of further information, a Bibliography, pace charts, and mile/kilometer conversion charts.

The pleasure and fulfillment of running are deep-rooted. Like many of life's most fundamental gifts, the importance of running to a real runner can be hard to articulate. Yes, I run for my health, for fitness, to channel my physical and emotional energy, and as a social outlet. Yet I know, too, that I'd be a runner even if it weren't good for me, and I weren't good at it. Because a runner is who I am.

CHAPTER I

▶ ▶ ▶ ▶ ▶ ▶ ▶ ▶ ▶ ▶ ▶ ▶ ▶ ▶ ▶ ▶ ▶ ▶ ▶ ▶ ▶ ▶ ▶ ▶ ▶ ▶ ▶ ▶ ▶ ▶ ▶

# You've Started Running—Now What?

When you first began running, you probably found lots of how-to-start advice. Yet despite this plethora of information, research shows that more than half of new exercisers (in all activities) quit by the six-month mark. Why is this so? People start exercise programs with the best intentions—why do so many fall by the wayside?

I believe it's because so many beginner exercise programs leave people high and dry. Naturally, getting started is the most important step. I know from my own experiences, and from listening to and reading people's stories, that new runners are asking their bodies to undergo vast changes. I know how discouraging those first workouts can be, when it seems as though the body will never cooperate, never feel fluid, never resemble the lean shapes that seem to be everywhere. I know it's important to give beginners precise instructions to help protect them from injury and overexertion, both of which can easily sabotage their efforts. Given the challenges and obstacles, perhaps it's not so surprising that half of exercisers drop out by the six-month mark.

## ▼ HOW THEY BECAME RUNNERS

Most people start running as a means to an end. They may want to stay in shape, have a healthier lifestyle in general, or lose weight. They may want to meet people, impress people, or spend more time in the company of a particular person or group of people. They may run as part of their conditioning program for another sport, such as skiing or soccer. It's rare that someone will tell me, "I started running because I wanted to be a runner." Even those people who take up running with the intention of doing it regularly and consistently may not consider themselves "runners" for months, even years.

When someone sticks with running, however, something happens. Running becomes an end in itself. It's not that the original motivations for running no longer matter. New runners lose weight and keep it off (often without dieting), lower their cholesterol levels, gain fitness, and make new friends, and they are pleased with these changes. But on top of all that, the activity of running itself becomes a reason for heading out the door. It may take a few days, or it may take months or even years. But at some point it dawns on the runner that she would do this even if it didn't help keep her slim, healthy, and connected to a close-knit group of friends. She is drawn to the simple activity of putting one foot in front of the other, breathing harder than normal, and feeling the wind in her hair and her feet rhythmically hitting the ground. She has become a runner.

Runners love to talk about their early running experiences. They share these stories before runs, on the run, after races, and at social gatherings. Running is almost always a wonderful, health-promoting, life-affirming pursuit. But for those who have made running a regular part of their lives, running is something more. It is a part of their essence. It is not just something they do; it is who they are. The stories that follow (starting with my own) illustrate how runners at all levels became real runners.

### Finding Myself

I spent my childhood developing a love of running, though I had no idea that's what I was doing at the time. I played very actively, roaming our wooded suburban neighborhood on foot from age six or seven on. Once when I was 10 or 11, my dad and I went together to plant bulbs in the courtyard of my elementary school as part of an ongoing school-beautification project. We arrived and realized we'd forgotten the trowel.

My dad was all set to drive home for it, but I offered to run home for the tool. I set off across the playground and through our neighbors' backyards, covering the half mile or so to our house without stopping to walk. I dashed into the garage, grabbed the trowel, and ran back. I remember being in awe of myself. I was breathing hard and sweating, but it felt wonderful to move swiftly and silently through the woods, pausing only to climb over fences. I arrived back in the schoolyard panting and triumphant.

In the spring of my sophomore year in high school I started playing lacrosse. I'd joined the team because that was what the most popular girls did, and more than anything at that age I wanted to be popular. Unfortunately I had no eye-hand coordination, so although I could run up and down the field all day doing drills, when it came to tossing and catching and cradling and scoring, I was hopeless.

In the middle of the season, we had a fund-raising event for the team. We all got sponsors to donate money for each 100-yard lap we ran up and down the field while cradling the ball in our sticks without dropping it. I signed up my sponsors and showed up with my ball and stick. Predictably, I dropped the ball on about the eighth lap, well before most of the other girls. Glumly I watched the others run up and down the field, lap after lap in the warm spring sunshine, while I fretted over how little money I'd raised. Amazingly, one girl ran 17 miles without stopping or dropping the ball, raising more than $200 (a lot of money in those days!) for the team.

That summer I decided to run to get in shape for field hockey in the fall, a sport in which I was similarly limited by my lack of coordination. I ran for 30 minutes at a time around our neighborhood, wearing tennis shoes. I imagined I was doing at least four miles, but when I clocked my run on the car's odometer, it was less than three miles. Discouraged, I ran new routes and purposely didn't measure them to avoid disappointing myself, and eventually worked up to running close to an hour at a time.

I failed to make varsity that year, and performed poorly in lacrosse again the following spring. I simply didn't have the skills, no matter how much I practiced. That fall the coach finally put me on the varsity field hockey squad, but I spent most of my time warming the bench. I went to her office once after practice and announced I wanted to quit and go out for cross-country. She gave me a well-meaning lecture about the virtues of perseverance and determination, and I ended up sticking it out. As soon as the season finished, I asked my friend Amy, who'd captained the girls' cross-country team, if I could start running with her. Amy had done winter track the previous year and hated it (she preferred running outdoors, and three seasons of competition was too much), but was delighted to have someone to help her stay in shape for the spring track season.

We lived about a quarter mile from each other, so our plan was simple: meet at the corner midway between our homes every weekday morning at 6:30 and run for 30 to 45 minutes. That first late-November morning it was pitch black in my bedroom when my alarm clock jangled me awake at 6:10. I burrowed deeper under the covers, planning to go back to sleep for another hour. But then I thought about Amy out there waiting for me in the cold and dark. I knew she'd be there, and would do the run whether I showed up or not. I thought about her voice on the phone the previous evening: "Okay, see you in the morning!" I hated letting anyone down, and I hated the thought of what Amy might think: that I wasn't reliable or, worse, that I was a wimp.

So I got up, stumbled around looking for socks, shoes, sweats, hat, and gloves, and tiptoed downstairs and out the door. Amy was waiting for me at the corner, her breath clouding the air as she gripped the pole of the stop sign and stretched. "Hi. Where do you want to go?" she asked. We ran slowly toward the elementary school, then cut across the playing fields, coated with thick white frost. My eyes teared, my fingers and the tip of my nose tingled. At first I worried—about being too cold, about keeping up with Amy, about how tired I'd feel later in the day, about how I'd manage to get up again tomorrow. But a funny thing happened as we ran and talked and watched the sun rise: Gradually my worries started to feel trivial and insignificant. It was as though I could look at them sitting there in a place in my mind called "worries," but they had nothing to do with what I was really experiencing in that moment: the rhythm of my breathing, the sound of our feet hitting the sidewalk, the sights of passing trees and houses and an occasional dog-walker or car. By the time we'd circled back to our corner, I couldn't even remember what I'd been worrying about.

Amy and I kept running every morning. A few times those first few weeks I did let her down—either sleeping through my alarm or hearing it and going back to sleep. She let me slide at first. Then one morning I awoke to a "ping, ping" sound. Tiny pieces of gravel were hitting my window. I jumped up, parted the curtains, and peered out. There was Amy, standing in the driveway tossing stones up at me. I dressed in a flash, flew downstairs and outside. "Thanks!" I gasped, much to my surprise. Thanks? Thanks for rousing me from a sound sleep before dawn on a freezing cold winter morning so I could stumble around the neighborhood while everyone else was sleeping?

Yes, thanks. I was grateful that Amy had come to wake me up. I *wanted* to run. I *liked* being out there in the silent dark with that alive, tingling feeling. It didn't make me tired, or cold, or sore. It felt great—I felt great. I'd do it whether Amy met me or not. I'd do it even if I decided not to go out for spring lacrosse. I loved it for its own sake.

We ran all that winter, every school morning. Sometimes we did longer runs on Saturday or Sunday afternoons, around the lake, across town to the Revolutionary War battlefield, or out into the country. That spring I skipped lacrosse and went out for track. Amy and I graduated in June and headed off in different directions. Running was to play vastly different roles in our lives, but I'll never forget those runs. They transformed me from someone who ran into a *runner*. My life would never be the same.

—*Gordon Bakoulis*

### My Midlife Breakaway

In 1965, at 147 pounds, I deduced that a future spent bashing heads with 222-pounders in high school football practice would not be bright. While I still had my wits about me, I switched to the cross-country team, and won a 5k junior varsity race less than three weeks later. Eventually, I would set a school record in the two-mile.

Life in the counterculture, travels around the world in bohemian style, and a series of 80-hour-a-week jobs took me light-years away from the sport. Then, in 1976, on a flight from Los Angeles to Cleveland, I read Kenny Moore's *Sports Illustrated* article about John Walker and Filbert Bayi, who had both set world records in the mile and were expected to be Olympic rivals in Montreal (Bayi's home country, Tanzania, ended up boycotting, so the showdown never took place). The article connected with every pleasant residual memory I had about running. I was ready to do interval training right there in the aisle of the plane. In accordance with FAA rules, I waited until I got home to New York, and into Central Park.

I've been running on and off for 25 years now. The highlights are many: the blissful four-mile road race I ran in the Berkshire foothills by the 8:30 P.M. light of a full moon; the Thanksgiving five-miler I managed to win even though I was about the seventh best runner in the event; the day I greedily entered—and won—two races in two states.

Running uniquely combines the lyrical and contemplative with the analytical and quantitative. What other endeavor can give such a sense of empowerment—while no one else is getting hurt? No judge or coach determines your value; race results speak eloquently for themselves. At 50, I no longer compete, but running enables me to stage a bit of a breakaway every day, and hopefully assists me in being ... well ... less fiftyish.

—*Peter Gambaccini, 50, New York City*

### Life-Affirming Steps

As a child and teenager, physical fitness was never a priority for me. I was quite overweight and I started smoking at age 12; in addition, I lived in a household where fitness wasn't important and in a neighborhood where, at that time, an evening jog wasn't safe, especially for a female. However, at age 25 I got a wake-up call in the form of precancerous lesions in my mouth due to 13 years of smoking. I knew that I had to take control, and I knew I could do it because 10 years earlier I'd lost (and kept off) 60 pounds through sensible dieting and light calisthenics. As part of my strategy to stop smoking, I started exercising a little more seriously. I began using an exercise bike, then graduated to a real bicycle. I jogged a little and did weight training for variety, but cycling was my activity of choice.

Less than a year after I smoked my last cigarette I took part in a 35-mile bike ride to raise funds for multiple sclerosis research. When I finished with lots of energy to spare, I was so proud of how far I'd come! By then I'd realized that I needed to make exercise a permanent part of my life, given the work it took to lose weight and stop smoking, as well as a long family history of obesity and heart disease. And I was determined to have fun in the process.

A couple years later, my employer was recruiting for the Corporate Challenge, a 3.5-mile running race, and I signed on. I started training and entered a four-mile fun run as a dress rehearsal. I was amazed—a free T-shirt, a number to pin on, and best of all, folks who didn't even know me cheering on the sidelines! I finished in a time that is slower than my current training pace, but I didn't care very much about pace that day. Later that week I ran the Corporate Challenge on a hot, humid night. Not only did I run a faster pace than I had in the four-mile race, but I came in first of the women in my company. It was a heady feeling.

Running gradually replaced cycling as my favorite fitness activity. One of the things that helped was the New York Road Runners Club, which sponsored group runs that enabled me to run safely. The NYRRC's races also gave me opportunities to improve. In the next few months my race times improved dramatically. I ran the New York City Marathon the following year. Training for and finishing that first marathon was so wonderful and empowering that I've been hooked ever since. One thing that keeps me going is remembering it's a privilege. Many people, due to inability and/or circumstances, can't run or perform any type of exercise, and thus miss out not only on the sheer pleasure that comes with being physically active, but on the opportunity to save and extend their own lives.

—*Adria Gallup-Black, 41, New York City*

### A Natural Progression

I started running when I was 13 years old. I can't remember exactly why, it's been so long. I started out by running around my block, which was about a quarter mile. I enjoyed it so much, I began running longer distances. My mother persuaded me to join the cross-country team in high school, which turned out to be a great idea. That turned me into a runner for life—I loved the regular workouts, the team spirit, and the challenging races. Running became part of my everyday routine.

When I went to college I didn't join a team, but I kept running on my own. Gradually I built up to running longer distances, always surprising myself at how far I could go—10 miles or more—without feeling bored or exhausted. I got to see parts of the surrounding towns and the city I probably wouldn't otherwise have seen, all the while turning into a better runner. After I graduated I continued to run. I kept on running when I moved several times to take jobs in different cities. It was a constant, no matter where I was living. I added more mileage each week, ran everlonger distances, entered races, and watched my finishing times get faster. Running had become a vital and constant part of my life, without my even stopping to think about it. I can't remember Saturday mornings without long runs, or how I used to fill my free time during the week that I now spend out on the roads. But I know this: I'm awfully glad I discovered the sport.

—*Matt Glynn, 30, Buffalo, NY*

### My Longest-Running Relationship

Running is my best friend. It's been with me longer than any adult relationship I've had, including my marriage of 26 years. Starting out in 1967, when I was 16, in a time and era when running was not popular—especially for women—nightly runs around the block consoled me from bouts with bad boyfriends, catty girlfriends, and the fear of going off to college. Running and I had a sort of secret liaison, because I didn't dare tell anyone except my dog who came with me. It was tough enough getting through the teenage years without being labeled a weirdo for running.

During college in the early seventies the running boom was still a few years away, but I kept up my nightly runs on and off—mostly off because guys were always hooting at me about my endeavors. To some degree that never changed. But, faithful as ever, my pal running was always there for me, welcoming me after long hours in the library, keeping me away from the dreaded "freshman 15," and on long runs whispering in my ear that my boyfriend was remaining true to me.

—*Gail Waesche Kislevitz, 50, Ridgewood, NJ*

### Reminiscences of a Would-Be Field-Goal Kicker

I started running in 1971, during the summer between my junior and senior years in high school. I ran to get in shape for football—I was going to be a field-goal kicker, and figured running was the best way to get strong legs. (I know now that I would have been better off biking and lifting weights, but I was young and ignorant back then.) I ran for about two weeks on trails wearing soccer cleats, then switched to sneakers—not running shoes, but gym sneakers, because back then only "serious" runners owned running shoes, usually Adidas leather-and-suede affairs. If you were *really* serious you had a pair of nylon Onitsuka Tigers.

I soon realized that I lacked the requisite strength and accuracy to be a kicker, so I figured I'd go out for cross-country, which in those days was more of a "counterculture" sport than football. I worked out with the team in August, ran the first time trial, and did not finish in the top seven (which was required to make the varsity squad). The coach told me, "You can be a bigger help to the team writing about us than running for us," so I began writing articles for the school newspaper. I then went to the sports editor of the local weekly and offered to do the same for them. This was my first "real" byline, so in a sense running is what started me writing. I don't know if I would have wound up where I am today otherwise.

During my first two years of college at the University of Pennsylvania I partied and played rugby (had to get that football thing out of my system, I guess). I got back into running during my junior year, when I started training with the Penn track team. I had a goal of running the Penn Relays Marathon (a standard 26.2-mile marathon held around the time of the Penn Relays) in the spring of my senior year, so I trained for close to a year, then ran the marathon in April. I believe that was my first road race. I dropped out of the marathon, but I came back the following year and finished it in 2:56. I really had little clue how to train for a marathon—I just hung around some guys in the area who were road racers and did what they did.

Basically I've been going at it ever since. I had a "streak" period in the early eighties when I didn't miss a day of running for four years. I can't remember what broke my streak, but I'm still a committed runner, out there nearly every day.

—*Jim Gerweck, 47, Norwalk, CT*

### A Fast Girl Who's Stuck With It

My earliest memory of running is taking the President's Physical Fitness Tests in the late 1960s. I was always the fastest girl at the various distances. About that same time, the era of girls' and women's sports arrived, and my President's times caught the attention of the P.E. teachers, who sought me out for the school's first-ever girls track team. I did as many running events as was allowed, plus long jump and discus (we were a small team). It turned out I was pretty good and as a high school sophomore I ran 2:15 for the 800, tying the state record. I was unbeaten for two years.

Despite that promising beginning, I stopped running completely when I got to college. I guess I was overwhelmed with schoolwork, part-time jobs, and various other college activities. I didn't run again until a year after graduation when a boyfriend suggested training for a 10k road race. I was immediately hooked (on running, not the guy), and 22 years later I have not stopped. My motivations for running have changed a lot over the years. In high school, it was my identity: I was the girl who ran really fast. I've used running to win trophies. I've used it to test my endurance—mental and physical—by training for and running marathons.

I've used it to feel less bloblike during two pregnancies, and to get my body back in the aftermath of pregnancy. It has also served as a sanctuary during periods of personal and professional stress. As I enter middle-age, running allows me to outdistance the thirtysomethings who only know my race number, not the birth date on my driver's license.

—*Sharon Linstedt, 45, Buffalo, NY*

### In Grandfather's Footsteps

I started running in the seventh grade, during the winter of 1973. My grandfather had been the track coach at Grinnell College in Iowa from the mid-1920s until about 1945, and served as the head starter at several big Midwestern track meets until about 1970. He inspired my interest in running, and I also remember following track and field keenly during the 1972 Munich Olympics. About the same time Grinnell built an indoor P.E. facility with a 200-yard track, and as a faculty kid I was allowed access to the building. I embarked upon a "fitness routine" which I followed several times a week. It consisted of running a mile or two around the indoor track and then sneak-ing into the weight room—where only college athletes were supposed to venture—and pump-ing rather minimal amounts of iron. I also occasionally watched the college track teams practice and learned of an indoor all-comers meet some of the dis-tance runners were organizing. I entered the mile race and fin-ished in 7:17, and recall being completely demoralized by such a slow time.

During high school I be-came a pretty good tennis player and gave that sport most of my athletic attention. But I secretly yearned to try cross-country, having enjoyed my oc-casional runs on the local golf course and college practice fields. I doubted, though, that I would be a strong runner. In my senior year I joined the cross-country team, and sure enough I was strictly junior varsity material, never breaking 11 minutes for two miles. But at the end of the season our coach took us to a six-mile road race. I finished second among my teammates and decided I liked longer distances.

I attended Grinnell, where I ran cross-country all four years and track as a junior and senior. At first I had no intention of joining either team, despite my grandfather's background there, but the cross-country coach talked me into it, and I will forever owe him a debt of gratitude. Participating on those teams was a great experience. We worked pretty hard but kept things in perspective. I made considerable improvement during those four years and was number-three on the cross-country team by my last season.

During the winter of my freshman year I trained for my first marathon (Drake Relays). To my surprise I discovered that running 50–75 miles a week through an Iowa winter is not only possible but also fun. There wasn't much to read about marathon training back then (1979), but I prepared pretty well and my training log from that year is one of my most prized possessions. On race day I ran a very steady pace and finished in 3:07. By that time I was hooked, and so I've remained ever since.

—John Kissane, 41, Athens, GA

### The "Now What?" Factor

Certainly, some new exercisers give up within days of starting, due to soreness, fatigue, and lack of time. I've found, however, that there's another point beyond this initial stage, when the will to keep moving can wane. This second stage occurs sometime during the three to six months following. For runners, it often corresponds with the completion of a 12-week or 16-week beginner running program, a typical schedule offered by running clubs. These programs are often timed to culminate by participating in a local race, such as a 5k (3.1 miles), a reasonable goal for most people.

The problem is this: The runner finishes the 12-week class, does the race, or is able to finally run a mile without stopping to walk. The accomplishment feels amazing and transcendent while it's happening.

Yet afterward, the runner wonders, *Now what?*

I wrote this book with that runner in mind. I don't want any runner, anywhere, to give up on running at any point because they aren't sure what to do next. Running is one of the simplest and most natural physical activities in the world. Almost anyone can do it, with minimal equipment. However, what is not so simple and often is far from obvious is how to run to maximize your enjoyment of running and the benefits you derive from it. It took me many years to fully integrate running into my life. I found there was a big difference between *running* and *being a runner*. This book exists to bridge the gap between those two states of being.

## QUESTION AND ANSWER

**Q.** What is *fartlek* running?

**A.** If you hang around runners long enough, you'll eventually hear the word "*fartlek*." This, unfortunately, is a Swedish word meaning "speed play." It refers to a type of speed training in which runners alternate faster and slower running within their run in a less-structured pattern than they would at a track or other workout setting. They might run hard segments of various times (30 seconds, 1 minute, 2 minutes, etc.), or use landmarks such as streetlights or telephone poles, or simply alter their pace when the coach or group leader tells them to. The result is a workout that's tough in a fun, invigorating, and spontaneous way. (See this chapter and Chapter 3 for more on setting up training programs.)

## STARTING FROM SCRATCH

The primary purpose of this chapter is to help you elevate your training from the level many runners have reached after about three months of running or walk/running. If you are not there yet, this box offers basic guidelines that will help most healthy people get to that point.

Most running clubs and many health clubs and gyms offer guidelines on starting a running program or other kind of aerobic-exercise program. Some people join a club or participate in a group workout for the camaraderie, motivation, and instruction, and this program can be an adjunct to that. If you can't or don't want to run with a group, the program outlined here is a simple, safe, and effective alternative. (If you are over 35 or have any personal or family history of heart disease, or any other health problems that could possibly make running a health hazard, it's wise to get your doctor's okay before starting an exercise program.)

Commit to at least 30 minutes of activity, three to four times a week. Run on alternating days, such as Monday, Wednesday, and Friday, or Tuesday, Thursday, and Saturday, rather than cramming all your running into the beginning or end of the week. On the other days, you can either do no formal exercise (though a short stretching session can be of great benefit; see Chapter 5 for more information on stretches for runners), or do some light cross-training, supplemental training, or active-rest activities. (See Chapter 9 for more on how these activities can enhance your running program.)

Most people who have never run or who are returning to running after six months or more of relative inactivity should start with a combination of walking and running. Spend the first five minutes walking at an easy pace. This will warm up and loosen the muscles. If you feel stiff, then stop to stretch the muscles in your legs and hips. (For more on stretching, see Chapter 5.) Then run for one minute at a pace you can maintain without getting out of breath, and walk briskly for four minutes. Repeat four times for a total of 20 minutes of running/walking. Then walk the final five minutes at an easy pace to allow your heart rate to gradually return to normal.

This workout will be too easy for many people. Try it on two separate occasions, at least two days apart, and if you don't feel challenged either time, try increasing the ratio of running to walking, up to 4:1 (that is, 4 minutes running/1 minute walking, for 20 minutes). Don't eliminate the five minutes of warm-up walking and five minutes of cool-down walking. These segments are *supposed* to feel easy. Warming up helps your body and mind prepare for a physical challenge, and cooling down helps prevent post-workout stiffness and fatigue.

Gradually increase the ratio of running to walking within the workout until you can run for the full 20 minutes without stopping. Follow a pattern of adding 30 seconds from walking to running for each of the run/walk blocks that make up the 20-minute core of your workout. Thus, your Week 2 workout would be: warm up for 5 minutes; run for 1:30, walk for 3:30 (repeat four times); cool down for 5 minutes. For Week 3 you'd increase to a run two minutes, walk three minutes pattern, and so on. Continuing on this schedule will lead to 20 minutes of continuous running by Week 9. You can then either hold steady at this level (continuing to include the five-minute warm-up and five-minute cool-down), or extend your runs by up to 10 percent per week, which will mean adding about two minutes to each run initially, or five minutes to a couple of your three to five weekly runs.

## BEGINNER WALK/RUN SCHEDULE

| Week | Warm-up | Run Segments | Walk Segments | Cool-down | Total |
|------|---------|--------------|---------------|-----------|-------|
| 1 | 5:00 | 1:00 | 4:00 | 5:00 | 30:00 |
| 2 | 5:00 | 1:30 | 3:30 | 5:00 | 30:00 |
| 3 | 5:00 | 2:00 | 3:00 | 5:00 | 30:00 |
| 4 | 5:00 | 2:30 | 2:30 | 5:00 | 30:00 |
| 5 | 5:00 | 3:00 | 2:00 | 5:00 | 30:00 |
| 6 | 5:00 | 3:30 | 1:30 | 5:00 | 30:00 |
| 7 | 5:00 | 4:00 | 1:00 | 5:00 | 30:00 |
| 8 | 5:00 | 4:30 | :30 | 5:00 | 30:00 |
| 9 | 5:00 | 20:00 continuous | | 5:00 | 30:00 |

The most important goal for beginning runners is consistency. The best way to establish consistency is to enjoy what you are doing. I don't mean that every moment should be pure bliss—it won't be—but that on the balance, the positives should outweigh the negatives. Although our bodies are built to run, running is a major physical challenge for many people in 21st-century Western society. You'll be stressing your muscles, joints, and cardiovascular system much more than the average person. Covering ground swiftly under your own power may also be a big emotional step. If you're dreading your workouts, or if they challenge you to the point where you're in pain or can't converse, laugh, or sing a line or two, you're working too hard. Slow down, even if that means walking for the full 30 minutes. Take a day off if you need a break, then try again. Remind yourself that nothing worthwhile comes easy. You will progress—everyone does. It's better at this stage to feel slightly underchallenged than to push yourself to the point of injury or burnout.

### Your Early Experiences With Running

Let's assume that the "now what?" factor has occurred at about three months into your running career. There are three basic paths that most people travel to arrive at this point. The route you choose to follow will depend in part on which path you've taken thus far.

**1. The Solo Runner.** You decided on your own to start running, and pursued it primarily as a solitary activity. Although you may have taken occasional runs with other runners, your schedule, temperament, or other logistical or personality issues have dictated that you are more often than not running on your own.

**2. The Partner or Small Group Runner.** You began running with a friend, either another beginner or a more experienced runner who acted as your guide and mentor. Although you occasionally run by yourself, you love running for the camaraderie and companionship it offers. You and your partner(s) wonder where to go next with your running.

**3. The Class/Clinic Route.** You took a class or clinic for instruction and motivation. Now the class is over. Perhaps you've "graduated" by completing a 5k or other race. You feel dressed up with nowhere to go. You desperately want to keep running, but you are worried that without the group-running setting, you'll have a hard time maintaining your routine.

At this point you may be:

- uncertain what to do next;
- feeling bored and/or unchallenged with your routine;
- lacking motivation;
- in search of a goal;
- worried that you'll risk injury or burnout if you try and push yourself;
- full of questions about all aspects of running, from training to equipment to nutrition.

### Five Foolproof Ways to Survive the End of the Honeymoon

If you are reading this book, you've already taken a step toward moving your running in the right direction. Here are some other suggestions for continuing the process of shifting your mind-set from one of "running" to "being a runner." Many novice runners have yet to absorb the value of these steps.

• *Join a running club (if you haven't already).* This is probably the most productive step you can take to ensure your long-term involvement with running. There are running clubs in virtually every city and many towns and rural areas across North America. A running club can help you meet other runners; find classes, clinics, group training runs, and races; get race discounts in your area; connect to other runners when you travel; and more. The Road Runners Club of America, the largest grassroots running association in the United States, is an umbrella organization of 675 chapter running clubs in 48 states and Guam, representing 190,000 runners. The RRCA represents and promotes the common interests of its member clubs and individual members through education, leadership, programs, and other services. (See Resources for more information on the RRCA.) Go to *www.rrca.org* to find an RRCA-affiliated club in your area. If there isn't one, ask local runners; check at health clubs, gyms, running-specialty or sporting-goods stores, and universities; or consider starting your own club.

• *Find a coach.* Many runners think that coaching is only for high school and college athletes, along with a handful of super-serious elite types who run professionally. Actually, many running coaches work with runners at all talent levels and from all backgrounds, who share a goal of getting the most from their running (including maximum fun and enjoyment) in the context of a busy life. Although most coaches operate mostly in group settings, many also work one-on-one. (See Resources for information on finding a running coach in your area.) In choosing a coach, look for someone who understands your needs and priorities, who asks about your goals and listens to what you say, who does more than simply present you with a one-size-fits-all training program from a book or handout, and who is connected with local medical and health resources to assist you in areas that may be outside of his realm of expertise, such as injury treatment and nutrition (though some coaches do have expertise in these areas).

• *Set a long-term goal, with interim short-term goals.* I cannot overemphasize the importance of goal-setting as a motivational and organizational tool for runners. The schedules that I present later in this chapter and elsewhere in this book are organized around goals that you set for yourself before completing your first workout. In setting up programs for myself and other runners, I always consider goals first, then work backward to the present to establish interim benchmarks in the form of tune-up races, time trials, and other workouts.

• *Read, read, read.* I firmly believe that by learning about running from as many different sources as possible, you will be in the best position to develop your running potential. You'll find no shortage of reading material on running in magazines, journals, and books. In addition, there's a plethora of information and advice on the Internet. (See Resources for some of the most useful running-related books, magazines, journals, Web sites, and other sources of information.)

• *Make sure you have the proper equipment.* Nothing can derail a running program faster than an injury or persistent discomfort, and poorly chosen or worn-out equipment (usually shoes) is one of the most common culprits. Chapter 4 is devoted to finding and using the right gear for your running, from shoes to sweat-proof sunscreen. Seek general advice from other runners, but keep your own particular needs in mind.

• *Talk honestly with the non-runners in your life.* If you and your nearest and dearest are not on the same page as far as the role of running in your life is concerned, you'll face countless, and ultimately fruitless, battles about integrating running into your life. I've been fortunate that, overall, those around me have understood, respected, and appreciated the depth of my commitment to running, but at times it's taken considerable work. In my case, I am married to a runner who is, if anything, even more dedicated to running than I am. More often than not I'm the one pushing for a greater balance between running and other interests and activities, and a "lighten up" attitude toward running. Because it's important to me that my entire life doesn't revolve around running, I make every effort to see to it that we cultivate other interests, both individually and as a family. If you are a runner in a family or community of non-runners or less-committed runners, a give-and-take attitude works best. Set aside the needed time for your Saturday-morning long run—but then pitch in with chores on Saturday afternoon, and join in on the family trip to the museum on Sunday. Getting the balance right is a trial-and-error process, and you'll no doubt stumble around a bit before coming up with patterns and priorities that work for you. (See Chapter 10 for more on integrating running into your life.)

## WHY KEEP A RUNNING LOG?

For years I didn't keep track of my runs. I thought that if I started writing down how far, how often, or how fast I ran, I'd feel compelled to keep building up my mileage or maintain a certain standard. What if I just didn't feel like running one week? I was sure I'd feel terribly guilty about having nothing to write down. Besides, other runners obsessed over mileage and pace—but not me. I couldn't be bothered with such trivial concerns. When I ran my first marathon at age 23, New York City in 1984, my training partner, a veteran runner, asked me once during a training run how far I ran, how fast, and what I did to "taper" before races. I had no idea. "You should keep track," he suggested. I must have paid heed, for I remember spending a few minutes the night before the race staring at some penciled notations of my mileage and long runs over the past couple months. I was nervous, and seeing in black and white that I had done the necessary training helped me calm down and realize that I would be able to get out there and perform the next day. I also enjoyed looking at those simple markings ("9/30: 21 with Paul—tired!") and reminiscing about the runs themselves.

The following spring I joined a running club and my coach asked me about my training schedule. I made up something vague about my mileage, and started keeping a detailed log that very night. I've done so ever since, in one form or another.

What goes into a running log? That's up to you. Most runners include the distances and/or times of their runs (and other workouts), along with a few other related factors such as the weather, their training partners, and how they felt. Hence: "8 easy w/Jim in 64:09; light rain; dead legs." You might also include the terrain, your heart rate, your resting pulse, your mental state ("tense about big presentation at work"), injuries or illnesses, and any other factors that might have affected the run ("up all night with baby"). Some runners note information about their diet, or record their weight once a week or once a month. You can find software programs that help you calculate energy expended in terms of calories or other measures and assign values to specific workouts to help you train at an appropriate intensity level and duration. I tend to record information in my log only if it's pertinent to planning my future training and racing. That means some days, "4m easy" says it all, while other days I might scribble something like "2m warm-up, $8 \times 800$ in 2:52–2:46 w/Jenn & Patty, 2.5m cool-down; hot; needed more $H_2O$; still feeling Sunday's 10k in legs."

Here are a few tips for successful log-keeping:

- *Keep it simple.* You'll be more likely to stick with regular log-keeping if it's not a major production. Record your workouts either as hard copy or electronically—whichever is easier for you. Unless you're showing your log to a coach or advisor, it doesn't matter whether it makes sense to anyone else, so use whatever shorthand works for you. My husband's log, even after half a dozen patient explanations, is a complete mystery to me, but it works for him and that's what matters.

- *Get it down quickly.* I record my workouts as soon as possible after finishing them, and always the same day, so they're fresh in my mind. You can store up to hundreds of workout times on a chronograph watch with a storage function, but you may forget other important information if you wait too long to transfer the data to your log. It takes only a minute to write down most workouts.

- *Keep it honest.* You may discover that keeping a log tempts you to, if not outright lie, at least "fudge" the numbers a bit. You'll neglect to mention a nagging pain in your heel because if you ignore it, maybe it'll go away. A 4.8-mile run gets recorded as 5 miles to make things look nice and tidy. These decisions are yours, but keep in mind that the more accurate and honest your log is, the more it can help your running.

• *Resist compulsive tendencies.* Remember that your log is a means to an end, not an end in itself. The ultimate goal of log-keeping is to become a better runner, not to produce a perfect training week. It's inevitable that your running will have its ups and downs, due to injury, illness, other life stresses, and necessary adjustments you make based on your physical and mental feedback. That means if your ankle hurts, you cut a workout short and write down "4 × 800; sore ankle" even though "8 × 800" would look much better in the log. It means that you don't pull crazy stunts like running 5 miles at 11 P.M. on Saturday night for the sole purpose of recording 100 miles of training for the week. It means that after a marathon, you fill seven days with "0; resting"—and don't feel guilty about it.

Once you start logging your runs, you'll find there are many reasons for keeping accurate, up-to-date records. Here are the main benefits:

• *Motivation.* Recording your runs makes them real. This can provide motivation and validation, which are important to any runner. Exercise physiologist Robin Stuhr of the Women's Sports Medicine Center at the Hospital for Special Surgery in New York City urges women starting an exercise program to put their log in a prominent place—the refrigerator door often works well—and record every workout in a visual, even celebratory way, such as with a gold star. It sounds corny, but if it makes you get out there and run even when you're tired or pressed for time, then it's doing the job.

• *Reassurance.* A log is proof: I accomplished this. That evidence was what I needed the night before my first marathon, when I doubted my ability to run around the block, let alone 26.2 miles. And my log provided it: There was my two months' worth of long, hard training. I knew I had put in the work because I could see it all there in front of me. In the same spirit, I often look back at the previous season's worth of training when I'm beginning my buildup for the next season. When coming off a rest-and-recovery period, I can easily fall prey to how-can-I-do-this self-doubt. Again, my log reassures me that yes, I can do it, because I've done it before.

• *Feedback.* A log allows you to see patterns in your training and racing that you might otherwise miss. For example, if I have a string of bad races, my log will most likely tell me why. Have I overtrained? Am I expecting too much, too quickly coming off an injury or when establishing my base? Do I tend to run relatively poorly at certain times of year—such as in the early summer before my body acclimates to the heat? Remember to include significant details in your log, including your fatigue level. Note feelings of illness even if you don't have a fever or other obvious signs that you're unwell. You'll be providing yourself with clues that can help you train and race optimally.

• *Restraint.* A funny thing happened once I became a regular log-keeper. Though I'd feared my log would make me compulsive about my running, unable to relax and enjoy it due to fearing I wouldn't have "enough" to record each day, the opposite happened. My log became a check on my impulse to do too much, the feeling that "if five miles is good, six miles is even better" that I'd fallen prey to in the past. A log is just so honest. If I started recording "junk miles" (running done for no purpose other than to boost mileage), they would just stare back at me accusingly from my log.

• *A blueprint.* The information you record in your log is there to be used anytime you need it. Let's say you've run the marathon of your dreams. You rest and recover, then get ready to plan your training for the next one. This time, much of the work is removed because a successful training plan is mapped out for you, right there in your log (though there is no guarantee, of course, that it will work as well a second time).

Keeping a running log is so intuitive for me at this point that it's like brushing my teeth—a part of every day and something I can't imagine giving up. I feel lost without my log. If you're keeping a log, keep it up. If you're not, start one now.

### Beyond the First 12 Weeks

If you can run for 20 minutes without stopping, you are ready—and probably eager—to increase the challenge. This can be done in two ways: by increasing the total distance of your running; or by introducing segments of running at a higher intensity than you are used to. The two programs later in this chapter direct you how to move forward in both ways, at two different rates.

Both of these programs will help you improve your running on the roads, track, trails, and/or cross-country courses. Each program can be adapted in a number of different ways, depending on your needs and preferences. You can accelerate either program if you find it less challenging than you'd like, or scale back as needed. I suggest, however, that once you embark on either program, you stick to it in principle—barring injury, illness, or other extraordinary circumstances—for the full 12 weeks. This will provide essential structure to your running. Keep in mind that no single running program is perfect for every runner. After completing either of these schedules, you will most likely find things you'd have done differently. However, if you start out using some aspects of the program without others, or taking a "mix and match" approach with this and other schedules, you will be less likely to make the progress you desire. Even if you do improve and thrive, you won't know which elements of which program are helping and which are hindering you.

It's not necessary to follow either schedule to the letter, but keep in mind the following principles:

• *Follow the hard/easy rule.* In Chapter 2, you will learn that fitness gains actually take place during the rest period that follows hard physical work. During the day or two after a hard workout, you are actually less fit than before you started, due to the breakdown of muscle tissue, the depletion of fuel stores, and other factors. This means that hard workouts should be followed by rest periods or easy efforts (termed "active rest," a concept discussed in detail in Chapter 9) so that fitness gains can be realized. Most runners shouldn't run fast, or long, two days in a row. For example, if you do a hard workout on Tuesday, take Wednesday off or go for an easy run, waiting until at least Thursday before your next hard or long run. It's particularly important to go into races well rested in order to reap the benefits of all your hard training.

• *Heed your body's feedback.* Your body will "talk" to you constantly throughout your training and racing, and you must listen to it in order to continue progressing without injuries or other setbacks. You will learn to read levels of fatigue, degrees of soreness, the differences between normal and unhealthy pain and fatigue, stages of hunger and thirst, and other crucial cues to your physical well-being. Failing to read—and respond to—these signals can mean the difference between progressing gradually and steadily with your running and becoming injured or overtrained. This is what's meant by adapting a program to meet your individual needs. It's not easy. Even the best runners in the world sometimes misread their bodies' messages, or even deliberately ignore them. For novice runners, the best strategy is to back off and rest when in doubt. As you advance and gain experience, you will learn that there are times when you can perhaps take more of a gamble—for example, by running an important race when a particular injury is not quite healed.

• *Don't increase volume more than 10 percent per week.* This is a time-honored standard that allows your fitness to progress at a gradual, steady rate. For example, if you run 20 miles one week, you should run no more than 22 miles the following week. Some coaches recommend an even more conservative rate of progression, such as 10 percent every three weeks. The 10-percent figure serves as a general guideline, which you definitely should not exceed.

### Levels of Speed Training

In Chapter 2 we will discuss the body's three energy-delivery systems: the ATP-CP system for high-intensity/short-duration activity; the lactic-acid (or anaerobic) system for less-intense activity lasting longer than that which the ATP-CP system can sustain; and the aerobic system, for intensities that can be fueled predominantly by oxygen. In distance running (800 meters and longer), we rely primarily on the aerobic system to deliver energy to working muscles. This means that the bulk of training for distance runners consists of developing the aerobic energy-delivery system.

Most—though not all—exercise scientists and distance-running coaches agree that beginning and novice runners should spend *all* their time developing the aerobic energy-delivery system. This means that all running should be done at an aerobic pace—one that can be sustained while carrying on a conversation without becoming breathless.

I agree with this advice to beginner and novice runners, for three main reasons. One, starting a running program is challenging enough, physically and mentally, without the added stress of putting the body into oxygen debt, the state in which it can't meet its energy needs aerobically. Oxygen debt leads to breathlessness, lactic-acid burn, occasional nausea, and other discomforts. A beginning runner doesn't need any of that. Two, training at a moderate aerobic pace is easier on the muscles, joints, and bones, which need to gradually adjust to the demands of high-level activity, especially something pounding like running. And three, aerobic-level running is carried out at "conversation" pace—that is, an intensity at which participants can converse with one another. This ability to talk during training can greatly enhance the pleasure to be derived from running.

The programs outlined here add segments of running designed to challenge and develop the anaerobic (lactic-acid) energy system. Runners generally refer to this level of training as "speedwork." It's a catchall term for any running done at a higher intensity than "conversation" pace, and I'll use it from here on to refer to training at the lactate-threshold level or above.

You'll see that on the Challenging program, these elements are added after Week 4; they appear after Week 6 on the Moderate program. Workouts designed to develop the ATP-CP system, often referred to as "pure speed" or "raw speed," are introduced in Week 9 of the Challenging program and Week 10 of the Moderate program. Such workouts are used very sparingly in these programs, and in most other training programs followed by distance runners. To me, they are like hot pepper: They can wonderfully enhance a recipe if used in tiny amounts, but overwhelm and ruin a dish if used in excess.

## QUESTION AND ANSWER

**Q.** Is it okay to run every day?

**A.** Even some of the world's best runners don't run every day, for various reasons. Most significantly, daily running without a break increases the risk of injury and burnout. As a result, you may end up having to take off many days, and not by choice. Another reason not to run daily is so you can incorporate cross-training, supplemental training, and active rest into your fitness program (see Chapter 9 for more on these components). I recommend that all but the top elite take off at least one day a week, and either cross-train, train supplementally, or rest on the "off" days. Rest allows the body to consolidate fitness gains, and for muscles, joints, and connective tissue to recover from the pounding stresses of running. If you get antsy take a walk, meditate, do yoga, or find another way to relax or distract yourself from the fact that you are not running.

## THOSE ENDLESS QUESTIONS ABOUT RUNNING

Has this ever happened to you? You're at a party, in a meeting, or even in line for the movies, and the subject of running comes up. You mention that you run, and the questions begin. Certainly you're glad to hold forth on one of your favorite topics of conversation, and you don't mind the attention either. It's just that, well, don't people know *anything* about your favorite sport?

Chances are pretty good that no, most people don't. As you've probably noticed, running, though steadily increasing in popularity, isn't yet on par with baseball or even figure skating in terms of its position on the North American radar screen. While it would be hard to find a United States resident who'd never heard of a fly ball or a field goal, most people's knowledge of running stops with the wind sprints they were forced to do in high school gym class. They don't know a 5k from a first down. Mention the word "marathon" and you will probably see a glimmer of recognition, but start tossing around terms like "negative split," "midsole," and "tempo training," and you'll lose your audience completely.

You don't want to be rude, of course, and non-runners' questions, no matter how unenlightened, can be an entrée into sharing your running passion and possibly even winning some converts. The trick is to answer the questions warmly yet concisely, and not overwhelm your listeners with jargon or anything likely to scare them off. (You might not want to mention, for example, that a marathon is about 105 laps on their local outdoor track.) The following are questions you're most likely to hear from non-runners, and some suggested responses.

*"How many miles a day do you run?"* I'd be retired in Palm Springs if I had a dollar for every time I've been asked that question. The easy response is to spout off the number you get when you approximate your current weekly

mileage and divide by seven. But that answer is so misleading I can seldom bear to give it. The fact is, it rarely makes sense for any runner, no matter what her level or goals, to run the exact same number of miles every single day, throughout the year. For starters, few runners run daily. Second, whether they do or don't schedule a daily run, their day-to-day mileage varies based on factors such as the weather, their schedule, and upcoming races. For competitive runners, it's essential to vary mileage in order to allow the body to rest between the hard efforts needed to reach performance goals, and for everyone else, it's necessary in order to develop a wide array of running skills and fitness components. If I ran five miles a day, I'd get good at running five miles a day—and that's all.

I don't know why non-runners get so fixated on the miles-a-day question. My guess is, it's simply that the numbers aspect of running is one thing they think they can relate to. Often, they're probably just trying to make conversation. More than once I've given a long-winded response about training thresholds and recovery rates, etc., only to see a how-do-I-shut-her-up expression settle on the face of the listener. I've learned to keep my reply short and sweet: "At least 40 miles a week, up to 60 or 70 when I'm marathon training." If that answer elicits more questions, I'm off on a discussion of the merits of a hard-easy training program (see pages 28, 41, 42 in this chapter) and the importance of training in cycles (see Chapter 3 for more on this training pattern).

*"How far is that marathon?"* All marathons are 26 miles, 385 yards, period, end of story. (If your listener shows continued interest after you've imparted this information, you might mention a bit of historical trivia: The distance was standardized at the 1908 London Olympics when it was lengthened from about 25 miles so that the Princess of Wales could start the race in front of Windsor Castle and still have it finish at the Olympic Stadium. Before that the distance ranged from 24 to 26 miles. See Chapter 8 for more on marathons.)

It doesn't surprise me that most people have no idea how far a marathon is. (If I can live with their ignorance, though, why can't they accept the fact that I don't know the penalty for clipping in football, or the intricacies of baseball's designated-hitter rule?) It doesn't help matters that the term "ultramarathon" is used to refer to any distance greater than the 26.2-mile marathon. Answering the how-far question, though, may be complicated by the fact that to a surprising number of people, any footrace in which the competitors don't sprint from starting blocks on a track, Carl Lewis–style, is a "marathon." You may find that after you've stated the marathon distance, your questioner says something like, "My cousin ran one last month—I think it took her about an hour." Be prepared for some disappointment on the part of your listener, who probably delighted in referring to his friend or relative or coworker who just completed a 5k fun run as a "marathoner."

*"How many marathons have you run?"* As indicated above, you should probably first determine what's meant by "marathon" before answering this question. Another caveat: If your answer is "I haven't run a marathon," be prepared for the conversation to go dead in the water. The marathon is the glamour event of distance running. To the non-runner, any runner who admits to not having run a marathon is not actually a runner at all, but rather some sort of impostor. The number of people completing marathons (an estimated 451,000 in the United States in 2000) has grown steadily over the past 15 years—and over the past five years in particular—thanks in large part to a massive influx of participants running to raise money for a charity and having no performance or competitive goals (see Chapter 8 for more on racing and races at all distances). Suddenly, everyone has run a marathon, from President Bush to Oprah. So it's reasonable for the average runner to look askance at a so-called "runner" who hasn't. You can talk until you're blue in the face about the challenges and pleasures of racing at other distances, but with most people you might as well save your breath. It makes no difference to the average non-runner whether your time was a world-class 2:15 or a walking-pace five and a half hours.

*"Don't your lungs freeze in the winter?"* This question really and truly drives me crazy, to the point where it's often hard to give a polite answer. Of course lungs don't freeze. How could our prehistoric ancestors have evaded mastadons and saber-toothed tigers for millions of winters if our lungs froze every time we exerted ourselves in subfreezing weather? Don't ask me to explain the physiology (it has something to do with all the mucus and tiny hairs that line our airways), but Mother Nature took care of the freezing-lungs issue several hundred millennia ago. For those who are still unconvinced, there's always Gore-Tex.

*"Doesn't running bother your knees?"* This one at least makes some intuitive sense. Running is a pounding activity, and the knee is an inherently unstable joint. However, the scientific literature offers strong evidence that running can help rather than harm your knees—even if you have so-called "bad" knees. In a study of 3,600 women ages 25 to 74 by the National Center for Chronic Disease Prevention and Health Promotion, one third had been

diagnosed with arthritis. Those women who were overweight (according to a ratio known as the body mass index, or BMI), and therefore less likely to be exercisers of any kind, had a higher risk of osteoarthritis than those whose BMI was in the normal range. Obese women were the most likely to suffer from the condition. One of the many health-promoting benefits of running is that it can help maintain a body weight in the normal range. According to John Klippel, M.D., a rheumatologist and the medical director of the Arthritis Foundation, being overweight by even 10 pounds can significantly increase a person's risk of osteoarthritis.

Although overuse of joints in sports such as football and golf can increase the risk of osteoarthritis, there is no research linking running to an increased incidence of the disease. That said, running (and other pounding activities, such as step aerobics) *can* aggravate an existing knee injury, weakness, or imbalance. A knee injury can be very serious for a runner, but rarely does it permanently prevent someone from running. More often, a runner with injury-prone knees will have to take such measures as cutting back on mileage, or running primarily on soft surfaces such as dirt and grass. All runners can reduce their risk of knee pain and injury by wearing correctly fitted running shoes, replacing them regularly, avoiding hard, unyielding surfaces such as concrete, and wearing a supportive knee brace if needed. (You'll find this, and other injury-related information and advice, detailed in Chapter 5.).

To some extent, having healthy, injury-resistant knees is a matter of picking the right parents. I have run for more than 23 years and haven't always followed my own knee-preserving advice, but have never had a knee injury or even significant knee discomfort from running. Thus, my short answer to the question above is, "No." Chances are good that yours will be, too.

*"What do you think about while you're running?"* This question seems to come up less often than it did in the past. Perhaps due to my advancing age, my peer group now sees greater value in the art of thinking about nothing. My thoughts on the run range from the mundane (What's for dinner?) to the ecstatic (Look at that sunrise!) to the disturbing (Why didn't Alan kiss me good-bye this morning?) to the off-the-wall (If I were a princess, what would I want my castle to look like?). Really, what passes through my head on a run is little different from my thoughts at any other time of day, though I may free-associate more and tend to be calmer and more introspective. The longer or tougher my workout, the more I tend to focus on the act of running to the exclusion of all else.

The less tactful might ask, "Don't you get bored?" to which I've learned an effective reply. I remind my questioner that the French translation of "I am bored" is "I bore myself." Whether running, having sex, or taking out the garbage, we're only as bored as we choose to be.

*"Oh, do you jog?"* First of all, there's nothing to get a runner's dander up like the "j" word. It totally diminishes the sport and activity of running (and besides, it's way too seventies). Unfortunately, I can never think of a clever comeback to this question. Usually I just smile and say, "Yes, as a warm-up," or "Yes, except when I'm running." If this results in a sincere apology or inquiry for more information, I'll explain that a real runner wouldn't be caught dead "jogging."

If you've answered this question just a few too many times, and know a bit about the background of the questioner, you could answer with a version of the following (delivered with a sweet smile, of course):

To someone who has climbed Mt. Everest: "Yes, I do. Do you hike?"

To someone who has competed in the Tour de France: "Yes, and do you bike?"

To someone who has swum the English Channel: "Do you swim?"

You get the idea.

### Gauging Your Effort

"How do I know how hard I should be working?" is one of the most common questions I hear from runners starting a running program that involves speedwork. Indeed, gauging and monitoring your running effort is the crux of training as a distance runner at any level. There are several effective ways to determine your effort at the three levels of training (ATP-CP, lactate-threshold, and aerobic).

**Gauging effort by pace.** At first glance, this would seem to be the most accurate, and simplest, way to tell runners how hard they should be working—by how fast they are running. After all, running 6 miles per hour is running 6 miles per hour, right? Well, yes, but it turns out that all 6 m.p.h. training paces are not created equal. Many different factors can affect the effort that goes into maintaining a certain pace, including:

• *Air temperature and humidity.* Extremes of heat and cold both increase the energy required to maintain a certain pace. Running in the heat (especially when combined with humidity) causes an increase in sweating; the resulting dehydration forces the body to work harder to maintain the same pace because blood volume diminishes. Recall that blood carries oxygen to the working muscles, so with less blood circulating, less oxygen reaches the muscles with every heartbeat. Extremely cold weather forces the body to expend energy by shivering to keep warm, taking energy away from the task of running. Cold can also cause stiffness, slowing performances.

• *Wind.* Running into a headwind requires more energy to maintain the same pace than running with no wind or with the wind at your back (tailwind). This is one reason that world records in the marathon are recognized only on "loop" courses (in which the start is more than 30 percent of the marathon distance away from the finish). Even on a loop course the wind can slow the pace because the fatigue that results from battling the elements on the headwind segments never seems to be fully regained on the parts where there's the benefit of a crosswind or tailwind. When coaching athletes at a track on a windy day, I tell them to allow themselves at least an extra second or two per lap (400 meters). See Chapter 4 for more on training in various weather conditions.

• *Terrain.* It takes more energy to maintain pace over hilly terrain than on a flat course. Even on a hilly loop course, pace will be slower for the same effort than on a flat course, due to the energy required to "shift gears" between running uphill and downhill.

• *Time of day of run.* Most runners can maintain a quicker pace with less effort when running later in the day than first thing in the morning. This is primarily because muscles are less elongated in the morning (even with stretching and warm-up), making for a shorter stride. For this reason, many runners choose to do their harder workouts of the day in the afternoon or evening (although with a warm-up, you can do hard workouts whenever your schedule permits).

**Gauging effort by heart rate.** Heart rate monitor training has become very popular with runners and other endurance athletes over the past 10 to 15 years. This is thanks in large part to the development of sophisticated, yet simple, portable devices for measuring heart rate. An athlete can strap a heart rate detector to the chest, which generates data that's read by a monitor worn like a wristwatch. A heart rate monitor can be an excellent training tool. They are particularly useful for the runner who has a hard time "going easy"—that is, running at a pace that truly allows for recovery. There are a number of different formulas, based on age, fitness level, and other factors, for calculating optimal heart rates for various training efforts. Most coaches and exercise scientists define aerobic-intensity (conversation-pace) running as taking place at about 60 to 75 percent of maximum heart rate, lactate-threshold running at about 85 to 92 percent of maximum heart rate, and ATP-CP-intensity running as upward of 95 percent of maximum heart rate.

You can monitor your heart rate without a heart rate monitor by simply taking your pulse. This is best done by placing a finger lightly either on the wrist or against the carotid artery, just in front of and below the ear. Count the number of beats in 10 seconds and multiply by six to get your heart rate in beats per minute. The disadvantages of taking your pulse instead of using a heart rate monitor are that you must stop exercising to take your pulse, which interrupts your workout and immediately starts to slow the heart rate. Also, some people have a hard time finding their pulse, counting beats, and doing the math. The advantages are that it is free, and uses no equipment.

**Gauging effort by "feel" (perceived exertion).** As a coach, I often tell runners to "just run how you feel," particularly on their recovery days. Some runners are baffled by this advice. What do I mean, exactly? How can I give them such imprecise guidelines? Actually, running "by feel" is one of the best ways to teach a runner to tune in to the feedback from his or her body and respond accordingly. I have never trained by heart rate, and rarely by pace, because I strongly believe that learning to tap into and respond to the feedback from my body is the most precise and useful way to train as a distance runner. I am convinced that my running has benefited from learning to gauge my running effort on any given day by how I feel. On recovery days, when my effort is supposed to be aerobic in order to recover from hard workouts or races, I simply run at a pace that feels comfortable. Depending on a number of factors, including my fatigue level, the weather, the terrain, and the length of my run, my actual speed will vary by up to a minute or more per mile. That's okay. After 23 years of running, I can gauge my effort without a heart rate monitor or watch. The same goes for harder workouts. I time most of them out of habit and curiosity, but often I don't really have to. For example, when doing a set of 400-meter repeats at the track, my pace will seldom vary by more than a second or two per lap. After the first three or four, I usually turn off my watch.

Exercise scientists have quantified the "training by feel" philosophy using a tool called the Borg Scale, developed by Swedish scientist Gunnar Borg to study runners in laboratory settings. The scale is used to assist subjects in rating their effort level on a scale ranging from very, very light (6–8) to very, very hard (18–20). The numbers relate to the range of heart rates the subjects are likely to attain at corresponding levels, divided by 10. The Borg Scale has proven to be extremely accurate in predicting effort levels in endurance exercise.

Several coaches and exercise scientists urge athletes to tune in to their breathing to gauge their effort. I follow the advice of coach and scientist Jack Daniels, Ph.D., who suggests keeping aerobic effort to a 2-2 footstrike count; that is, breathe in for every strike of one foot (right, 2, right, 2) and out with every strike of the other foot (left, 2, left, 2). Running at lactate-threshold effort, for me, gets a 2-1 count (giving an in-out breathing cycle to every third step), and all-out ATP-CP effort is assigned a 1-1 count.

## QUESTION AND ANSWER

**Q.** What should I do if my running partner is slower than I am?

**A.** It depends on your goals for running, and whether you feel that running at a slower pace than you'd like is a sacrifice worth making in order to enjoy your friend's company. Once I had to make this decision. For years I'd run every day with the same friend, meeting every weekday morning at 6:30 for at least an hour's run. Some days I was slower, some days she was. We both valued the time together so much that neither of us ever minded slowing down for the other. Over time, I became more serious about my running, while she took a more recreational approach. Though neither of us ever said anything, we gradually went from being daily running partners to running together a couple times a week, to meeting only on weekends, to running together only once every few weeks. Our goals have completely diverged now, and though we don't run together we are still friends. But making the transition was tough. Looking back, I wish I'd been more straightforward with her about my goals and needs. It might work to try a compromise, and run together every other day. Don't suggest that he or she speed up, and don't run significantly slower than what feels comfortable to you; such compromises can result in injury.

## YOU KNOW YOU'RE A REAL RUNNER WHEN . . .

Runners, like any subspecies, have their quirks. You may not yet know all the idiosyncrasies of real runners, but little by little you're learning them, and perhaps coming up with some of your own. Here are a few unmistakable signs that you can count yourself among the company of real runners:

- You know how far a kilometer is.
- You don't have to ask where the sports drinks are stocked in your local supermarket.
- You own more than one pair of running shoes.
- You've run while it's raining or snowing—and enjoyed it.
- You have a favorite energy bar.
- You've set up a clothes-drying rack on which to hang your sweaty gear after a run.
- You've stopped worrying about your cellulite.
- You've purchased at least one issue of *Runner's World* or *Running Times*.
- You're training for your first marathon—or at least thinking about it.
- You own at least three race T-shirts.
- You've tried an energy gel.
- You just hate it when someone asks you if you "jog."

If you can identify with most of the points on the list above, move on to the next list. These are signs that you have become truly hardcore. (Even I don't meet the criteria for most of these!)

- You use words like "interval" and "split" in conversation, and are surprised when others don't know what you're talking about.
- You've attended a running camp.
- You've got Bill Rodgers' autograph.
- You have an e-mail address or car license plate that incorporates the word "run" (examples: gordonruns@aol.com; IMARUNNR).
- You know the Boston Marathon qualifying standards for your age division.

- You own more than half a dozen pairs of running shoes.

- Your first thought when someone mentions Chicago, Rotterdam, or Berlin is, "fast marathon course."

- At least one of your dresser drawers is filled to capacity with race T-shirts.

- You've seen the films *Personal Best, Without Limits,* and *Endurance.*

- You have a well-articulated opinion on why the Kenyans are unbeatable.

- You've been asked by other members of your household to find someplace (other than looped around the doorknob) to store your finisher's medals.

- You can explain the difference between Supplex and CoolMax.

- You wake up to a gloomy 45-degree day and think "great racing weather."

- You think Gatorade is a perfectly acceptable beverage to serve at parties.

- You've worn custom-fitted orthotics.

- You blow your nose without a tissue while running, and think nothing of it.

- You can utter the word *"fartlek"* in conversation without embarrassment.

- You've learned to program your VCR to record running events that are broadcast on cable channels in the middle of the night.

- You'll happily spend 20 minutes discussing the merits of various brands of energy gel.

- You know what "Go Pre" means.

### Applying "Training by Feel" to Speed Workouts

The workouts outlined in the charts on pages 20, 43, 44 refer to three different effort levels: "easy" for aerobic running; "comfortably hard" for lactate-threshold-level running; and "very hard" for ATP-CP-level running. Some coaches use formulas to predict the paces or heart rates at which runners should be running these efforts. Such predictions are valid and can be helpful to some runners. However, for the reasons I've outlined in this chapter, I prefer not to rely on them. Every runner is different, and the conditions under which every runner is going to be running every workout (weather, terrain, etc.) are all different as well. But an individual runner's perception of effort remains constant. Over time you will learn what "easy," "comfortably hard," and "very hard" running feel like, and your pace at these intensities will increase as your fitness improves, while your heart rate may vary due to ambient conditions, your fatigue level, and other factors.

You can use a stopwatch and/or heart rate monitor to help keep you "on track" with your training. Just don't become a slave to them; rather, learn to read and respond to the signals your body is passing along to you.

### The Nuts and Bolts

I've designed the schedules that follow for the runner who has been running regularly (at least three times a week for 20 minutes or more per session) for at least 10 to 12 weeks. Both programs pick up where the "Starting From Scratch" beginner running program on page 20 leaves off. That program builds up from a point of minimal fitness to running 20 minutes continuously without a break.

Both the Moderate and Challenging programs outlined here start with three 20-minute steady aerobic-intensity running workouts per week, and build from there over the ensuing 12 weeks. If it has taken you approximately 12 weeks to reach this point, starting from a level of minimal fitness, the program will take you to the five- to six-month mark of your fitness program—a crucial point at which, research tells us, approximately half of all new exercisers have already stopped working out. My hope is that at this five- to six-month point, you will have established a fitness routine to the point where it will be harder to quit than to continue to exercise! My aim is to present a program that's fun, interesting, varied, and challenging enough that you'll want to keep going, yet manageable enough to prevent injury and burnout.

There are two different schedules, which I call Moderate and Challenging. Both are safe and reasonable for a person in good health, and both are based on the principles of steady, progressive improvement with minimal risk of injury.

For the beginner program, I suggest that you precede your 20 minutes of continuous running with a 5-minute walking warm-up, and follow it with 5 additional minutes of walking to cool down. The purpose of the warm-up is to raise your body temperature and heart rate, and gradually elongate your muscles. These gentle adaptations to an increased activity level help keep the early stages of your workout comfortable and reduce the risk of overstressing muscle and connective tissue, which can cause a pull or tear. With the warm-up and cool-down, you are exercising for 30 minutes continuously. At this point, you may find that you can gradually eliminate your walking warm-up and cool-down, especially if you exercise later in the day, when your body is already "warmed up" from daily living. Just run the first mile or so of every run at a slow, easy pace—at least a minute per mile slower than your warmed-up pace. For example, my first mile is usually about 8 minutes, 30 seconds (8:30) per mile, after which I gradually increase the pace to about 7:30 per mile. This serves the same purpose as the walking warm-up, yet saves time. If you want to continue with a walking warm-up and cool-down, that's fine. (For simplicity's sake, the schedules here do not include a walking warm-up and cool-down.)

All running is at an "easy" effort level unless otherwise specified. At this intensity you should be able to talk comfortably, but not whistle or sing without a bit of a struggle.

## MODERATE PROGRAM

| Week | Day 1 | Day 2 | Day 3 | Day 4 | Day 5 | Day 6 | Day 7 |
|------|-------|-------|-------|-------|-------|-------|-------|
| 1 | 30 | 30 | off | 30 | off | 30 | off |
| 2 | 30 | 30 | off | 30 | off | 35 | off |
| 3 | 30 | 35 | off | 30 | 30 | off | 30 |
| 4 | 30 | 40 | off | 30 | 30 | off | 35 |
| 5 | 30 | 40 | off | 35 | 30 | off | 40 |
| 6 | 30 | 40 | off | 35 | 30 | off | 40 |
| 7 | 30 | AW-1 | off | 30 | 30 | off | 40 |
| 8 | 30 | AW-2 | off | 30 | 35 | off | 45 |
| 9 | 30 | AW-3 | off | 30 | 40 | off | 50 |

| Week | Day 1 | Day 2 | Day 3 | Day 4 | Day 5 | Day 6 | Day 7 |
|------|-------|-------|-------|-------|-------|-------|-------|
| 10 | 30 | RS-1 | off | 35 | 40 | off | 55 |
| 11 | 30 | AW-4 | off | 30 | 35 | 30 | 55 |
| 12 | 30 | RS-2 | off | 30 | 35 | 30 | 60 |

## CHALLENGING PROGRAM

| Week | Day 1 | Day 2 | Day 3 | Day 4 | Day 5 | Day 6 | Day 7 |
|------|-------|-------|-------|-------|-------|-------|-------|
| 1 | 30 | 30 | off | 30 | off | 30 | off |
| 2 | 30 | 35 | off | 30 | off | 35 | off |
| 3 | 30 | 30 | off | 30 | 30 | off | 30 |
| 4 | 30 | 40 | off | 30 | 30 | off | 40 |
| 5 | 30 | AW-1 | off | 30 | 30 | off | 40 |
| 6 | 30 | AW-2 | off | 35 | 30 | off | 45 |
| 7 | 30 | AW-3 | off | 40 | 30 | off | 45 |
| 8 | 30 | AW-4 | 30 | 30 | 30 | off | 50 |
| 9 | 30 | RS-1 | 30 | 30 | 30 | off | 50 |
| 10 | 30 | AW-5 | 30 | 35 | 30 | off | 55 |
| 11 | 30 | RS-2 | 30 | 40 | 30 | off | 60 |
| 12 | 30 | AW-6 | 30 | 45 | 30 | off | 70 |

All figures are in minutes. All training is at conversation pace unless otherwise noted.
AW = anaerobic work; RS = raw speed.

Workout descriptions (all workouts are preceded by a 10- to 12-minute warm-up and followed by a 10- to 12-minute cool-down):

AW-1: 2 minutes comfortably hard, 2 minutes easy
    (repeat 5 times)
AW-2: 3 minutes comfortably hard, 3 minutes easy
    (repeat 4 times)
AW-3: 4 minutes comfortably hard, 3 minutes easy
    (repeat 4 times)
AW-4: 5 minutes comfortably hard, 4 minutes easy
    (repeat 4 times)
AW-5: 2 minutes comfortably hard, 2 minutes easy
    (repeat 4 times) + 4 minutes comfortably hard, 3
    minutes easy (repeat 2 times)
AW-6: 6 minutes comfortably hard, 4 minutes easy
    (repeat 3 times) + 2 minutes comfortably hard, 2
    minutes easy (repeat 2 times)
RS-1: 1 minute very hard, 2 minutes easy (repeat 8 times)
RS-2: 90 seconds very hard, 2:30 easy (repeat 6 times)

### Where and How to Do Speed Workouts

My first speed workouts were done on a track, in high school. When I joined a road-racing team after college, I assumed we'd be heading to the track for all our speed workouts. As it turned out, only about 10 percent of our speedwork took place there. The rest of the time we took to the roads, paths, and dirt trails of New York's Central Park. I learned that speed workouts can be done anywhere you can run. You can measure courses or not, and use your stopwatch, landmarks, or some other parameter to determine when to increase and decrease your effort. It's a matter of choice and availability.

For example, the first anaerobic workout (AW-1) calls for alternating 2 minutes of comfortably hard with 2 minutes of easy running. You can do this workout in any of the following ways:

- Set your stopwatch (chronograph) to beep every 2 minutes, and adjust your intensity on the signal.

- Measure a course so that each comfortably hard segment can be run in approximately 2 minutes, followed by each easy segment in about 2 minutes.

- Run on a track for specific amounts of time; after one workout, you can note the distances you are covering and train by distance in the future, though if your fitness increases significantly, at some point you'll want to remeasure the distances covered.

- Program a treadmill to alternate working at comfortably hard (2 minutes) and easy (2 minutes) intervals.

- Pick landmarks that are spaced to allow you to alternate the hard and easy running approximately as instructed.

- Find a hill that you can run up in about 2 minutes at a comfortably hard pace; recover (the easy segments) by running back down the hill between efforts (this will give you a slightly longer recovery time, but it will not be significant for this workout).

Your body doesn't know whether you are training by the stop-watch, landmarks, or other parameters. Find a system that works well for you, and be prepared to make adjustments as needed. For example, if you usually work out at a track, but are traveling on business during your scheduled speedwork session, use a stop-watch or treadmill for that workout.

### A Note on Minutes vs. Miles

As both a runner and coach, I train and conduct most workouts based on time rather than distance. I'm not absolute in this rule, but I find it useful when designing workouts for large groups of people, especially when their fitness levels vary. A distance is precise, but the effort required to cover it can vary depending on numerous factors—weather, terrain, fatigue, etc. Time, on the other hand, always is what it is. Tell a runner to run for 30 minutes at conversation pace, and there's no ambiguity. It's a "you can take it with you" training method that's worked well for me and the runners I have coached over the years.

The schedules in this chapter, along with the advice on basic principles of planning your running program, gauging your effort, and integrating running into your life, should set you on the road toward becoming a runner rather than simply someone who runs. The chapters that follow will help you solidify the role of running in your life, and help you build a framework that supports and enriches that lifestyle.

▶▶▶▶▶▶▶▶▶▶▶▶▶▶▶▶▶▶▶▶▶▶▶▶▶▶▶▶▶▶▶▶▶

# CHAPTER 2

# *The Science of Running, and Running Well*

*I* often think of running as the purest sport: The more you put into it, all else being equal, the more you get out of it. Running to your potential is all about effort—your own effort, not that of teammates, support crew, or a piece of machinery. On any given day, among runners of equal inherent ability and barring freak mishaps (which, it must be admitted, can and do happen), the best-trained, most levelheaded athlete generally will win. The message to the runner who wants to improve is: Train hard, and stay healthy. You will reap the rewards; the laws of exercise science dictate it.

Because so much of running is pure physical effort (as opposed to technique), it is wise for runners to learn something about what goes on inside the body during training. What exactly happens to transform a man or woman who can't jog 100 yards without feeling faint into a lean, mean running machine capable of covering 26.2 miles or more? I view the changes as nothing short of miraculous. In this chapter we'll look at the basic physiological adaptations the body makes to running.

### How Running Improves Cardiovascular Fitness

Having a strong, well-functioning cardiovascular system allows runners to pump ample amounts of blood efficiently to the muscles used for running, then back to the heart for reoxygenation. Large-scale epidemiological (population) studies have linked cardiovascular fitness to lower rates of death from heart disease, hypertension, and other causes.

Cardiovascular fitness is the most important component of successful running. Runners are more efficient than sedentary people and nonendurance athletes at transporting oxygen in the bloodstream to the working muscles, which carry the body forward on the run. This process is outlined below.

When we breathe, air is drawn into the lungs through two large tubes called bronchi, which subdivide into many smaller tubes, terminating in hundreds of millions of tiny, saclike projections called alveoli. It is in the alveoli that oxygen is transferred to the bloodstream, passing through a microscopically thin barrier between alveolar cells and those in the smallest blood vessels (capillaries). Carbon dioxide is returned from the blood back to the lungs in the opposite direction through this same thin barrier. At rest, approximately 250 milliliters (ml) of oxygen per minute leave the alveoli and enter the bloodstream, while about 200 ml of carbon dioxide per minute diffuse back into the alveoli. During heavy exertion by a trained runner or other endurance athlete, the rate of exchange can increase up to 25-fold.

Most of the oxygen transported in the bloodstream attaches to hemoglobin, an iron-rich protein compound that is the main component of the body's 25 trillion red blood cells. When the blood reaches the capillaries, several of which border each of the millions of tiny fibers in a working muscle, oxygen is transferred from the hemoglobin in the red blood cells to another substance called myoglobin. The myoglobin in turn carries the oxygen from the muscle fibers' outer surface to millions of microscopic, semicircular structures within the muscle cells called mitochondria.

The function of the mitochondria, which have been called the "powerhouses" of the cells, is to produce energy for the muscles. To do this, they draw upon the energy in food, and convert it into the body's own energy currency, called adenosine triphosphate (ATP). Enzymes within the mitochondria speed up and enhance this process. The exact way in which the mitochondria produce energy is not fully understood, though it's known that they cannot function without oxygen.

Too much biology here for you? Don't worry, I'm not a scientist either, and the first time I tried to absorb this material, I found it complex and overwhelming. While it's true that these amazing processes will take place within your body, transforming you into a faster, fitter runner, whether you fully comprehend them or not, this stuff is worth learning. Why? For the simple reason that it can deepen your respect for what your running-fit body actually accomplishes during training and racing.

The cardiovascular adaptations to running are many, including:
- a larger and stronger heart capable of pumping more blood with each beat;
- an increase in the proportion of blood sent to the working muscles during exercise;
- an increase in the number of capillaries that deliver oxygen-rich blood to each muscle fiber;
- greater overall blood volume;
- an increase in the number of red blood cells;
- more myoglobin to deliver oxygen directly to the muscle fibers;
- an increased number of mitochondria in the muscle cells, and an increase in the size of the mitochondria;
- an increase in the activity of the enzymes within the mitochondria that produce aerobic (oxygen-fed) energy.

All these adaptations mean that the more you run, the better equipped your body is to fuel your muscles while running. Over time, the changes are what allow you to transform yourself from a couch potato into someone capable of running smoothly and efficiently, for 30 minutes, an hour, 2 hours, or longer without stopping.

## R-E-S-T IS NOT A FOUR-LETTER WORD

Runners train to get faster and stronger—to become better runners. Therefore, the longer and harder you run, the stronger and faster you will become, right? No, not exactly. Exercise scientist David Costill and his colleagues were among the first to show, in laboratory studies conducted in the 1960s, that trained athletes actually performed worse after a period of hard training than after a period of rest. In Costill's studies, the peak muscle power of swimmers was *lowest* when the subjects were training the most. The power increased progressively during a seven-day taper, or reduction in training, leading up to a competition.

How can this be? After all, we know that the best runners in the world train incredibly hard, and that the effort of preparing to run a 10k race at even a relatively moderate pace can challenge most ordinary mortals. How, then, can *not* training result in gains in fitness?

Here's how getting stronger and faster as a runner works: Running provides a stimulus to the body that prompts the many, varied physiological changes that are discussed in this chapter. The body perceives this stimulus as a stress, which it strives to meet as best it can as long as the stress continues. During this time the body is actually damaged and depleted, so that it becomes less capable of physical exertion. Fluid and fuel stores are diminished, and muscle fibers are broken down. At the end of a hard workout or race, you may feel as though you can't run another step—and in some cases, that may be literally true.

It is only when the exercise stops that the body can go to work repairing the damage inflicted and preparing to meet the next stimulus. Anticipating another stress of at least the same intensity as that which it has just undergone, the body adapts by making itself stronger: by increasing its stores of fluids and energy-generating glycogen, by building up the size and number of muscle fibers, by boosting blood volume, by creating more and larger mitochondria in the muscle cells, and by building more capillaries to transport blood to the working muscles. The point is, the body needs its "downtime" in order to complete the task. If it's hit with another stress before it's completed—or at least made progress on—the recovery and building processes, it will not be able to respond with the increase in fitness the runner is seeking. Perhaps you've experienced this yourself: You go to the track for a session of repeated 400-meter runs at your racing pace. The next day you run with a friend who didn't do the track workout, and he pushes the pace. This is a strain for you, not because you are unfit, but simply because you are still recovering from the previous day's effort.

The trick to training well and improving in running is to figure out just how hard you are capable of pushing your body—and thus stimulating gains in fitness—without crossing the line into the breakdown zone. Every runner is different in terms of finding that optimum level. The top runners in the world, and their coaches, are constantly walking that very thin line between peak fitness and overtraining. Getting the formula right is as much art as science, but there is one rule that is universally accepted and must be adhered to: You must rest—daily, weekly, from month to month, and from year to year. The world's most successful distance runners are often seen to lead pretty lazy lifestyles outside of running. When they are not working out, they tend to do very little besides sleep, eat, get massages and physical therapy, and try to relax. In reality, all that lounging about isn't laziness at all. Rather, it's allowing their bodies to absorb the stimulus of training and apply it to the next workout, and ultimately, to competition.

Though most of us have many other physical and mental stresses in our lives outside of running, we can all benefit from a running program that keeps rest front and center. We can do this by following the training advice and schedules presented in Chapters 1 and 3, which incorporate taking days off from running, and alternating long or hard efforts with short, easy runs. We can listen to our bodies and shorten or slow down our runs when we feel abnormally tired, without feeling like we're wimping out. We can include cross-training, supplemental training, and active rest. Doing these things will allow the body to recover so that fitness gains can be absorbed and used to our advantage.

Chapter 3 includes a complete discussion and guidelines on setting up training and racing programs that include time for rest and recovery. You'll learn how to incorporate rest into your training and racing schedule on a day-to-day, week-to-week, month-to-month, and year-to-year basis. This strategy will lead to gradual, steady improvement with a minimal risk of injury, illness, or burnout.

## QUESTION AND ANSWER

**Q.** What exactly is "fitness"?

**A.** The American College of Sports Medicine (ACSM), the largest

national organization of sports and fitness professionals in the United States, defines "fitness" using five basic components:
- cardiovascular-respiratory endurance
- muscular strength
- muscular endurance
- body composition
- flexibility

Of these, the first, cardiovascular-respiratory endurance, is considered the most integral to overall health. Also known as aerobic fitness, it refers to the capacity of the cardiovascular system—heart, lungs, and circulatory system—to deliver oxygen-rich blood to all areas of the body. Running is considered one of the best exercises for improving and maintaining cardiovascular fitness. By causing the heart, lungs, and circulatory system to work harder than they do at rest, running results in adaptations such as greater blood volume and others (which are discussed throughout this chapter) that allow these organs and systems to perform more efficiently both at rest and when working to capacity. A person with a strong cardiovascular system—that is, one able to stress the heart and lungs above resting level for extended periods—is generally termed "fit," even though he or she may be lacking in other fitness components.

The cardiovascular adaptations that improve oxygen delivery to the muscles are generally considered good for overall health as well. Numerous population studies have found that people who are cardiovascularly fit tend to live longer lives, as well as suffer fewer cases of heart disease, hypertension, cancer, and other life-threatening illnesses.

Running also improves muscular strength and muscular endurance, as discussed on pages 61–65 in this chapter. It can alter body composition by increasing the amount of lean tissue (muscle) and reducing fat stores. Chapter 7 offers more information on body composition and fueling your body for running.

### The Body's Three Energy Delivery Systems

The body has three basic systems that it uses to access the energy it derives from food sources and deliver it to working muscles during exercise.

**Adenosine Triphosphate–Creatine Phosphate (ATP-CP) System.**
Every cell in the body uses an energy-rich compound called adenosine triphosphate (ATP) to power biologic activity within that cell. Only a small amount of ATP is stored within each cell, so ATP must be constantly regenerated as it is used. ATP, often referred to as the body's "energy currency," provides the fuel for sudden, high-energy bursts, such as leaping into the air or running 60 meters at top speed. Although ATP is immediately available for use, its quantity is limited to activities lasting no more than a few seconds—at which point the body must call upon another energy source.

ATP cannot be supplied from an outside source, such as oxygen in the bloodstream. Instead each cell must continuously resynthesize its supply. This is done primarily via the transfer of chemical energy from another high-energy compound, called creatine phosphate (CP). The reserve of CP in cells is about three to five times that of ATP; thus, the ATP-CP delivery system can fuel high-energy activities lasting up to about 30 seconds. In running, this system is used to fuel events such as a 100-meter or 200-meter sprint. During these events, most competitive runners literally do not breathe, because ATP-CP alone, without oxygen, provides sufficient fuel.

Although ATP-CP stores are limited, they regenerate very quickly. For a runner, this means that with brief rest periods, it is possible to sprint all-out for short distances, as long as these bouts are followed by rest intervals. This allows runners to perform multiple-interval workouts, such as repeat 200-meter sprints. The ATP-CP system also comes in handy in a variety of sports—soccer, hockey, football, tennis, weight lifting, etc.—that require quick bursts of explosive energy alternated with periods of rest or low-level activity.

**Lactic-Acid (or Anaerobic Energy) System.** For strenuous exercise to continue beyond about 30 seconds, the body must tap into other energy systems. The body's most readily accessible extracellular energy source is glucose, which is stored in the cells throughout the body, with concentrations in the muscles and liver. (The storage form of glucose is called glycogen.) When a cell needs to meet energy demands beyond what ATP can supply, a glucose molecule enters the cell and undergoes a series of chemical reactions known as glycolysis. A substance called pyruvate is formed, and when pyruvate levels accumulate more rapidly than they can be used to fuel activity, the resulting by-product is called lactic acid, or lactate. Lactic acid helps fuel work that outstrips the demands of oxygen. This lactic-acid system (also known as the anaerobic energy system) allows the body to sustain a high level of activity for approximately 30 seconds to 3 minutes. However, during this intense period, levels of lactic acid in the bloodstream accumulate more rapidly than they can be taken up by the muscle cells. At a certain point, known as the lactate threshold, the accumulation of lactic acid shuts down enzyme activities in the cells that produce energy. This generally leads to a reduction to a level that can be sustained aerobically (using oxygen as the primary energy source).

For untrained runners, the lactate threshold occurs at between 55 percent and 70 percent of the body's maximal capacity for using oxygen (known as $VO_2$ max), the level at which the body takes full advantage of all available oxygen. The lactate threshold of highly trained endurance athletes can be as high as 80 percent to 90 percent of $VO_2$ max. (This chapter and Chapter 3 include more detailed descriptions of lactate-threshold training and $VO_2$-max training.)

## THE LACTATE THRESHOLD

As the body's exercise intensity level increases within the aerobic range, lactic acid (lactate) begins to accumulate in the blood. This is known as the onset of blood lactate accumulation (OBLA), or, more commonly, the lactate threshold (or sometimes, anaerobic threshold, though this term is less technically accurate). As a runner, you will experience the lactate threshold as a mild burning sensation in the muscles that becomes progressively more intense as exercise effort increases. You'll also notice a marked rise in your breathing rate, and a sense of having an increasingly difficult time meeting your body's energy requirements by breathing alone.

And that is exactly what is happening. Runners in laboratory settings show a sudden, dramatic buildup of lactate in the bloodstream precisely at the point when they report feeling as if they are "huffing and puffing" to keep up with the demands of the intensity of their running. If their running

continues at this level, their breathing becomes more labored. More significantly, the burning in their running muscles progresses to the point where they feel a sense of "rigging" or "tying up." This is the result of lactic acid flooding into the blood that is supplying the working muscles. Lactic acid inactivates the energy-producing enzymes in the blood, leading to a sharp reduction in the muscles' work capacity. The "rigged" or "tied up" feeling serves as a signal to the runner's body to either supply more oxygen to the muscles (impossible at this point without growing a third lung) or reduce the demands of the muscles by slowing the pace.

For a distance runner, the lactate-threshold level is probably the most powerful predictor of athletic performance, although it took years for exercise scientists to realize this. Previously it was thought that the maximum oxygen uptake (known as $VO_2$ max), the highest level of oxygen (in milliliters) the body could process to fuel one minute of exercise, was the primary measure of an endurance runner's fitness. It turns out that the lactate threshold is a more telling predictor of potential than $VO_2$ max in distance running and other endurance events. By training the lactic-acid energy system, even veteran distance runners can significantly boost their performance. This is because so much of running takes place at a sublactate threshold level, and because $VO_2$ max is largely dependent upon your heart's ability to pump blood to your working muscles (and therefore is in large part genetically determined), whereas the adaptations that occur due to an increase in lactate threshold take place throughout the body—not only in the heart, but also in the muscles and at the cellular level.

As you will see in Chapter 3, the most effective way to do this is by training at your lactate-threshold level (which is approximately the pace at which you would run a competitive 10-mile race), thereby getting the body accustomed to working at a level that stresses but does not overwhelm it.

**Aerobic Energy System.** Energy is released quickly by glycolysis, but because of the rapid accumulation of lactic acid that follows, activity fueled primarily by the process cannot continue beyond several minutes. Therefore another energy system must come into play to fuel longer-term activity—which makes up the bulk of that done during training and racing by distance runners. This system is known as the aerobic energy system.

Exercise is defined as *aerobic* if its demands can be met primarily by oxygen carried in the bloodstream to the working muscles. Most of the running you do from day to day in training, and a fair amount in longer races, is fueled by the aerobic energy system. (See Chapter 3 for more information on setting up training programs to improve aerobic fitness.) Like anaerobic exercise, glycogen provides a substantial proportion of the energy used to fuel aerobic exercise (the rest comes from the breakdown of fat and small amounts of protein). As noted above, lactic acid is produced as a by-product of the breakdown of glycogen for energy (glycolysis), but at aerobic levels the accumulation of lactic acid does not exceed the body's ability to continuously use it to fuel the body's activities.

As an energy source, oxygen is available in unlimited quantities as long as breathing continues. Therefore, in theory, aerobic exercise can continue indefinitely. In the real world, of course, this is not the case. We can't run forever, even if we would like to, because of the losses of fuel and fluid, which cannot be replenished quickly and completely enough for the exerciser to make use of them. In addition, the breakdown of muscle fibers due to the pounding activity of running can be a severely limiting factor—you simply can't keep going due to the stress on the muscles and connective tissue. Over time, however, a runner can train himself to complete distances that are truly extraordinary, such as multiday races and transcontinental runs.

## EFFECTS OF PERFORMANCE-ENHANCING DRUGS

You have probably heard about runners getting "busted" for taking drugs or engaging in practices that illegally and artificially enhance their performance potential. The specter of illegal drug use casts a pall over running and other sports in which performance differences are measured in hundredths of a second, and in which some unscrupulous athletes, and the coaches, doctors, trainers, and others who advise them, will sully their reputations—and endanger their health—by trying to gain a pharmacological edge.

As has been noted throughout this chapter, success in distance running depends largely upon the body's ability to deliver oxygen-rich blood to the working muscles. Therefore, attempts at cheating among runners—as well as cyclists, cross-country skiers, rowers, and other endurance athletes—have focused on enhancing the oxygen-carrying capacity of the blood. (Of course, training accomplishes this in a perfectly legal manner.) Many runners live or temporarily train in high-altitude locations—also a legal and widely accepted training method—where the body naturally responds to the lower oxygen content of the air by creating more red blood cells, thus increasing blood's oxygen-carrying capacity and creating a significant potential for improvement. A more recent trend (also legal) has been the use of "altitude chambers," which create a high-oxygen environment for training and/or everyday living, either as a low-oxygen tent or by removing oxygen from the air of an ordinary room. All these methods assist the body in its task of shunting as much energy-promoting oxygen as possible to working muscles.

Most people—as well as the national and international governing bodies of running and other sports, including the International Olympic Committee—draw the line at using drugs or invasive techniques. In the 1970s and '80s a common technique among some runners was "blood doping." An athlete would withdraw and store a quantity of blood, thus stimulating the body to produce more red blood cells to counter the loss (as it does after you give blood). Then, prior to competition, the stored blood would be reinfused, giving the athlete a boost in the form of greater blood volume and red blood cell count. Though banned by international sporting federations, "blood doping" was and still is undetectable, and thus a constant source of suspicion in high-level running circles. It was considered risky, too, what with the dangers of infection and contamination from blood removal, storage, and reinfusion, and the fatigue that would follow upon the initial withdrawal of blood.

Thus, in the early 1990s a more refined technique started to come into use. A substance known as recombinant erythropoietin (rEPO, now commonly referred to as EPO) came on the market to treat kidney patients and others with severe anemia. EPO is a hormone found in the body, where it stimulates the production of red blood cells. Taking the drug EPO increases the amount of natural EPO in the blood; the body is thus able to transport more oxygen in the bloodstream to the working muscles. By taking EPO, athletes are able to work out harder and longer at a high level, and to recover more quickly between hard workouts and race efforts.

Though EPO eliminates the hazards of infection, contamination, and debilitating fatigue associated with "blood doping," it has its own dangers. Chief among them is that it must be administered at very precise levels because too much can cause excessive thickening of the blood, drastically raising the risk of blood clots and heart failure. A cluster of deaths of young European cyclists in the early 1990s has never been explained and is widely thought to have resulted from EPO misuse. The cycling world was shown to be rife with EPO use during the 1998 Tour de France, in which the drug was found in the possession of several team doctors and trainers.

Like blood doping, EPO is banned in international competition. Urine and blood tests for EPO were developed prior to the 2000 Sydney Olympic Games and used there in limited testing. The newly formed World Anti-Doping Agency has among its goals to continue the development and implementation of EPO testing in Olympic and other international competition.

Other drugs and techniques known or suspected of being used by some endurance athletes, including distance runners, are:

*Stimulants.* Scientists once thought amphetamines and other drugs increased performance in endurance events by delaying the onset of fatigue due to their glycogen-sparing properties. Amphetamine testing was conducted as early as the 1964 Olympics. Many amphetamines and other stimulating drugs are banned from competition, meaning that athletes who are subject to testing must be very careful about their use of decongestants, asthma-controlling drugs, and other classes of medications, lest they inadvertently commit a doping violation. Even ordinary caffeine is banned at high levels, though a person would have to consume the equivalent of five to eight cups of coffee in the two to three hours prior to testing in order to fail a drug test.

*Testosterone.* Runners of both genders, but women in particular, can benefit from drugs and techniques that increase levels of the male hormone testosterone, which is found naturally in the human body. Testosterone, injected by athletes seeking a performance edge, helps contribute to muscle growth and development and reduce fat stores. It has masculinizing side effects, such as deepening of the voice and the growth of facial hair.

*Anabolic steroids.* Though of greatest benefit to sprinters, lifters, throwers, jumpers, and others competing in events that require explosive power, steroids can improve performance for endurance athletes as well. They help the body increase muscle size and strength, and reduce fat stores. Anabolic steroids are universally banned in international competition. Like testosterone, steroids have masculinizing side effects.

*Human growth hormone (hGH).* Like EPO and testosterone, hGH is a substance found naturally in the body. By artificially introducing it at higher-than-normal levels, runners and other endurance athletes can stimulate the growth of lean tissue (muscle) and reduce fat stores.

*Genetic manipulation.* Considered the "new frontier" of performance enhancement, genetic manipulation alters a person's genetic makeup (remember the TV series *The Bionic Woman?*). This could increase an athlete's performance potential in ways previously unimagined. Recent scientific advances are bringing the techniques of genetic manipulation—once the stuff of science fiction—ever closer to reality.

## QUESTION AND ANSWER

**Q.** What causes muscle soreness?

**A.** For a long time, exercise scientists didn't understand the precise cause of the muscle soreness that often follows exercise. It was once thought that lactic acid (lactate) accumulation was responsible. Now it is known that all of the lactate your body produces after even the longest and hardest efforts, such as running a marathon, is eliminated from the body within a few hours after exercise.

Most of the muscle soreness caused by running results from microscopic tears to the muscle fibers caused by intense, repeated contractions of the running muscles. The most serious damage results from eccentric (lengthening) contractions, such as those that occur when running downhill. This explains why downhill marathon courses, such as the Boston Marathon and Utah's St. George's Marathon, typically result in more soreness than courses that are flatter or include more uphill running (particularly late in the race, when muscles are fatigued and thus most susceptible to damage).

When muscle fibers are damaged, the body responds by increasing blood flow to and enzyme activity in the area of the injury. This response causes inflammation and mild swelling, stimulating the nerve endings, which causes the feelings of soreness and discomfort. This soreness—which is often accompanied by stiffness in the muscles and connective tissue around the joints—is known as delayed onset muscle soreness (DOMS) because it typically occurs not immediately after exercise but 12 to 96 hours later. Runners generally find they are the most sore about two days after a long, hard effort such as a marathon, and that the soreness has started to dissipate by the fourth or fifth post-marathon day, as the muscles begin to repair themselves.

In general, runners can minimize soreness by not overtraining, by avoiding excessive downhill running (particularly at fast speeds), by wearing the right shoes, and by running on soft surfaces. (See Chapter 5 for more on ways to minimize muscle soreness.) However, most beginning runners will experience at least mild DOMS after their first few runs no matter how cautious they are, due to their muscles being unaccustomed to running. As long as it's not extremely painful or debilitating—thus causing the runner to alter form—it should not prompt a reduction in training. The soreness should gradually lessen, then disappear within a few weeks of starting a progressive running program.

There's considerable debate over how to best treat serious DOMS, such as after a marathon or other long race. Some experts recommend very slow running, or a nonpounding activity such as walking, swimming, pool-running, or cycling, to stimulate blood flow, thus speeding the repair of damaged muscle. Others counsel no activity at all, because of the increased risk of tearing damaged muscle. I tend to avoid running when I'm excessively sore, but I enjoy running in the pool at a relaxed effort level, or taking leisurely walks (see Chapter 9 for more on these and other forms of "active rest"). My suggestion is to do what feels comfortable and works into your schedule.

### How Running Improves Muscular Strength and Endurance

How do muscles get stronger? Through a chemical, biological, and biomechanical process. The body contains three major types of muscles: heart (or cardiac) muscle; smooth muscle, which forms the muscular lining of many internal organs; and skeletal muscle, which controls most voluntary movement, including running. Each skeletal muscle is made up of many muscle fibers, and each fiber is composed of individual muscle cells. The cells are fed by a blood supply delivered by capillaries and carrying oxygen and nutrients to the muscles. Each cell also has its own nerve supply through which it receives neural impulses.

All skeletal muscles work by contracting in response to a stimulus. Stimulating or overloading a muscle or group of muscles sets in motion a complex series of electrical and chemical events that results in a contraction, or shortening, of the muscle. When muscles are repeatedly overloaded, the body is prompted to recruit more motor units, or to increase the size of individual muscle fibers, in order to facilitate the contraction. The multitude of contractions of muscle cells adds up to the muscle movements that allow us to perform all sorts of physical activities.

### Fast-Twitch and Slow-Twitch Muscle Fibers

Skeletal muscle (which is connected to bones and controls the body's voluntary movements) consists of two different types of fibers, fast-twitch and slow-twitch. Fast-twitch fibers have physical, chemical, and electrical properties, which give them the ability to generate energy rapidly in order to produce quick and forceful contractions. These fibers, which are pale or whitish in color, are therefore activated in short-term activities that depend on anaerobic energy, such as running sprints, accelerating quickly, changing direction rapidly, lifting heavy weights, or leaping long distances. Slow-twitch fibers, on the other hand, generate energy mainly through the aerobic energy system. They are physically, chemically, and electrically adapted to prolonged aerobic endurance exercise such as distance running, swimming, and cycling. They have a slow contraction speed compared to fast-twitch fibers, but contain more mitochondria and larger quantities of the protein myoglobin, which transfers oxygen carried in the blood to the working muscles.

Studies have shown that the muscles of sprinters, jumpers, lifters, and throwers contain higher than normal proportions of fast-twitch fibers, whereas the fibers of endurance athletes, such as distance runners, cross-country skiers, distance swimmers, cyclists, and triathletes contain higher proportions of slow-twitch fibers. To a great extent these differences are genetic, and a person's ultimate potential to succeed in a sport may be determined in part by his or her proportion of fast-twitch or slow-twitch fibers.

However, the activities that the muscles engage in regularly also further enhance the differences in proportions of fiber types. Developing slow-twitch fibers enhances the endurance of the muscles—that is, their ability to contract repeatedly for long periods without performance-reducing fatigue. Slow-twitch fibers tend to increase in number rather than grow in size. Thus, the best distance runners in the world have higher proportions, on average, of slow-twitch fibers than do matched groups of recreational or even subelite-level athletes. Fast-twitch fibers, on the other hand, may grow significantly larger through high-level training. This explains why the muscles of athletes in sports that rely upon fast-twitch fibers, such as weight lifting, throwing, jumping, and sprinting, tend to be quite well developed, whereas the muscles of distance runners and other endurance athletes appear normal in size.

Slow-twitch fiber percentage is not, of course, the sole determinant of performance potential in distance running and other endurance sports, and it is not yet known just how important it is.

---

## SUMMARY OF FITNESS ADAPTATIONS TO RUNNING

As running fitness improves, the body is able to supply increased levels of oxygenated blood to the working muscles. This change is accomplished via the following adaptations:

- *Greater blood volume.* The liquid content of the blood is higher in runners than non-runners. This helps to ensure proper hydration and cooling during running, and helps the blood carry nutrients throughout the body and remove waste products. (For more on staying hydrated while running, see Chapter 7.)

- *An increase in the number of red blood cells.* Having more red blood cells increases the blood's ability to deliver oxygen to the working muscles.

- *An increase in the number of capillaries.* Capillaries are the tiniest blood vessels, which carry oxygen and nutrients to the muscle cells and remove waste products. Having more capillaries leads to more efficient delivery of oxygen to the muscle fibers.

- *An increase in muscle mass and strength.* Running causes muscles to become larger and stronger. The increased strength makes running—as well as other activities, from pushing a shopping cart to walking up stairs—easier and more efficient, and can lead to improvements in appearance. Strong running muscles tend to be lean and streamlined, not bulked up.

- *An increase in the number and size of mitochondria, the "energy powerhouses" of the cells.* Having more and larger mitochondria enables the muscles to draw upon oxygen as an energy source at higher levels of intensity, thereby extending the length of time that the body can run at a high level (fueled primarily by oxygen).

- *An increase in energy-producing enzyme activity within each cell.* Running stimulates an increase in enzyme activity within cells, enabling muscles to produce more energy aerobically. This allows the body to exercise aerobically at a higher level without the accumulation of lactic acid.

In addition, running causes an increase in the body's overall rate of metabolism (energy generation and expenditure), a decrease in fat stores, and in most cases, an improvement in running economy (the ability to use energy efficiently).

All these improvements, while not necessarily correlated with better health, can help runners perform better and often feel better, both while running and at rest. From time to time, I'm asked by non-runners to describe the feeling of being supremely fit as a runner. How do I feel, they want to know, compared to someone who doesn't run? I've been a regular runner for so long, it's hard to answer that question. The only significant breaks I've had from running in over 23 years have been during my two pregnancies. These times allowed me to reflect on how running makes me feel. For me, the feeling of being a very fit runner includes:

- A sense of strength of the muscles in my legs, especially my hamstrings (back of thighs) and calves.

- Strength of energy and will. I feel like I can handle many tasks and a high stress load each day. Little things don't overtax me, whether it's climbing a flight of stairs or telling my preschool-aged son that he can't have chocolate cake for breakfast.

- High energy (fuel) demands. My appetite definitely increases the more I run. I need to eat more, and more often.

- A sense of calm, probably resulting from a lower resting heart rate (which occurs in runners and other endurance athletes thanks to the increased efficiency of the cardiovascular system).

Running makes me feel like a finely tuned machine. The only downside is that the fitter I become, the closer I am to the possibility of getting injured. A sports medicine friend of mine compared high-level training to sharpening a pencil: The sharper it gets, the more likely it is to break. I often have a sense of being "on the edge" when my mileage and training intensity are high, and I keep in mind how fine the line is between peak fitness and overtraining. (For more on injury prevention and risk reduction, see Chapter 5.)

▶ ▶ ▶ ▶ ▶ ▶ ▶ ▶ ▶ ▶ ▶ ▶ ▶ ▶ ▶ ▶ ▶ ▶ ▶ ▶ ▶ ▶ ▶ ▶ ▶ ▶ ▶ ▶ ▶ ▶ ▶

# Setting Up a Running Program

Running regularly for six months or longer demonstrates a commitment to the running lifestyle. I define "regularly" as at least three times a week, for at least 30 minutes at a time—though many runners, of course, run considerably more often and for longer stretches of time.

For most runners, moving forward from this point involves shifting to a pattern of training in cycles. I have been a regular runner for more than 23 years, and for me, organizing my running by training cycles has become almost instinctive. I tend to forget that not all runners organize their running in the same way. Many have a tendency to get into a pattern of running a certain number of miles or for a certain time, and do nothing but that. For example, many runners in New York, where I live, frequently run the six-mile loop around Central Park. They run six miles, four or five times a week, at roughly the same pace, for weeks, months, or even years on end. If they get bored, injured, or busy and take time off, they return to the same program. This isn't the best way to improve as a runner, or to maximize your enjoyment of running.

I was recently reminded of the need to instruct runners in setting up a cyclical training program when I got an e-mail from my sister Anne. She had just intensified her running by hooking up with a neighbor who shares her desire to run consistently and to get faster and stronger. Despite periodic back pain caused by a herniated disk, Anne has been a regular runner for 12 years. She wrote:

> I want to hit you up for some training advice because I'm not exactly sure what I'm doing. I'm running about 25 miles a week with no particular plan, just keeping fit. My neighbor and I are probably running nine-minute miles—faster or slower based on how we feel. I guess the goal is to increase mileage and decrease our times. We'd like to do some races; she has targeted a half-marathon in early September. She used to run competitively but hasn't in a long time, and doesn't really know how to get back in the swing of things. Do you think you could get us pointed in the right direction?

As noted in Chapter 1, so many runners, like Anne, find themselves stuck at this "now what?" stage with their running. In fact, for many of them, running without a plan—just muddling along from day to day, letting the weather, their mood, work schedule, and countless other factors dictate their running schedule—becomes a way of life. They aren't necessarily thrilled with the status quo, but they imagine there's no real alternative short of becoming overly rigid, methodical, and maniacally disciplined about their running.

There is a better way. While I applaud anyone who has remained committed to running for six months or longer—and certainly would agree that what they are doing is healthy and life-affirming—I believe they are shortchanging their enjoyment of running and prohibiting themselves from advancing their fitness and any competitive goals they might have. In this chapter you will learn to train with a plan, one that will keep you moving forward with your running—healthily, steadily, and consistently—for as long as you wish.

## TAKING DAYS OFF

As outlined in the Training Charts in Chapter 1, it is not necessary—nor even wise—for most runners to run every day. For one thing, daily running represents a significant time commitment for most people. More importantly, however, for all but the most highly conditioned athletes, daily running allows the body insufficient time to recover between running efforts. Chapter 9, on cross-training, supplemental training, and active rest outlines the many ways runners can complement their running with other activities that are less stressful to the body (particularly to the joints, due to the pounding nature of running) and enhance their fitness in other ways, and explains how runners can use very easy running, walking, and rehabilitative activities such as stretching, massage, and water exercises to maintain their fitness and soothe their muscles and joints between running workouts.

However, even with cross-training, supplemental training, and active rest worked into the running schedule, and a training program that includes planned days off at least once or twice a week, you may occasionally face the question, "Should I run today?" If a run is on your schedule, you may well have a hard time deciding whether to go ahead with that run or not, despite the difficulties of running that day, and despite commonsense arguments not to run. Here are instances when the "to run or not to run" decision may be a particular challenge, and suggestions for resolving the issue.

- *You feel ill.* The basic rule of thumb to determine whether you are too sick to run is this: If your symptoms are confined to above the neck, a run most likely won't hurt (and may even help); if symptoms are below the neck, it's probably better not to run. Above-the-neck symptoms include nasal congestion, sinus blockage without fever, and headache without fever. Running, especially a short, easy outing, generally will not make these symptoms worse. (If you feel symptoms worsening during your run, then cut your run short.) Symptoms below the neck include a fever of 101 degrees or higher, body-wide muscle aches and fatigue, upset stomach, sore throat, and congestion in the lungs and chest. Not only will you probably feel terrible if you run with these symptoms, but running (or any type of vigorous exercise) will most likely make them worse. Take the day off from running and other strenuous exercise. Return to your training program—gradually, if it ends up being an extended time off running after your symptoms are gone. You'll learn from experience whether to run or not when you feel under the weather. In general, it's best to err on the conservative side.

- *You have a crazy schedule.* Say you have a run planned for 5:30 P.M., after work, but you get stuck in a late meeting, and you promised your family you'd be home for dinner by 6:30. Then you have to put the kids to bed, return phone calls, wash the dishes, check e-mail, and before you know it, it's 10:00. You're finally free—but does it make sense to run now, an hour before bedtime? Or let's say you're scheduled to leave on a 7:00 A.M. flight. This means getting up at 5:00—even without planning to run. Your spouse says you're crazy to set the alarm for 4:00 to fit in your run, but when else are you going to have time? Only you can make these judgment calls. Consider the following when making your decision: Safety, what you're giving up (such as sleep), and the purpose of the day's run. If it's an easy recovery day, consider skipping it. If it's a long run or speedwork session, try to switch it to another day.

- *You feel wiped out.* There is a difference between physical and mental fatigue. When you feel exhausted at the end of a long day of work, school, or caring for children, a run may be the perfect antidote. If you're tired at the start of your run, give it 5 to 10 minutes. If you're not overtrained or ill, the fatigue is most likely more mental than physical, and you'll realize that a run is just what you need. However, if after 5 to 10 minutes you're still dragging to the point where you hate every step and want to walk, then call it a day. Look at your training log: Chances are, you're overdoing it and need to cut back. Or you may be coming down with something. Either way, the run is doing you more harm than good.

- *The weather isn't cooperating.* I've lived almost all my life in the Northeast, and run in blizzards, heat waves, and hurricanes. So my bias is toward not letting the weather get in the way of my running. That said, there are plenty of times certain people, in certain weather conditions, definitely should not run outdoors. *No one should run during an electrical storm, or any other time their safety is threatened by the elements.* However, thanks to advances in clothing fabrics and construction (see Chapter 4 for more on choosing and using the right running apparel), running in the heat, cold, wind, snow, and rain—without thunder and lightning—is easier these days than ever before. Just make sure to have the right gear with you, or it won't do you any good. If you choose to run on very hot, cold, windy, rainy, or snowy days, dress appropriately, concede to the conditions by slowing your pace, and be prepared to cut your workout short if necessary. As a coach, I'll cancel hard speed workouts on extremely hot days due to the risks of heat stroke and heat prostration, but this has happened only a handful of times in the past 16 years. Runners with asthma or allergies may not be able to run without severe discomfort and even health risks under certain conditions. Consult a medical professional for guidance—preferably someone who works with runners or other athletes. In all these cases, working out indoors on a treadmill is an option worth considering, as is a cross-training or supplemental training workout.

Fitness does not decline significantly due to one or two days of missed running. The effects are not noticeable until at least four to five days of exercise have been missed, and even then the losses are negligible. Put your health, safety, and sanity first in making the "to run or not to run" decision. In fact, the rest may do you good.

### The Importance of Training in Cycles

"Periodization" is the technique of effectively varying the timing, intensity, and duration of workouts to maximize gains in strength, speed, power, and endurance. Athletes know that it's impossible to be "at the top of your game" all the time. Typically, a professional athlete in any sport, from tennis to pole vaulting, will aim to peak for several important competitions per year. These peak-performance efforts are likely to be followed by periods of rest and regeneration before beginning a buildup to the next pinnacle of effort.

As early as the 1940s and 1950s, coaches of endurance athletes, including New Zealand coaching legend Arthur Lydiard, were starting to formalize periodized training programs. Lydiard, influenced by the ideas of Australian swimming coach Forbes Carlile, experimented with and refined the concept of training to peak for an important race or series of races once or twice during the year. He developed a semiannual training cycle that prepared his distance runners to peak twice a year, at most. When Lydiard's methods resulted in Kiwi runners bringing home Olympic gold medals in 1956, 1960, and 1964, other runners, coaches, and scientists took notice. (Now in his mid-eighties, Lydiard continues to preach "the Lydiard way," which has been adopted by innumerable runners and coaches around the world.)

Eastern bloc athletes were other early converts to highly rigid, systematic periodized training programs. Romanian exercise scientist Tudor O. Bompa, Ph.D., first developed the concept of "periodization of strength" when working with Eastern bloc athletes in the early 1960s. Since then, periodization has become a standard method of conditioning top-level professional athletes, particularly in endurance sports. Typically, these athletes will aim to peak one to three times per year.

The programs that most elite-level runners follow are highly systematized. It's not necessary for most nonelite runners to adhere to such strict schedules. However, runners at all levels will benefit from following a cyclical training program, for the following reasons:

• *Cyclical training leads to peak performance.* Lydiard's athletes were but the first to reap the benefits. Perhaps the most dramatic example of outstanding performances attained through cyclical training to culminate in a peak is that of Finnish distance runner Lasse Viren, who won double gold medals (5,000 and 10,000 meters) at both the 1972 and 1976 Olympics. These accomplishments were noteworthy because Viren raced infrequently—and relatively poorly—between these efforts. Instead, he and his coaches concentrated all their energies on Viren's quadrennial peaks. The sports world is replete with other examples of athletes who have seen dramatic improvements by training cyclically to peak for specific events. As noted in Chapter 2, the body actually increases its fitness level not during hard training, but during the rest and recovery periods that follow. This physiological reality dictates that in order to attain peak fitness, cycles of rest must be incorporated into training, both on a day-to-day and season-to-season basis.

• *Cyclical training prevents boredom.* For most of us, peaking so that we can win an Olympic gold medal is beyond our wildest dreams. The main reason most runners follow cyclical training methods is that training this way is more interesting than the same-thing-every-workout pattern followed by many runners. If I ran the same time, distance, pace, and route every day, I'd be bored out of my mind. Varying these parameters makes training much more interesting. It can also help pull you through the tough segments in a workout. When I'm finishing a set of 800-meter repeats on the track, for example, one thought that often motivates me is, "Tomorrow is my easy day—just four miles at conversation pace!" Similarly, after finishing a marathon, I'm thrilled to be able to enjoy a month or more of easy running—or no running at all if I choose.

• *Cyclical training can reduce the risk of injury.* Training in cycles allows the body to rest and recover between hard efforts—both on a day-to-day basis (you do a speed workout or race today, then run easy tomorrow) and from week to week and month to month (racing seasons are followed by weeks of rest and recovery with easy running). This pattern prevents the sort of continual buildup of physical stress that can cause the body to break down.

• *Cyclical training can follow the natural rhythm of the seasons.* In many areas, weather extremes in the summer and winter months make it a challenge to continue training at a high level year-round. Thanks to cyclical training, you don't have to. Many runners who train cyclically aim to peak twice a year (see "Peaking Twice a Year," below), in the spring and fall. Not coincidentally, this is when the majority of marathons are run, along with the bulk of road races at shorter distances. For years, I've trained for a spring marathon in February, March, and April, run the marathon in April or May, done a few short races in June, rested in July, trained for a fall marathon in August, September, and October, run the marathon in October or November, done a few short races in December, and rested in January. This pattern has kept me fresh, motivated, and relatively injury-free. It has also allowed me to relax and not worry about lost training during the months when the weather makes running at a high level particularly difficult.

### Making the Transition

You should make the shift from running without a plan to follow a cyclical program gradually and with care. The goal isn't so much to train harder (though you will improve your ability to put forth harder efforts at specific times) as to train smarter. It's quite common to become overtrained on a program that is not cyclical and does not work toward a peak performance. In other words, you can be suboptimally prepared for an important race, and at the same time exhausted and at high risk of injury and illness due to overtraining!

If you decide to shift your running from a noncyclical pattern to a cyclical program, I suggest taking the following steps:

• *Start maintaining a log if you're not already doing so.* See "Why Keep a Running Log?" in Chapter 1 for specific guidelines. A log will help you identify exactly how much running you are doing, and see patterns you are following.

• *Try to establish a consistent plan for your running and stick to it for several weeks.* As you've probably noticed, any number of things can—and do—get in the way of running: work, family responsibilities, etc. You can't always put running first. All runners struggle to maintain their training, not so much due to lack of fitness or motivation, but because life is unpredictable. Still, to become the best runner you can, you need to make room in your life to run regularly—in the morning, at midday, in the evening, whenever works for you. Write down what you think you can do (it should not differ drastically from what you are already doing), and try to stick to that plan for four weeks. If it's too much for your schedule, scale back until you find a pattern that works.

• *Think about your goals.* Where would you like to be with your running in three months, six months, a year, or even four or five years? Your goals may include specific race times you'd like to aim for, race distances you'd like to complete, or training goals, such as "run an average of 35 miles per week and feel comfortable doing it." Setting goals is an essential part of the process of establishing a progress-oriented training program.

## QUESTION AND ANSWER

**Q.** Tell me exactly what to do the week before a marathon.

**A.** Your premarathon week training depends on how you have trained and your previous experience running a marathon. The tapering schedules that are included with the two training programs on pages 83 and 84 are both sensible blueprints. If you have done a marathon before, look back at your log and judge what worked and what didn't. Some people like to take a few days completely off (no running or other exercise); others like to run a bit on all but the day before just to keep the feel and habit of it. Keep in mind that very few people reach mile 25 of a marathon thinking, "I must have tapered too much because I'm not tired enough!" It's also important to take care of yourself in other ways during premarathon week. To the extent that you are able, sleep well, eat healthily (for more on premarathon eating, see Chapter 7), and minimize stress. Don't do anything new or different, such as lifting heavy furniture, cleaning the gutters, or trying a new step-aerobics class. You'll feel the week's sum-total of fatigue and stress during the race, so try to husband as much of your physical and mental energy as you can.

## WHAT IS TAPERING, AND HOW DOES IT CONTRIBUTE TO A GREAT PERFORMANCE?

Tapering is the process of reducing your training before an important race. It allows your body to rest and stock up on fuel and fluid, and your mind to relax and focus on the task at hand without the distraction of regular hard training. The more important the race, the greater attention you must pay to your taper. In general, the longer the race distance, the longer the taper. Marathon and ultramarathon races in particular require a long and careful taper due to the need to stock stores of glycogen, the storage form of carbohydrate, which will be the body's primary fuel source during the race. (See Chapter 7 for more information and advice on prerace fueling.)

Most tapering plans encourage runners to cut down on the total volume of running and any other training and to reduce both the frequency and intensity of hard workouts. The training schedules included with this chapter follow this pattern. The main reason for reducing training volume is to allow the muscles to stock up their glycogen stores, while the main purpose of cutting down the frequency and intensity of hard workouts is to rest the muscles in preparation for the supreme challenge of race day.

Many runners find it hard to taper because it goes against their belief that the harder they work, the greater their chances of running well in their goal race. This planned rest is vital to success, in order to allow the body to realize fitness gains. To runners who do not fully understand the purposes of tapering, and who are inexperienced in doing it, tapering may not feel right. They may get antsy having so much extra time on their hands—time that would otherwise be spent running. They may begin to brood, and to second-guess their training and fitness level. They wonder whether they have logged enough miles, run enough interval sessions at the track, and chosen the optimal combination of tune-up races. They may suddenly have questions about other aspects of race preparation, such as fueling, hydrating, injury prevention. On top of all that, it seems that suddenly, everything hurts.

You must trust that tapering will allow you to race to your potential. You can do little to nothing to improve your fitness in the two to three weeks prior to your big race, and you may in fact sabotage all the hard work you've put in to get where you are. If you are less fit than you would like to be going into a race, then use that as motivation to train better during your next cycle. For this race, you should aim to consolidate the gains you've made during this cycle, and the best way to do this is with a well-planned taper.

### The Basic Cyclical Training Pattern

Runners and their coaches have devised innumerable ways of organizing training cycles to lead to peak performance with minimal risk of overtraining, illness, or injury. Every sound program with which I'm familiar includes the following five elements:

- building an aerobic base
- developing speed and running economy
- focusing on your specific race distance
- sharpening for peak performance(s)
- resting to recover after a peak effort

## HOW I PEAKED FOR A GREAT RACE

I had been running competitively at a high level for more than 10 years when I decided to have a baby. Because I'd had an irregular menstrual history (a common condition among elite women runners), I knew I'd have to sharply cut back on my running to conceive. In the spring of 1996 I shifted from heavy training and racing to running only 10 miles per week, along with some walking and water exercise. In late 1996 I found I was pregnant. I ran about 20 miles a week through most of the pregnancy, and gave birth to my first child in July 1997.

I was in no hurry to resume high-level running until I went to Houston in January 1998 to cover the women's national championship marathon. That race inspired me to start training seriously again, in an attempt to qualify for the 2000 U.S. Women's Olympic Marathon Trials, which required running a sub-2:50 marathon. (My best marathon ever is 2:33:01; in my most recent marathon before getting pregnant I'd run 2:39:08, so my work was cut out for me.) I chose the Vermont City Marathon, held in Burlington on May 24, as my target race, which gave me 18 weeks to prepare.

I had a solid aerobic base, so I was ready for the next phase of training: developing speed and running economy. I began by picking up the pace for 30 to 60 seconds at a time during my aerobic-intensity runs, just to get my legs used to moving quickly again. For two weeks I did this two or three times a week. I also entered two short races, a 5k and a 5-miler, to see exactly how fit (or unfit!) I was, so that I could plan my upcoming speed workouts accordingly.

Over the next three weeks I replaced my mid-run pickups with more structured short-speed workouts. It was winter, and therefore difficult to work out on an outdoor track, so I used measured 200-meter and 400-meter (about one quarter mile) areas on a cinder surface near my home. I raced again and found my fitness had improved, so I increased my mileage and the intensity of my short-speed workouts. Once or twice I went to an indoor track where I could run in shorts, with plenty of light, and in the company of other runners. I felt my speed coming back. My longest run during this phase was two hours (about 15 miles) at aerobic-intensity pace, which I found very challenging, as it was by far the longest exercise session I'd done in two years.

By mid-February I was ready to shift gradually to the next phase, focusing on the specific race distance. For the marathon that meant more long runs, and a shift in speed workouts from short and fast to longer and slightly slower. This was the toughest phase of training for me, because it had been two years since I'd done such high-level training. I listened carefully to my body as I ran long runs of up to 3 hours (once every week to two weeks), interval-intensity speed workouts of 3, 4, 5, and 6 minutes of hard effort interspersed with slightly shorter recovery intervals, and lactate-threshold intensity runs of between 8 and 25 minutes. I gradually increased my mileage and held it at about 70 miles for three weeks. I made my recovery days very easy (three or four miles at conversation pace) to allow my body to absorb this training without breaking down. I raced only twice during this phase (a 5k and a 10k), which lasted eight weeks. My race performances continued to improve.

By mid-April I was ready to begin intensifying my training. I cut back my mileage by about 20 percent, and chose three races in which to test my fitness and race-readiness: a 4-mile, a 10k, and a half-marathon. The first two went according to plan and showed me I was on target to run a marathon time that would qualify me for the Olympic Trials. I did a couple more long runs, continued with my interval-intensity and lactate-threshold intensity workouts (but less frequently than during the previous phase), and rested up for the half-marathon I'd scheduled for three weeks before the marathon.

This race did not go according to plan. The course was hillier than I'd anticipated, and the weather was unseasonably warm and humid. In addition, having suddenly felt that I had not trained hard and long enough for the marathon, I didn't rest adequately before the half-marathon, making it a physical and mental struggle just to finish. I ran 1:20:42, which predicted a marathon time that was slower than the Trials qualifying standard.

In the three weeks before the marathon I cut back my mileage by about 20 percent, then 35 percent, then 50 percent during the week before the race. I did two hard interval-intensity workouts, which went well. Feeling that my goal was still within reach, I started the marathon at a pace that would give me about a two-minute "cushion" to meet my goal of sub-2:50. I felt that I'd made the most of the 18 weeks of structured training by following a careful plan geared toward meeting a specific goal. I was lucky on race day in terms of the weather and other factors. I ran 2:42:51 and met my goal with plenty of time to spare. The performance showed me that peaking for a specific race does indeed work!

The main differences among the programs I've seen is in the ordering of the second and third elements. Some coaches and runners believe in waiting to focus on speed and running economy (accomplished primarily with short, fast intervals) until after developing the ability to run longer distances at a slower yet still sustained, hard pace (the skill that's most important for success in racing distances of 5k or longer). I've trained using both patterns, and prefer the former, which is the approach I outline in the program recommended here.

**Building an aerobic base.** In this stage runners develop their aerobic energy-delivery system. This is probably the most important phase of training. During this phase the focus is on aerobic-intensity running at "conversation pace." Some running at lactate-threshold pace is also included along with a very limited amount of high-intensity running to stress the ATP-CP system. Racing is kept to a minimum during this time, and done in a low-key manner. Though some programs give this phase 12 weeks, it typically lasts 6 to 8 weeks in most programs.

**Developing speed and running economy.** This phase introduces some fast running for short distances, with full recoveries, to develop the ability to move the legs quickly. Although most running is still done at aerobic intensity, once or twice weekly training will include repeated short runs (up to 400 meters for most runners) that allow the runner to work on proper form (for more on running form, see Chapter 5 on staying healthy). There's a long rest interval after each hard effort to allow the runner to fully recover for the next one. These workouts can be done on a track or other measured course, with a stopwatch, or up short hills. While this training is more challenging than aerobic-intensity running, it's not meant to be exhausting or to stress the lactate-threshold system. It introduces runners to the concept of running hard, yet controlled, and allows them to practice their form and get in touch with what it feels like to ask the body to move quickly on a regular basis. Racing is still not the focus here; although it's fine to race for fun and as a measure of progress, runners shouldn't expect to see their best results at this point. This phase lasts four to six weeks in the majority of training cycles.

**Focusing on your specific race distance.** In most programs, this is the toughest phase of the training cycle. Though aerobic-pace running still makes up the bulk of training, this phase focuses on workouts of repeated fast running at a slower pace but for a longer duration than the repeated short and fast runs emphasized during the previous phase. Runners can do this training in a variety of ways: on a track or other measured surface, with a stopwatch, up and down long hills, or as part of a training run using a watch or landmarks. The workouts focus on developing the lactate-threshold system, which is the energy-delivery system most crucial to success in races of distances 5k and longer. These workouts are done once or twice a week in most programs. In addition, the total volume of training increases during this phase. The frequency of racing may also be increased in preparation for the upcoming peak-racing season. However, peak performances don't usually occur at this point due to the heavy volume and intensity of training. This phase lasts six to eight weeks in most training cycles.

**Sharpening for peak performance(s).** At this point there is a gradual cutback on the volume and intensity of training in order to allow the body to rest and produce peak racing performances. This phase is the most fun and enjoyable because the bulk of the hard training work is done, and the runner now gets to reap the results. Most programs cut total training volume by at least 20 percent, and occasionally by as much as 50 percent for non-marathon-focus programs. The short, fast speed sessions emphasized in the second phase are eliminated or sharply reduced. Lactate-threshold running continues in most programs, though it's generally less frequent. Instead, the runner does mostly easy recovery running between peak-effort races. Resting to recover after a peak effort. This phase is essential—and often short-changed. During a peak racing season, a runner is most vulnerable to injury and illness due to the high-level demands on the body. Racing is also psychologically stressful. Runners vary greatly in their ability to sustain a racing peak—generally the range is two to six weeks, depending on the race distance emphasized and the fitness, background, and preferences of the runner. Most coaches urge runners to end this phase while they're still feeling great—as if they could do at least another great race or two—and before injury or illness strikes (see Chapter 5 for more on staying healthy).

**Resting to recover after a peak effort.** After you've put in a complete training cycle culminating in a peak racing season, the vast majority of coaches recommend pulling the plug, and taking four to six weeks off from racing and high-intensity training. During this phase focus on running simply for enjoyment and basic fitness maintenance. If you've trained and raced well, you'll probably welcome this break, and revel in it. If the results of your cycle have not lived up to your expectations, it may be harder to relax and take it easy. All runners struggle with this frustration. We tend to be driven people, and we tell ourselves that the reason we didn't meet our goals was that we just didn't work hard enough. That may be so, but this phase is not the time to try and rectify the situation. Training cycles seldom play out to perfection, but they are still physically and psychologically stressful. A rest period is a time for niggling pains to go away, muscle tissue to rebuild, and joints to heal. It's also a time for many runners to catch up on sleep, pursue other interests, and indulge in a slice of cake after dinner without worrying about whether their training will suffer. I recommend taking it easy for four weeks at the end of your racing season, and if you don't yet feel an enthusiasm for running at this point, take another couple of easy weeks.

### Two Examples of Training in Cycles

The two schedules below are reasonable for runners who must balance their training with a full-time job, student load, and/or homemaking and child-care responsibilities—nonprofessional runners, in other words. If your lifestyle, fitness, and goals are similar to those of the hypothetical runners presented under each schedule, you can use either of these programs as a training blueprint. Adjust the volume and intensity of training, and the frequency and pattern of racing, as needed. Remember, these programs are suggestions; though you should stick to them in principle you do not need to follow either to the letter to see progress in your training and success in your racing. If you have not run a marathon you need not plan to do two marathons a year, but you should train and prepare for your first marathon with a program lasting from 16 to 26 weeks.

### Implementing the Schedules

To implement either program, count the weeks back from the race or series of races for which you have chosen to peak. If you have a solid aerobic base you can jump into either program after the first four to seven weeks of the base-building phase. The other phases can be shortened by as much as 50 percent each if necessary. A four-week period of rest and recovery is recommended after completing either schedule. These four weeks will precede your next aerobic base-building period.

## QUESTION AND ANSWER

**Q.** I had to take a week off from running because of a hectic schedule. What should I do to come back?

**A.** Taking up to three days off from your regular running routine requires no special comeback routine; simply pick up with your normal schedule, without trying to "make up" the days you've lost. For a four- to eight-day break, most people should do short, easy runs for at least two days before doing any long or fast running. Be extra careful to warm up before and cool down after running as you come back, and if you feel pain in your muscles or joints, back off. If you race, do so conservatively, modifying your time goals. Never try to make up for lost running time; this could lead to injury or excessive fatigue.

### What About Mileage?

Recommended mileage is not included in either schedule, for several reasons. One, runners vary widely in their mileage needs and preferences. Some thrive on a high-mileage program that would cause injury, illness, or burnout to a runner of similar background and ability. Others need relatively little mileage in order to meet their goals, and view additional mileage as a waste of their time and energy. Two, runners also vary in the time they have to devote to running. Some runners can devote only a fraction of the amount of time to their running as other runners with similar goals. Trying to follow a training program that calls for a specific number of miles to be run each week—especially if the program calls for running those miles on specific days—when you simply don't have the time can be frustrating and ultimately counterproductive. Three, runners vary in the proportion of their training that they devote to cross-training. Trying to adhere to rigid mileage guidelines when you're spending a significant portion of your training time in the pool or on a bike can be challenging and unnecessary. (See Chapter 9 for more on cross-training.)

All this said, a runner must put in a minimum amount of mileage in order to perform adequately as a distance runner, particularly in longer races. Therefore, I've included recommended mileage guidelines with each schedule. Also, at the end of each week is a recommended percentage of maximum weekly mileage for that week. For example, if you are aiming for a maximum weekly mileage of 50 during the training cycle, and the figure in this column is 90 (percent), you will aim to do 90 percent of 50, or 45 miles that week. (All workouts should be preceded by a warm-up and followed by a cool-down. If you run the warm-up and cool-down, count them as part of your weekly mileage.)

Generally, the higher your training volume, the fewer "off" days you will have on your schedule. Thus, the "off" days on both schedules are suggested guidelines. If you are following a high-volume program, you should do short, easy runs (or cross-training) on most of these days—though I recommend that every runner take one day completely off from running and other exercise at least once every three weeks. If your training is relatively low-volume, add more "off" days on days marked "A" on the schedule.

This schedule is designed to work most easily for those who

work or have other responsibilities Monday through Friday, leaving more time available to train and race on the weekends. Thus, Day 1 corresponds to Monday, with Days 6 and 7 corresponding to Saturday and Sunday. Of course, Day 1 could correspond to any day of the week you wish, depending on your schedule.

## CHART #1: PEAKING TWICE A YEAR: POST-COLLEGIATE ROAD RACERS AIMING TO PEAK FOR MARATHONS

This is a suggested six-month (26-week) cyclical training program for a runner who is focusing on road racing at distances between 5k and the marathon, and intending to peak in a marathon twice per year. It is best used by someone who has successfully completed at least one marathon in under five hours, and is aiming to complete the next in four and a half hours or faster. If this is your first marathon, you do need this amount of time to properly prepare.

To start training, count back 26 weeks from your goal marathon. For example, if your marathon is scheduled for mid-April, Week 1 of this schedule would begin in mid-October of the previous year. I recommend a minimum average of 30 miles per week of running (or the equivalent in cross-training; see Chapter 9) in order to complete a marathon in 4:30 or faster. The schedule here works best for runners already averaging between 40 and 50 running miles per week, though it can accommodate a runner training at higher levels.

The schedule allots the following numbers of weeks to the training phases outlined in this chapter, with gradual transitions between the phases:

Establishing an aerobic base—8 weeks
Developing speed and running economy—4 weeks
Focusing on your specific race distance—8 weeks
Sharpening for peak performance—4 weeks
Tapering—2 weeks

| Week | Day 1 | Day 2 | Day 3 | Day 4 | Day 5 | Day 6 | Day 7 | %Max |
|------|-------|-------|-------|-------|-------|-------|-------|------|

**Building an aerobic base:**

| Week | Day 1 | Day 2 | Day 3 | Day 4 | Day 5 | Day 6 | Day 7 | %Max |
|------|-------|-------|-------|-------|-------|-------|-------|------|
| 1–3 | off | A | A | off | A | A | A | 40–60 |
| 4–5 | off | A | A/S | A | off | L | A/S | 50–65 |
| 6–7 | off | A/S | LT | A/S | A | L | A/S | 55–70 |
| 8 | off | A | AC | A/S | A | LT or R | A/S | 55–70 |

**Developing speed and running economy:**

| Week | Day 1 | Day 2 | Day 3 | Day 4 | Day 5 | Day 6 | Day 7 | %Max |
|------|-------|-------|-------|-------|-------|-------|-------|------|
| 9 | off | AC | A/S | A | LT | A | L | 60–75 |
| 10 | off | AC | A | A | AC | A | LT | 60–75 |
| 11 | off | AC | A/S | A | A | AC or R | A/S | 65–80 |
| 12 | off | I | A | A/S | AC | A | L | 65–80 |

**Focusing on your specific race distance:**

| Week | Day 1 | Day 2 | Day 3 | Day 4 | Day 5 | Day 6 | Day 7 | %Max |
|------|-------|-------|-------|-------|-------|-------|-------|------|
| 13 | off | I | A/S | A | AC | A | I or R | 70–85 |
| 14 | off | LT | A/S | A | I | A | L | 70–85 |
| 15 | off | I | A/S | A | A | L | A/S | 75–90 |
| 16 | off | I | A | LT | A | A | I or R | 75–90 |
| 17 | off | AC | A | A | I | A | L | 80–95 |
| 18 | off | LT | A | I | A | L | A/S | 80–95 |
| 19 | off | I | A | LT | A | A | I or R | 85–100 |
| 20 | off | AC | A | I | A/S | L | A | 85–100 |

**Sharpening for peak performance:**

| Week | Day 1 | Day 2 | Day 3 | Day 4 | Day 5 | Day 6 | Day 7 | %Max |
|------|-------|-------|-------|-------|-------|-------|-------|------|
| 21 | off | A | I | A | A | R or L | A | 80–95 |
| 22 | off | I | A | LT | A | R or L | A | 75–90 |
| 23 | off | A | I | A | A | R or L | A | 70–85 |
| 24 | off | I | A | LT | A | R or I | A | 65–80 |

**Tapering:**

| Week | Day 1 | Day 2 | Day 3 | Day 4 | Day 5 | Day 6 | Day 7 | %Max |
|------|-------|-------|-------|-------|-------|-------|-------|------|
| 25 | off | A | LT | A | off | A | A | 55–65 |
| 26 | A | A | I | off | A | off | GOAL | 25–35* |

* not including marathon

## CHART #2: PEAKING THREE TIMES A YEAR: POST-COLLEGIATE TRACK OR ROAD RACERS COMPETING YEAR-ROUND

The following 4-month (17-week) schedule trains a moderately fit runner to progress through the phases outlined in the chapter's main text, to a peak of running one to four 3000-meter to 10,000-meter track races, or 5k to half-marathon road races. The lengths of the phases can be adjusted based on the distance of the goal race(s): Those wishing to peak for the half-marathon or 10-mile distance probably should have a longer buildup period (up to eight weeks) and a longer taper (up to three weeks).

This schedule can be repeated up to three times per year. To start training, count back 17 weeks from your goal race or race series. For example, if your goal race is mid-June, Week 1 of this schedule would be mid-February.

This plan is best used by someone who has successfully completed at least two or three 5k or 4-mile and one 10k, 15k or 10-mile races without walking breaks, and who is aiming to complete a 10k in an hour or faster, a 10-mile in 1:42, or a half-marathon in under 2:10. I recommend a minimum average of 20–25 miles per week of running (or the equivalent in cross-training) to complete a 10k in one hour or faster. The schedule here works best for runners averaging between 30 and 45 running miles per week, though it can accommodate a runner training at higher levels.

The schedule allots the following numbers of weeks to the training phases outlined in this chapter:

Establishing an aerobic base—4 weeks
Developing speed and running economy—4 weeks
Focusing on your specific race distance(s)—4 weeks
Sharpening for peak performance—4 weeks
Tapering—1 week

| Week | Day 1 | Day 2 | Day 3 | Day 4 | Day 5 | Day 6 | Day 7 | %Max |
|------|-------|-------|-------|-------|-------|-------|-------|------|
| **Building an aerobic base:** | | | | | | | | |
| 1–2 | off | A | A/S | A | off | L | A/S | 50–65 |
| 3–4 | off | A/S | LT | A/S | A | L | A/S | 55–70 |
| **Developing speed and running economy:** | | | | | | | | |
| 5 | off | AC | A/S | A | LT | A | L | 60–75 |
| 6 | off | AC | A | A | AC | A | LT | 60–75 |
| 7 | off | AC | A/S | A | A | AC or R | A/S | 65–80 |
| 8 | off | I | A | A/S | AC | A | L | 65–80 |
| **Focusing on your specific race distance:** | | | | | | | | |
| 9 | off | I | A/S | A | A | L | A/S | 75–90 |
| 10 | off | I | A | LT | A | A | I or R | 80–95 |
| 11 | off | AC | A | A | I | A | L | 85–100 |
| 12 | off | LT | A | I | A | L | A/S | 85–100 |
| **Sharpening for peak performance:** | | | | | | | | |
| 13 | off | A | I | A | A | R | A | 80–95 |
| 14 | off | I | A | LT | A | R or L | A | 75–90 |
| 15 | off | A | I | A | A | R | A | 70–85 |
| 16 | off | I | A | LT | A | R or I | A | 65–80 |
| **Tapering:** | | | | | | | | |
| 17 | A | A | I | off | A | off | GOAL | 35–50* |

(this week can be repeated up to three times, if race performances remain consistent)

* not including goal race

## Key (see main text for more complete descriptions of training elements)

*A = aerobic-intensity running or cross-training*
These are training sessions designed to promote recovery and maintain basic aerobic fitness. They should last from 30 to 90 minutes, depending on total training volume, and are done at a "conversational" pace.

*AC = ATP-CP intensity running*
These sessions are designed to increase speed without overtaxing endurance. They consist of runs lasting up to two minutes, with

recovery intervals (walking or slow jogging) after each run long enough to complete the workout at a consistent intensity.

### I = Interval-intensity running

Interval-intensity running is not as fast as ATP-CP intensity running, but faster than lactate-threshold intensity running. For most runners this is the intensity at which they race the 5k to 10k distances. The training intervals last from about 2 minutes to 7 minutes for most runners, and are separated by rest periods of 90 seconds to 4 minutes, depending on the workout composition and the runner's background and fitness.

### L = long run

Long runs increase endurance and condition the body to keep working when fatigued. In this program, long runs should be 20–30 percent of total weekly mileage, done at an aerobic intensity. For most runners who are training for a marathon, the longest run is two to three-and-a-half hours of continuous running. For most runners who are training for 10k, 10-miles, or the half-marathon, the long run is one-and-a-half to two-and-a-half hours. The longer runs should be concentrated toward the end of the cycle, with the longest run done only once or twice (not in successive weeks) during the cycle.

### LT = lactate-threshold intensity running

Lactate-threshold intensity running conditions the body to work at an intensity that produces lactate in quantities that contribute to a gradual, steady buildup of fatigue. This training increases the lactate threshold (the point at which lactate buildup increases dramatically), which is the single best way to build fitness for distance racing. Lactate-threshold runs of 7 to 30 minutes work best.

### R = race

Races can be either tune-up efforts with very little rest or tapering beforehand, or harder efforts with greater rest, as a way of testing mid-season fitness.

### S = strides

Strides are short (100 meters or less) intervals of running at a pace between aerobic intensity and all-out sprinting. They are designed to increase running efficiency and provide a transition in the training cycle between aerobic base-building and the more strenuous phases of training. Between 6 and 10 strides are recommended, separated by 30–60 seconds of walking or light jogging.

### Suggested Workouts

Choose from the following suggested workouts when planning your lactate-threshold, interval-intensity, and ATP-CP-intensity sessions. Vary your workouts from week to week to prevent boredom. If you run on a measured surface such as a track, you can adjust the workouts so that you're running distances rather than times, for the sake of simplicity. Always warm up before and cool down after workouts.

### Suggested LT workouts:
- 20–30 minutes at LT intensity
- 10–14 minutes at LT intensity, 1–2 minutes at A intensity, 8–14 minutes at LT intensity
- 7–12 minutes at LT intensity, repeated three times, interspersed with 1–2 minutes at A intensity

### Suggested I workouts:
- 6 minutes at I intensity, repeated three to four times, interspersed with 4 minutes at A intensity
- 4 minutes at I intensity, repeated five to six times, interspersed with 3 minutes at A intensity
- 3 minutes at I intensity, repeated 6 to 8 times, interspersed with 2.5 minutes at A intensity
- ladder of 1 minute, 2 minutes, 3 minutes, 4 minutes, 5 minutes, 4 minutes, 3 minutes, 2 minutes, 1 minute, all at I intensity, interspersed with equal recoveries at A intensity

### Suggested AC workouts (workout volume should be 4–5% of total weekly mileage):
- 2 minutes at AC intensity, with full recoveries (2–3 minutes)
- 1 minute at AC intensity, with full recoveries (2–3 minutes)
- alternating 2 minutes/1 minute at AC intensity, with full recoveries
- ladder of 30 seconds, 1 minute, 90 seconds, 2 minutes, 90 seconds, 1 minute, 30 seconds, all at AC intensity, with full recoveries

CHAPTER 4

▶ ▶ ▶ ▶ ▶ ▶ ▶ ▶ ▶ ▶ ▶ ▶ ▶ ▶ ▶ ▶ ▶ ▶ ▶ ▶ ▶ ▶ ▶ ▶ ▶ ▶ ▶ ▶

# *The Right Stuff*

*I* love the fact that I don't need a lot of fancy equipment to run well and derive pleasure from my running. The essential gear items are a good pair of running shoes, and clothing that offers protection from the elements.

That said, runners are no different from any other sports enthusiasts in that most of us like stuff. Our gear—from shoes to stopwatches to water carriers—defines us as runners. Proper equipment can also greatly enhance the joy of running, not to mention running performance.

This chapter offers guidelines for finding and regularly updating your running gear. Without going into detail about specific products and brands, it's a "real world" guide to what is available to the runner concerned with having the most functional, safest, and (in some cases) most stylish running gear. (Product resources and contact information are included in the Resources section.)

### What You Need to Know About Running Shoes

The one absolutely necessary piece of equipment for any runner is a pair of high-quality running shoes that fit properly and address the individual runner's unique biomechanical needs. Entire books have been written about running shoes, and most running magazines regularly include guides to choosing and purchasing shoes for both training and racing. Here is a guide to the key information you need to select, purchase, and care for shoes for all of your training and racing needs.

### A Short History of Running Shoes

The present-day running shoe is an outstanding example of a product that has evolved over time to meet the unique needs of its users. Running shoes allow runners of all sizes, shapes, foot types, and fitness backgrounds to withstand the rigors of running hundreds, if not thousands, of miles per year in relative comfort and safety. To be sure, some running shoes have qualities and features that are silly at best, and injurious to the runner at worst. Still, even the most inferior running shoes these days is a far sight better than those worn by runners—even those at the world-class level—a generation ago.

Before the 1960s, it was not unusual for runners, even in

Olympic and other championship-level events, to fail to finish, or finish in agonizing pain, due to the poor quality of their shoes. Most running shoes were flimsy canvas uppers attached to rubber soles, and came apart when subjected to pounding and slapping over long distances. Other shoes were leather contraptions that slowed the runners down because of their weight and construction. Miki Gorman, two-time winner of both the New York City and Boston marathons, recalls that when she started running in the late 1960s, "My first running shoes were a pair of leather Adidas that I had to cut because they were so heavy and painful." (She made cuts in the toe area to prevent blisters and removed parts of the soles to reduce weight.) Seams and other protrusions caused blisters so severe that runners were forced to abandon longer races such as the marathon. Shoes had little "give" when they came in contact with the ground, little or nothing in the way of arch support, and modest or nonexistent cushioning around the heel, on the top of the foot, and in the toe area.

The main reason more runners weren't injured by their shoes in those days is that running used to be much more of an elite sport. Those few people who pursued running seriously tended to be thin and have a very efficient running stride. This type of runner is the least likely to incur an injury, no matter how poor his or her equipment.

Starting in the early 1970s there was a huge influx of nonelite runners into the running ranks. This new running population was made up primarily of people who were pursuing the activity for the first time. For the most part they were out of shape, and knew little to nothing about running, including what to wear on their feet. They figured out quickly that running didn't always feel good. They didn't mind so much that it made them breathless and exhausted, but they minded a great deal when running hurt their feet, ankles, knees, hips, and back. Not to mention that it hurt their pocketbooks when their new running shoes fell apart after mere weeks of use.

Clearly, running shoes had to be drastically improved. The first efforts to produce better shoes were mixed. Most runners who were involved in the sport before 1980 owned at least one pair of shoes that frayed or split, were as stiff as a board, produced instant blisters, or simply fell apart.

As the industry matured, the overall quality of running shoes began to improve, and the number and range of choices available increased. Today, runners are more likely to complain that there are too many shoes available, rather than too few, and that shoe manufacturers persist in "updating" perfectly good models. In fact, today this practice of needless updating is the number-one complaint runners voice about running shoes, according to running shoe expert J. D. Denton, a senior writer at *Running Times* magazine. The problem is that as soon as a runner finds a shoe that works for him or her, the model is changed—updated—and the search must begin all over again.

Some experts also voice concern that today's running shoes provide an excess of support and cushioning, which prevents the foot from functioning naturally while running. In particular, they say, the built-up heels now common in running shoes have caused the Achilles tendons (located in the back of the ankle) in many runners to shorten, tighten, and weaken. This, they contend, has caused an increase in the number of running injuries, particularly in the feet and lower legs. Though there may be some merit to this argument, it's certainly no case for reverting to the running shoes of yesteryear. Most runners who purchase the correct running shoes for their feet (see guidelines below) need not worry about getting injured by their shoes.

### Why You Need Shoes Specifically Designed for Running

Raise your hand if you took your first run wearing something other than running shoes on your feet! I wore tennis shoes for my first few months of running in 1977. Although in those days running shoes weren't much better than tennis shoes, the ache in my shins did lessen after I switched to running shoes.

Runners should do all their running in running shoes *only*. In an emergency you may run short distances in cross-training shoes, walking shoes, moccasins, sports sandals, or other supportive, low- or no-heeled nondress shoes. You should, however, stop running as soon as you can. (Just think how embarrassing it would be to tell your running friends that you injured yourself running in dress shoes.)

Running shoes offer the following features (listed from the

ground up) that make them the only acceptable footwear for regular running for health, fitness, or competition:

• *Outsole.* This is the bottom of the shoe, the part that comes in contact with the ground. The outsole should have plenty of traction and be hard enough to resist wear, yet flexible enough to bend with the foot's natural roll from heel-strike to toe-off. It is usually made of carbon rubber or expanded rubber, durable materials that resist abrasion.

• *Heel plug.* Sometimes considered part of the outsole, the heel plug is the first part of the shoe to contact the ground on each footstrike. Almost always made of a hard carbon-rubber material, it can extend up to half the length of the bottom of the shoe.

• *Midsole.* More than any other component, the midsole makes the running shoe unique among sports shoes. Its function is to provide the shoe with cushioning, support, and flexibility. The primary material of most midsoles is either ethylene vinyl acetate (EVA) or polyurethane (PU), both of which are firm, yet flexible and shock-absorbing. A foam, gel, air pocket(s), or other material may be imbedded within the midsole. The exact composition, configuration, density, thickness, and weight of the midsole determine the most significant differences among the hundreds of running shoes on the market today. Compared to other sports shoe midsoles, the midsole of the running shoe is thicker and wider in the heel, lighter, more flexible, better cushioned, and offers less support for lateral (side to side) movement. All these properties help running shoes withstand the repetitive, pounding motions of running.

• *Last.* A shoe's last is the hard, molded form in the shape of the bottom of the foot. Running-shoe lasts fall into two general categories: straight and curved. The last may be left in the shoe (board lasted), partially removed (combination lasted), or completely removed (slip lasted). In running shoes, the designations curve lasted and straight lasted have become less meaningful over the years due to the increased importance of differences among midsoles. Some experts suggest ignoring the slip vs. board differentiations altogether. In my experience, the differences are not terribly meaningful.

• *Insole.* The insole is the bed inside the shoe on which your foot rests. It provides comfort and absorbs perspiration. Running-shoe insoles are lightweight, very flexible, and can be removed to allow the shoe to accommodate an orthotic device (see Chapter 5 for more on orthotic devices), and replaced for greater cushioning.

• *Heel counter.* The heel counter surrounds and supports the heel. Its purpose is to hold the heel in place, allowing for minimal slipping without squeezing the heel so tightly that it cannot move or hurts when you run. The heel counter also protects the heel from the impact of the foot strike. It is usually made of a hard plastic material imbedded within the upright part of the heel at the back of the shoe. When you squeeze the back of the shoe, the heel counter should yield only slightly to the pressure of your fingers.

• *Toe box.* This is the area surrounding the toes and the front part of the foot. Its purpose is to protect the front of the foot. The toe box should be roomy enough to allow your toes plenty of room to wiggle without feeling squeezed either on top or on the sides. Follow the "rule of thumb" when sizing the toe box by making sure there is at least a thumb's width between your longest toe and the front of the shoe.

• *Ankle collar.* This is the rim around the top of the shoe through which you slip your foot when putting on the shoe. The ankle collar should grip the ankle firmly, but not tightly.

• *Upper.* Technically, the upper is everything above the shoe's midsole, including the heel counter and ankle collar, the tongue, the laces or other size-adjusting system, and the toe box. Most uppers are made of a combination of lightweight, breathable materials such as nylon mesh, and more sturdy materials such as leather or suede for durability. Seams should be double-stitched, and there should be a strong seal between the upper and the sole.

### How to Select and Purchase Running Shoes

You've probably heard that runners should not "go it alone" when buying running shoes. The main reason for this is that running shoes are constantly evolving, with dozens of new models coming on the market every season. More importantly, the knowledge and perspective that a trained salesperson brings to the shoe-buying experience will help you find and select the best shoes for your unique biomechanical profile. Finally, trying on and running in a shoe is invaluable in making your purchasing decision. Keep in mind, too, that feet change over time, getting bigger and wider in most people. Even if you are "sure" you know your running-shoe size, type, and brand preference, making your purchases at a running specialty store will help ensure you are getting the shoes that are best for your feet.

Here's what matters most when selecting running shoes:

• *Fit.* This is far and away the most important factor. If a shoe does not fit and feel comfortable when you put it on, lace it up, and jog around in it, it's not the right shoe for you. A shoe's fit refers not only to the proper length (there should be plenty of room in the toe box for the toes to wiggle, and at least a thumb's width between the end of your longest toe and the front of the shoe) and width (many running shoes come in varying widths), but also to how it feels against the bottom of your foot, across the top of your foot, in the heel, and around the ankle. A shoe that feels too tight, too loose, or otherwise not right in any of these areas isn't the right shoe for you. Unlike street shoes, running shoes don't soften, stretch, and become more comfortable over time.

• *Foot type.* Foot type refers to how your foot moves through each running stride. All feet pronate, or roll inward, between the moment the heel first contacts the ground and when the toes push off. Part of a running shoe's job is to control that pronation. There are three main categories used to describe degree of pronation: severe overpronator, moderate overpronator, and underpronator. There are three main categories of running shoes that are best for the corresponding foot types: motion control/

stability, cushioned, and neutral/flexible. Feet that overpronate severely (that is, roll inward excessively) require shoes with the greatest degree of motion control and stability. Feet that pronate moderately require less motion control and stability, more cushioning, and some flexibility. Feet that underpronate require very little motion control and stability, and quite a bit of flexibility. Though the terms may vary—and this can cause confusion—the bottom line is that the more you pronate, the more you need a shoe that controls that motion. The less you pronate, the more you need a shoe that cushions your foot, then bends with it as it goes through its naturally efficient foot-strike-to-toe-off motion. If you buy your shoes at a running specialty store, a salesperson will probably observe your feet from behind as you stand and run, to determine your degree of pronation. He or she will then probably have you try on several models in your category and help you make your selection.

### DO YOU NEED A RACING SHOE?

For many runners, the primary reason for racing is to cover ground as quickly as possible. Therefore, runners often assume they should wear shoes designed to go fast when racing. However, the features of racing shoes that allow you to run fast—light weight and flexibility—make them unsuitable for many runners, even for occasional use. I ran for seven years before I wore racing flats for the first time. Even then, for the first three years I wore them solely for racing, and continued to do all my speed workouts in training shoes. When I switched to racing flats for speed workouts I did run the sessions faster, but I would feel particularly sore and beat up the next day. These days, as a 40-year-old runner, I'm back to doing many speed workouts in my training shoes.

Use the following guidelines when deciding whether or not to wear racing shoes (also frequently called racing flats) when racing:

- *Racing shoes offer less cushioning and support.* Compared to shoes worn for training, racing shoes have thinner and/or less durable outsole, often with some materials cut away, a less-cushioned midsole with a lower heel elevation, and lighter-weight upper materials. Heavy runners and overpronators are more likely to feel these differences. Nothing slows down your running more than an injury. The few seconds per mile that you may gain from wearing racing flats will be lost when you're forced to take time off for an injury to heal.

- *A lightweight trainer may be suitable for racing.* If you're a heavily built runner, an overpronator, or frequently injured, and don't want to risk wearing racing flats, consider training in a motion control/stability shoe, and using a neutral/flexibility trainer for your racing and speed workouts. The lighter weight and less-rigid construction may offer you a speed boost without significantly increasing your risk of injury. Consider also that racing flats designed for longer races, such as half-marathons and marathons, offer more cushioning and support than those designed for shorter races (10k and under).

- *Ease into using racing flats.* Try them for just a portion of your first few speed workouts. Be careful when wearing them on small or tight tracks and hard surfaces, such as concrete. Don't wear them in a race (especially an important peak competition), without first trying them in training.

- *Wear racing flats sparingly.* Warm up for races and speed workouts in your training shoes. If you are "running through" a race as a workout, and therefore not overly concerned with your time, wear your training shoes. Wear training shoes instead of racing flats when coming back from an injury. Consider wearing training shoes in longer races, such as half-marathons and marathons, and saving your racing flats for shorter races and speed workouts only.

• *Replace racing flats frequently.* To provide optimal support and cushioning, they need replacing after fewer miles than training shoes. Replace them as soon as you feel the support in the midsole start to go (see page 100) for more on determining when it's time to replace running shoes).

Here's what doesn't matter—or matters less than some runners, shoe manufacturers, and misinformed salespeople might lead you to believe:

• *Shoe weight.* Shoes vary in weight by no more than a few ounces. Shoe buying guides in most running publications usually list a shoe's weight, and I've never understood why. Motion-control/stability shoes tend to be heavier than cushioned shoes, which in turn tend to be heavier than neutral/flexible shoes. You may be tempted to buy a lighter shoe because you think it will help you run faster. Injury or discomfort may result at the very least. Besides, the difference in weight will not significantly affect your running. (When racing, however, you may want to consider a lighter shoe; see "Do You Need a Racing Shoe?" on page 96.)

• *Price.* Alas, running shoes are not cheap. The $100 mark was passed years ago, and shoes costing $150 and higher are not unusual these days. You will pay slightly more for shoes purchased at a running specialty store, but as noted above, the extra expense is well worth it for the service you will most likely receive. You should not buy a shoe based on its price. If a discounted shoe is not the correct size and type for your foot, do not buy it. On the other hand, more expensive shoes are not necessarily better than those costing less. Motion-control/stability shoes tend to cost a bit more than cushioned and neutral/flexibility shoes, not because they are "better," but because they have more materials and sometimes more sophisticated constructions. However, if your foot does not pronate excessively, wearing this type of shoe will be uncomfortable at best, and injury-inducing at worst. A friend who works in a New York City running specialty store tells of one regular customer, a well-known fashion designer, who always insists on buying the most expensive running shoes. "They cost the most, so they must be the best," he says. The Gucci crowd isn't likely to change its thoughts on such matters, but when it comes to running shoes, the reasoning doesn't hold.

• *Brand.* "Which brand of running shoe is best?" I'm often asked. Among those you will see displayed on the wall of most running specialty stores, there is no "best" company. All use the same basic technologies, materials, and constructions. Some runners develop loyalties to a particular brand because shoes of that brand have tended to work well for them over the years. Certainly, if a brand of shoe works for you, stick with it. If not, don't take another runner's advice, but rather seek out your own "best" brand and model. Remember, every foot is different.

• *Midsole enhancements.* Many midsoles include gel, air pockets, or other shock-absorbing materials. Although manufacturers claim that these features improve a shoe's cushioning, the most effective shock-absorbing materials in the midsole, EVA and/or PU, are present in all running shoes. The "extra" materials should not be the basis of your decision to purchase a certain shoe.

When purchasing running shoes, follow these guidelines to minimize your chances of wasting your money or—worse—ending up with a shoe that causes injury:

• *Visit a running specialty store.* This offers you the best chance of buying shoes that fit and meet your foot type. You may be tempted by the lower prices and convenient location of a general sporting goods store. However, the staff at such outlets generally are trained to sell running shoes to runners. Your salesperson will be unlikely to know much about pronation, motion control, stability, cushioning, and other factors that can help you select the best running shoe for your foot. If you purchase shoes from a catalogue or online, be sure you know your foot size and type, and have tried on the model you are buying. Running specialty stores are more likely than general sporting goods stores to stock a large variety of models and brands in a wide range of sizes and widths. The salespeople in running specialty stores usually are runners, and are trained specifically in selling shoes to runners. And, knowing the importance of word of mouth among runners, the owners and managers are more likely to respond positively if a problem develops.

• *Be prepared.* Bring along your old shoes for the salesperson to examine for wear patterns. Bring the socks you run in to help ensure proper fit. Know your shoe history—which brands and models have and haven't worked for you—and your injury history.

### How to Care for Your Running Shoes

The expense of running shoes, the comfort of familiar shoes, and the challenge of finding a new best pair for you can tempt many runners to hang on to running shoes for longer than they should. Runners make other mistakes that can cause shoes to decline in function, inviting pain and injury. Follow these guidelines in caring for your shoes:

• *Ease into wearing new shoes.* Though running shoes don't generally need an extensive "breaking in" period, wear them for short easy runs the first few times out to make sure the shoes really do work well on your feet. New running shoes should not hurt or cause cramping, blisters, or significant soreness. If you have a problem with the shoes on your first few runs, take them back. Most running specialty stores will offer you a new pair without charge.

• *Replace shoes at least every 500 to 600 miles.* Most running shoes lose their utility for running long before they look ready for the dustbin. Shoes are ready to retire when the midsole materials have compressed to the point where the shoes no longer offer adequate cushioning and support. A shoe with a compressed midsole will be noticeably thinner than a new shoe of the same model, and will lean inward slightly when placed on a level surface. They will also simply feel less cushioned and supportive. You can feel this difference if you buy two new pairs at the same time and wear one pair regularly, the other only occasionally. When you can feel a definite difference in the support and cushioning offered by the two pairs, replace the worn pair. Or you can buy just one pair, and replace it when you start to notice pain in your feet, ankles, or shins (this is risky if you have a high pain tolerance or a strong sense of denial). Another strategy is to make a note in your running log when you purchase new shoes, or write the date of purchase on the shoe itself, in ink. Keep track of your mileage as an indicator of when you need new shoes. Some runners, such as severe overpronators, should replace shoes about every 400 miles. The extra money you spend is only a fraction of what you would end up paying a doctor to diagnose and treat an injury caused by running in worn-out shoes.

• *Clean shoes sparingly.* Water can compromise shoe materials. If your shoes get really dirty or muddy, clean them with a damp cloth or small brush such as an old toothbrush. Dry shoes out of direct sunlight and away from heat sources such as heaters. Place wadded-up newspapers or paper towels inside shoes (remove the insoles) to speed drying. Do not place your shoes in an oven, microwave, or clothes dryer. Most runners have at least two pairs of shoes—a spare if one pair is wet.

• *Don't let the outsole wear down excessively.* Runners with a heavy heel strike may wear down the lateral side of the outsole in the heel area before the shoes are ready to retire. You can purchase a urethane shoe-repair product to shore up the outsole and get more wear from the shoe.

• *Donate old running shoes to charity, or recycle them.* Most used running shoes are still fine for wearing around. Keep a pair or two for gardening, lounging, etc., and give others to the Salvation Army, a homeless shelter, or another organization that can use them, or ask your local running specialty store about projects to recycle old shoes.

## TRAIL-RUNNING SHOES

Trail-running shoes have become extraordinarily popular in recent years. Like regular running shoes, not all trail shoes are worn for trail running. They're very popular among high school and college students, who wear them mainly for walking around campus.

If you run on trails, do you need a trail-running shoe? In most cases, no. Most trail shoes have more substantial ankle support than non-trail shoes, along with a water-resistant upper, a tongue and lacing system designed to keep out debris, and a reinforced toe box. These features protect the feet and ankles from rocky, uneven surfaces, water, and mud, but also make trail shoes heavier and stiffer than the average road-running shoe. If you do all or most of your running on trails that are rocky, rutted, uneven, wet, or muddy, then you will probably benefit from wearing a trail shoe in terms of being better protected and less susceptible to injury. The trade-off is extra weight and stiffness. If you are a part-time trail runner or you run on wide, smooth, well-maintained trails, then your regular running shoes are most likely just fine.

## QUESTION AND ANSWER

**Q.** What should I look for in a running bra?

**A.** The running—or sports—bra has developed remarkably since the 1970s, when one of the first manufacturers designed a prototype by sewing together two men's jock straps. Today's bras aim to fit, support, and flatter active women of all shapes and sizes without chafing, binding, or otherwise making their presence felt. Expect to pay $20 to $30 for a good sports bra, which should last six months to a year, depending on use, before the elastic starts to give and chafing occurs due to wear. Look for the following features:

- **Fit.** Running bras are sized either as S, M, and L, or by rib cage and cup size like traditional bras. Try on a bra before purchasing. Straps should not be loose, and the breast should fill out the shape of cupped bras (made primarily for C- and D-sized women). Expect a bit of shrinkage in a bra that contains cotton. Adjustable shoulder straps are a plus—they are not standard in most sports bras.

- **Support.** Look for a "high impact" label in the side panel, meaning that the bra is designed to support the breast in activities that include up-and-down movement. When you try on a bra, jump up and down while wearing it, run a few steps, swing your arms, and twist your body to make sure it

offers support. You may feel silly, but these are the activities you'll be doing when you wear the bra to work out.
- **Comfort.** You'll want a bra made of light, breathable fabric such as nylon mesh for warm-weather wear, and probably something warmer (which also means more supportive) in the cold. The inner lining and the fabric that encases the elastic around the chest should be made of a wicking material to help prevent moisture buildup that can lead to chafing. Look for wide shoulder straps that don't cut or bind. Seams should be soft and plush to minimize irritation to the skin. You can minimize chafing by applying a skin lubricant around the armholes and neck and under the elastic chest band.

## QUESTION AND ANSWER

**Q.** Is it ever too cold to run outdoors?

**A.** It can be, in extreme conditions. In deciding whether to run outdoors in the cold, you must consider not just the air temperature, but the windchill as well. The chart below notes, for example, that frostbite is unlikely to occur at a 10 to 15 degrees Fahrenheit if it's only slightly windy, but that it is likely to result at those temperatures if there is a wind of 35 m.p.h. or stronger. If you are running when frostbite is a risk, cover all exposed flesh and keep your run short and close to home, so you can bail out if necessary. Be careful of icy patches that can cause slipping and falling, and make sure to warm up thoroughly to minimize the risk of pulling or tearing of stiff, cold muscles.

## The Windchill Factor

"Windchill" is the term used to describe the rate of heat loss on the human body resulting from the combined effect of low temperature and wind. As winds increase, heat is carried away from the body at a faster rate, driving down the skin temperature and eventually the internal body temperature. Exposure to low windchills can be life-threatening.

### EQUIVALENT TEMPERATURE (F°)

| Wind Speed MPH | 35 | 30 | 25 | 20 | 15 | 10 | 5 | 0 | −5 | −10 | −15 | −20 | −25 | −30 | −35 | −40 | −45 |
|---|---|---|---|---|---|---|---|---|---|---|---|---|---|---|---|---|---|
| Calm | 35 | 30 | 25 | 20 | 15 | 10 | 5 | 0 | −5 | −10 | −15 | −20 | −25 | −30 | −35 | −40 | −45 |
| | | COLD | | | | | | | | | | | | | | | |
| 5 | 32 | 27 | 22 | 16 | 11 | 6 | 0 | −5 | −10 | −15 | −21 | −26 | −31 | −36 | −42 | −47 | −52 |
| | | | | VERY COLD | | | | | | | | | | | | | |
| 10 | 22 | 16 | 10 | 3 | −3 | −9 | −15 | −22 | −27 | −34 | −40 | −46 | −52 | −58 | −64 | −71 | −77 |
| | | | | BITTER COLD | | | | | | | | | | | | | |
| 15 | 16 | 9 | 2 | −5 | −11 | −18 | −25 | −31 | −38 | −45 | −51 | −58 | −65 | −72 | −78 | −85 | −92 |
| 20 | 12 | 4 | −3 | −10 | −17 | −24 | −31 | −39 | −46 | −53 | −60 | −67 | −74 | −81 | −88 | −95 | −103 |
| | | | | | EXTREME COLD | | | | | | | | | | | | |
| 25 | 8 | 1 | −7 | −15 | −22 | −29 | −36 | −44 | −51 | −59 | −66 | −74 | −81 | −88 | −96 | −103 | −110 |
| 30 | 6 | −2 | −10 | −18 | −25 | −33 | −41 | −49 | −56 | −64 | −71 | −79 | −86 | −93 | −101 | −109 | −116 |
| 35 | 4 | −4 | −12 | −20 | −27 | −35 | −43 | −52 | −58 | −67 | −74 | −82 | −89 | −97 | −105 | −113 | −120 |
| 40 | 3 | −5 | −13 | −21 | −29 | −37 | −45 | −53 | −60 | −69 | −76 | −84 | −92 | −100 | −107 | −115 | −123 |
| 45 | 2 | −6 | −14 | −22 | −30 | −38 | −46 | −54 | −62 | −70 | −78 | −85 | −93 | −102 | −109 | −117 | −125 |

### WINDCHILL CHART

Source: National Weather Service

## *What to Wear to Take on the Elements*

Unless you run exclusively indoors on a treadmill, running gets you up close and personal with the weather. As a runner I relish the chance to be out in the sun, wind, rain, snow, or whatever else Mother Nature feels like dishing out on a given day. However, I have cursed the elements on days when I wasn't wearing the right gear to take them on. Today, thanks to advances in the materials and construction of running gear, there's almost never a day you can't run due to the weather in most places. Here's what to keep in mind when deciding what to put on for your run:

### Staying Warm and Dry in the Cold, Wet, and Wind

• *Dress in layers.* Your mother probably told you this as she bundled you up to go out in the cold. It's great advice for running on cool and cold days as well. The reason: Layers of fabric trap warm air close to your skin. They also allow you to easily add and remove clothing if temperatures change during your workout. For the top half of your body, choose a base-layer garment with moisture-management or "wicking" properties to draw perspiration away from the skin; these materials are constructed of two layers to soak up, then disperse fluids. If needed, a middle layer made of fleece can provide lightweight warmth. On the outside, choose a garment that resists water and wind. Ask a salesperson at a running specialty store for advice, as the names and exact properties of various garments are constantly being updated. As for the bottom half of the body, most runners wear tights, which provide warmth without bulk and drag, if it's cold and dry. Look for tights with wicking properties to draw moisture away from the skin. In cold rain or snow, rain pants offer water resistance, and on extremely cold and windy days, tights underneath pants provide maximum protection.

• *Choose synthetics.* The explosion of warm, lightweight materials has rendered cotton, wool, and other natural fabrics obsolete for running. In fact, cotton is a poor choice on cold days because it's relatively heavy without offering much in the way of warmth or wind protection. And in wet weather cotton can be an absolute disaster because it soaks up water (both rain and perspiration) and holds on to it without dispersing it, so that it can more than double in weight while holding the cold, drenched fabric next to your skin. Wool, though it does provide warmth even when wet, is heavier and less durable than synthetic fabrics with superior warmth, wicking, wind-protecting, and water-repelling properties.

• *Protect your head, face, and hands.* Wearing a head-covering can reduce loss of body heat through the head by up to 50 percent. For most winter running and racing, I wear a lightweight, synthetic-knit cap that I can take off and stuff in a pocket or into my waistband as the temperature changes. Protecting your face in extreme cold and wind is vital for the prevention of frostbite.

Wear a scarf, balaclava (which covers the cheeks and neck), or hooded jacket that can tighten to cover all but your eyes. Keep your hands warm with gloves or, preferably, mittens. On bitter cold days I wear wool socks inside mittens to keep all my fingers (including the thumb) together for warmth. Mittens made from Gore-Tex or other wind- and water-resistant material offer better wind and rain/snow protection than woolen, cotton, or synthetic-knit mittens or gloves. Wear your normal running socks when running in the cold; extra-thick socks or two pairs of socks can alter your shoe fit.

• *Consider the windchill.* Windy days feel colder than days with no wind. When considering what to wear in cold weather, be sure to get a windchill reading, and plan your running route so that you head out into the wind, and come back with the wind behind you. Otherwise you may sweat excessively during the first half of your run, and then become chilled as the wind hits your sweaty body during the second half. You'll also have to work harder fighting the wind when you're most tired.

• *Don't overdress.* Remember, running works up a sweat. A good rule of thumb is to add 20 degrees Fahrenheit to the temperature when planning your running wardrobe. For example, if it's 40 degrees, dress as you would if heading out for a light stroll on a 60-degree day. Overdressing can cause excessive sweating, which can lead to dehydration and exhaustion. In general, the more protection against wind and moisture a garment offers, the less "breathable" it is. Wearing a 100 percent waterproof garment, such as a rain slicker, will cause excessive perspiration. It's better to trade a bit of dampness for breathability.

## QUESTION AND ANSWER

**Q.** What is the difference between waterproof and water-resistant?

**A.** Waterproof means that a fabric is literally impenetrable by water. No garment specifically designed for running is waterproof because it would also prevent the water molecules in sweat from dispersing into the air. (Try running wearing a rain slicker or garbage bag, and you'll get the idea.) Consequently, wet-weather running gear is designed to be water-resistant in varying degrees depending on its intended use. This means the fabric blocks some, but not all, of the moisture from the outside, which also allows perspiration to move to the fabric's surface for dispersion into the surrounding air. Of course, when it's pouring rain this system breaks down eventually, but not as quickly as it would without the water-resistance. Both a fabric's composition and the presence or absence of a laminate (and the laminate's thickness) can affect a garment's degree of water-resistance. As a rule, the thicker and heavier a garment, the more water-resistant it is likely to be.

### Staying Cool and Keeping Off the Sun

Hyperthermia (a rapid and uncontrolled rise in core body temperature) can be just as dangerous to a runner as cold-related hazards. On extremely warm days (especially with high humidity) consider running on a treadmill, water running, swimming, or skipping exercise. Otherwise, follow this advice to stay as comfortable and safe as possible:

• *Stick with synthetics.* As with fabrics designed to keep runners warm and dry, those intended to provide comfort on warm, sunny days have taken a quantum leap in effectiveness. The standard cotton T-shirt, though ubiquitous, isn't your most comfortable or sensible option on warm days because it will absorb perspiration, becoming heavy, sticky, and clammy. In contrast, shirts and singlets made from synthetics wick perspiration away from the skin, helping you stay cool and relatively dry. Mesh fabrics are extremely lightweight and breathable. A pair of synthetic shorts, a synthetic T-shirt or singlet, and (for women) a sports bra, are all you need for most warm-weather runs.

• *Protect yourself from the sun.* Besides wearing sunscreen on exposed skin when running in daylight hours (even when it's overcast), you can adjust your wardrobe to stay sunburn-free and reduce your risk of sun damage. Wear dark-colored clothing for more protection from the sun's rays than white or light-colored garments provide. Wear a hat with a brim to protect your head and face; a mesh cap or a visor will help prevent heat buildup.

Use sunglasses to keep the glare out of your eyes and minimize sun-related damage that can lead to cataracts. Apply sunscreen underneath mesh garments, which offer inadequate sun protection. Don't forget to protect the back of your neck, and your shoulders, lips, nose, and ears.

• *Wear socks.* You may be tempted to run sockless on warm days—but don't. Socks absorb perspiration, helping to prevent blisters. They also help protect feet in all types of weather. Look for very thin, lightweight socks if the heavier fabrics and construction bother you in warm weather.

### Gadgets, Gizmos, and Other Stuff

You may want to consider the following running gear:

**Treadmill.** A treadmill can cost upwards of $5,000, so it's not a purchase that even a serious runner should make lightly. The advantages of owning a treadmill include the freedom to run safely at any time of day or night, and the ability to control the pace, distance, gradient, and other parameters of your run. The disadvantages include the treadmill's cost, the risk of mechanical problems, and the fact that treadmill running doesn't precisely mimic running on a nonmoving surface.

Most experts recommend a motorized treadmill over a non-motorized version because running on a nonmotorized treadmill puts considerable stress on the hamstring and buttocks muscles and can alter your running form. Most motorized treadmills can be set to go at speeds of up to 10 m.p.h. (six-minute miles), and some can go as high as 12 m.p.h. You can program them to do all types of workouts, including steady runs, hills, intervals, and gradual accelerations.

I recommend working out on a treadmill regularly for at least a few sessions before considering a purchase. You'll then have a better idea of what you need. If you race, try to do at least some of your training on a non-treadmill surface because of the slight biomechanical differences in footstrike and toe-off between treadmill and non-treadmill running.

**Running watch.** Most runners wear a chronograph-type watch that can time and record the total duration of their runs and perform various other functions. You can pay as little as $20 for a bare-bones chronograph watch, and as much as several hundred dollars for a top-of-the-line model. Watches are available in sporting goods stores, running specialty stores, and online. They are designed to be clearly visible, relatively simple to operate, and with easy-to-punch buttons. Other useful features in a watch are listed below. Some may be useful to you; others you may be able to do without.

• *Lap counter.* This allows you to break your run into segments (usually referred to as laps or splits) and note the total elapsed and segmented times.

• *Memory and recall.* Most running watches have both these functions, which allow you to store up to hundreds of runs (including the laps) into a memory, then recall them at any time.

• *Download function.* This allows you to download information from your watch into a computer.

• *Alarms.* Most watches have at least one alarm; many offer multiple alarm functions (useful, for example, when you want to awaken at a certain time, be alerted to the time and hour before the start of a race, etc.).

• *Countdown.* This function lets you count down to an important time, such as the start of a race, with beeps at periodic intervals.

• *Programmable workouts.* This allows you to program the watch to beep at preset intervals, such as every two minutes, to facilitate workouts measured by time rather than distance.

• *Pulse calculators.* Not to be confused with a heart rate monitor (see below), this watch takes your pulse on the wrist (rather than picking up heartbeats), a reasonably accurate approximation of your heart rate.

• *Pace calculators.* An advanced function not yet standard on most watches, this tells you the pace of a run.

• *Distance calculators.* This is a relatively new function appearing on a few top-of-the-line models that accurately measures the distance of your runs.

**Audio headset.** Many runners like to run to the beat of music or use their running time to catch up on the news, and so use a small, portable headset. The Road Runners Club of America frowns on the use of headsets while running, for safety reasons (see Chapter 11 for more running safety tips from the RRCA). I agree with the RRCA's position, and believe strongly that no one should ever use a headset when running outdoors. However, I see no harm in using a headset at low volume while running on a treadmill. Models are getting more compact and lighter all the time, and play radio, audio tapes, and/or CDs. Expect to pay about $75–100 for a decent headset.

**Heart rate monitor.** A heart rate monitor actually refers to a heart rate sensor, which is strapped around the chest and picks up the electronic impulses of the beating heart. The monitor itself is worn on the wrist and picks up the transmitted data from the sensor. This provides an assessment of exercise intensity. (See Chapter 2 for more information on how heart rate reflects exercise intensity.) Today's heart rate monitors offer a variety of other functions, including programmable workouts, a beeper that sounds when preset heart rates are exceeded (so that you know when you are working too hard), and the ability to download the information into a computer. A decent heart rate monitor costs about $100, but you can easily pay two or three times that for a top-of-the-line model.

**Water carrier.** Those running where water and other fluids are scarce should carry fluids with them, especially when it's warm out. On my long runs during the winter, when the water fountains along my long-run route are shut off, I use a simple waist carrier that holds a 16-ounce water bottle at the back. A couple of times during the run I'll reach around, grab the bottle, take a few swigs, and stick it back in the carrier, all while barely breaking stride. For longer runs or in very warm conditions, you're probably better off with a more sophisticated and larger-capacity carrier worn like a backpack and with a small tube from which you can sip without removing the pack or reaching around. You can find water carriers in sporting goods stores, running specialty shops, and bike shops.

**Carrying pack.** If you use running for transportation, a back- or waist-pack can be useful for carrying gear. There are models designed specifically for runners, but any pack that's lightweight, water-resistant, fits close to the body, and allows you to tuck in loose straps will do the trick. Zippers are safer and more efficient than buckles or buttons, and nylon is probably the best material for most conditions.

**Running stroller.** At least half a dozen companies make strollers designed to be pushed by parents and other caregivers on the run. For safety purposes a stroller should have a wide wheel-base for stability and to keep it upright on turns, a deep seat, a secure seat belt or strapping system, a locking brake, a secure handle, and a leash to slip over your wrist to prevent it from rolling away. Other useful features include a carrying pouch, a detachable overhead canopy, extra shock absorption for running on trails or other rough surfaces, and folding ability for storage and transport. Expect to pay at least $200 for a new stroller of decent quality, though a used model may be a far cheaper alternative. Side-by-side twin models are also available.

CHAPTER 5

▶▶▶▶▶▶▶▶▶▶▶▶▶▶▶▶▶▶▶▶▶▶▶▶▶▶▶▶▶▶▶▶▶▶▶

# *Staying Healthy*

R unning causes many healthful changes. On average, runners live longer, healthier lives than non-runners, and are at a reduced risk of major diseases such as heart disease and some cancers. Thus, many runners are shocked when their first running injury strikes. How can this happen when they feel so fit, healthy, and practically invincible? Yet virtually every runner gets injured at some point, due to the physical demands of the sport and often runners' ignorance of (or refusal to recognize) the early warning signs of injury. This chapter will help runners recognize, avoid, and treat common running injuries, and offers guidelines on minimizing the risk of new or recurring injuries, illnesses, and other maladies related to running.

### What Causes Running Injuries?

There are those who believe that a running injury should never happen in the first place. After all, running is a natural human activity so why should it cause injuries? At the other end of the spectrum are those such as physician and exercise scientist Tim

Noakes, M.D., author of *Lore of Running*, who says that given the demands of running and the biomechanical structure of the lower body, "it becomes remarkable that any runner can escape injury." The truth is somewhere between these two viewpoints. Evolutionarily speaking, human primates have very little experience walking—let along running vast distances—on two legs rather than four. We may simply need another few million years to work out the kinks!

Running injuries have a broad range of more immediate causes. Though it can be helpful to categorize the cause of an injury as either genetic/structural (and therefore difficult, if not impossible, for the runner to control) or training/equipment/ lifestyle (and therefore within the runner's control, at least in theory), the truth is that most injuries have a combination of causes. For example, Runner A and Runner B may both over-pronate, which predisposes them to chondromalacia (runner's knee), but only Runner A develops the injury because Runner B wears shoes designed to control overpronation, replaces them regularly, uses orthotic shoe inserts, runs on soft surfaces, stretches, and cross-trains. Although some runners are genetically more predisposed to certain injuries than other runners, there is a great deal that every runner can do to control his or her susceptibility to injury, and the degree to which injuries disrupt his or her running.

Running injuries tend not to be sudden and traumatic, such as those caused by a blow, fall, sprain, or other violent occurrence. Rather, they come on gradually, in most cases due to the constant, repetitive motions of running. This affords the mindful runner the opportunity to pinpoint the root cause(s) of an injury and to make changes to correct the problem, such as replacing shoes, switching running surfaces, or reducing training intensity or volume. The problem, of course, is that many runners aren't mindful—due either to inexperience or, more often, stubbornness. Olympic gold medalist Frank Shorter wrote in 1984, "The same personality—independent, introverted, single-minded, self-reliant, self-confident, distrusting—that enabled me to excel as an athlete in full health hindered me when I became an athlete in pain."

The good news is that the vast majority of running injuries

can be treated and, if not cured, at least managed, allowing runners to continue to run. In most cases, however, the runner must be willing to change his or her running and lifestyle habits—at least temporarily, and sometimes permanently. This chapter offers guidelines for making those adjustments, be they large or small. With the goal of a lifetime of healthy running, the changes are usually worth making.

### General Strategies for Avoiding Injuries

There is plenty you can do on a day-to-day basis to minimize your risk of spending time on the sidelines. Here are some strategies.

• *Wear the right shoes and replace them regularly.* Incorrect or worn-out footwear is responsible for a large proportion of running injuries. See Chapter 4 for guidelines on choosing the best running shoes for your feet and replacing them before they increase your injury risk.

• *Run on soft, even surfaces.* Our ancestors may have evolved covering long distances on foot, but they didn't have to contend with concrete, asphalt, and other unyielding surfaces so common in the modern world. Running on soft surfaces such as dirt, short grass, hard-packed gravel or sand, and cinders spares the pounding of running and can go a long way toward injury prevention. Kenyan and other East African runners train almost exclusively on dirt and clay roads and trails in their home countries, and thus are able to handle mileage loads with much lower injury risk than runners putting in equivalent efforts on roads and sidewalks. Hit the dirt whenever you can. If you choose trails, look for those with a smooth, even surface, to minimize the risk of an ankle sprain or another mishap.

• *Heed an injury's early warning signs.* New runners—as well as many veterans—find it difficult to distinguish between normal and expected muscle soreness in muscles and joints, and the pain that can herald an injury. In their early stages, most injuries aren't acutely painful. The pain may occur at times other than while running; in fact, running may even relieve injury pain as muscles and tissues warm up and loosen. Unlike garden-variety soreness, though, the pain of an injury tends to persist and worsen over time, and to eventually cause changes in running form that may bring on an injury elsewhere. When in doubt about the cause of any pain, stop running (and any other activity that worsens the pain) for a day or two. Noninjury soreness should disappear or diminish, whereas an injury that's serious enough to warrant medical attention will probably still be with you after this period of rest.

• *Watch your form.* Poor running form predisposes the body to injury. Running with upright posture, a strong knee lift, a forward arm drive, a natural stride length, and little up-and-down movement of the head and shoulders will help keep your risk of injuries low.

• *Cross-train.* Many runners wait until after they are injured to cross-train. Cross-training *before* you become injured can reduce your injury risk by allowing you to train with less pounding than occurs with running. I cross-train—deep-water running with a flotation device and cycling—regularly, and therefore don't fear an injury as much as I might otherwise, because there are other substitute activities. Ease into cross-training activities to avoid injury; I know plenty of runners who have gotten a second injury by cross-training too intensely in new activities during an injury layoff from running. (See Chapter 9 for a full discussion of cross-training.)

• *Avoid sudden changes.* Injuries are an increased risk anytime you change something in your running—mileage, intensity, shoes, running surface, etc. Make changes gradually, paying attention to the feedback from your body.

• *Stretch and strengthen.* Running is one of the best fitness activities available, but it doesn't do it all. For total-body fitness and injury prevention, runners should strengthen their torso (back and abdominal muscles) and upper body with a regular strength-training program as well as cross-training, and maintain the flexibility of their running muscles. Loose, supple muscles and joints are less likely to pull and tear. See pages 216–217 in Chapter 9 for a total-body strengthening program for runners, and pages 128–130 for stretching exercises designed specifically for runners.

• *Treated is not cured.* Some injured runners, eager to return to training as quickly as possible, rush the healing process. Treating an injury with rest, icing, heat, massage, anti-inflammatory medications, and other methods is only the first step toward complete healing of an injury. Trying to rush back into running can lead to reinjury and often a longer layoff.

## WHAT'S UP, DOC?

When an injury doesn't respond to home treatment such as rest, ice, and self-massage, it's best to consult a medical professional. Ah, but what sort of medical professional? No matter what ails you, I recommend finding a doctor who treats runners regularly if your injury has been affecting you for more than a couple of weeks. Get recommendations from other runners, running clubs, and running specialty stores. (Also see Resources to help you find practitioners in your area.) The seriousness of your injury will not necessarily dictate the type of professional you should see, and you may end up consulting more than one person to treat various aspects of your injury.

The following professionals are among the most helpful to injured runners:

• *Sports medicine practitioner.* This is the type of professional many injured runners first go to for a diagnosis, evaluation, and treatment. A sports medicine practitioner may be either a medical doctor (M.D.), a doctor of osteopathy (D.O.), or a doctor of podiatric medicine (D.P.M.) who specializes in sports medicine. There is no board certification for the specialty of sports medicine, though a practitioner may become a fellow in the specialty through qualification and testing by the American College of Sports Medicine or the American Academy of Podiatric Sports Medicine. A Certificate of Added Qualifications in Sports Medicine is granted to those (not including orthopedists or podiatrists) who have met certain criteria and passed an exam administered by the American Board of Family Practice, the American Board of Pediatrics, the American Board of Internal Medicine, or the American Board of Emergency

Medicine. See Resources for a list of organizations that can help you find a qualified sports medicine practitioner in your area.

• *Orthopedist.* An orthopedist is a physician specializing in the treatment of bones. He or she is not the practitioner most injured runners see first unless they suspect a stress fracture. Even when bone problems are involved in a running injury, it may not be necessary to see an orthopedist, though for chronic bone-related injuries (such as repeated stress fractures) that resist treatment by other specialists, it may be wise to consider this option.

• *Podiatrist.* A podiatrist, whose title includes "D.P.M.," is a physician (though usually not an M.D.) who specializes in the care of the lower legs and feet. A podiatrist can become a fellow in sports medicine by qualifying and passing a test administered by the American Academy of Podiatric Sports Medicine. A podiatrist who treats runners regularly is often your best bet for dealing with injury problems below the knee.

• *Chiropractor.* Chiropractic is a medical practice that focuses on structural, spinal, musculoskeletal, neurological, vascular, nutritional, emotional, and environmental relationships. A doctor of chiropractic (D.C.) specializes in adjusting and manipulating bones, joints, and tissues, in particular the spine. Chiropractors do not perform surgery or prescribe drugs. For an injured runner, a chiropractor can be most useful in treating injuries involving the back and torso area. In addition, many runners rely on regular chiropractic adjustments to help achieve optimal fitness for running by maintaining structural balance.

• *Physical therapist.* A physical therapist (P.T.) is a professional who treats injuries and other functional and structural limitations with stretching, strengthening, massage, ultrasound, ice/heat, electrical stimulation, manual manipulation, exercise therapy, and other methods. In most states you must have a medical referral to see a P.T., who must hold an undergraduate degree in physical therapy (most also have a masters degree) and pass a state licensing exam in order to practice. Physical therapy can be extremely useful—sometimes essential—in injury treatment and the prevention of reinjury.

## QUESTION AND ANSWER

**Q.** How can I tell the difference between "normal" muscle soreness and an injury?

**A.** Muscle soreness from running results from the breakdown of muscle fibers caused by the motions of running—both the contractions of the muscles themselves and the contact between the body and the unyielding surfaces underfoot. Most beginning runners experience mild muscle soreness for one to two days after running because their muscles are unaccustomed to running. There are, however, ways for all runners to minimize this soreness, which will help reduce injury risk and allow you to gradually increase your fitness.

One, you should follow a structured training program to allow your muscles to rest and recover between hard efforts. Two, warm up before and cool down after your runs, especially hard efforts. Three, stretch after running, when the muscles are warm and loose. If localized soreness persists three days or longer, or changes your running form (such as causing you to limp), take a day or two off from running. If the soreness isn't better within two weeks, see a sports medicine practitioner.

### 12 Common Running Injuries and How to Recognize, Avoid, and Treat Them

The injuries listed below are among the most common to runners. Here are ways you can recognize and treat them, and what you can do to minimize your risk:

• *Chondromalacia (runner's knee).* Many sports medicine professionals consider this the most common running injury. The knee is a complex joint that relies on the balance, alignment, and interplay of dozens of muscles, tendons, ligaments, and bones to maintain stability during running and other activities. Chondromalacia, commonly referred to as "runner's knee," occurs when the patella (kneecap) does not track properly in the V-shaped groove behind it. This causes the cartilage under the kneecap to roughen and become irritated, leading to inflammation and pain. Runners will feel the pain during and after running (especially downhill and on hard surfaces because of the increased impact forces) and when walking up and down stairs due to the bending of the knee. In severe cases the rough cartilage can be felt rubbing and heard crackling.

Resting, icing, and taking anti-inflammatory medications can relieve the symptoms of runner's knee, but the problem will continue unless the underlying issue of poor tracking of the patella is addressed. Wearing a motion-control shoe can improve tracking by controlling overpronation. If that doesn't help, a sports medicine professional may prescribe custom-made orthotic devices (shoe inserts) to better control pronation. Replacing shoes regularly, running on soft surfaces, cross-training, and stretching and strengthening the quadriceps, hamstring, and calf muscles, all of which support the knee, can help keep symptoms in check (see page 128–130 for specific strengthening exercises).

• *Plantar fasciitis.* The *plantar fascia* is a band of thick, fibrous tissue that extends along the bottom of the foot from the heel to the base of the toes. Running stresses it, and too much stress may cause small tears, which become inflamed, causing pain and the gradual buildup of scar tissue. All of this makes the *plantar fascia* less flexible, and results in a continuing cycle of pain and stiffness. Causes of *plantar fasciitis* include overpronation, tight calf muscles, overtraining, excessive speed training or hill training, running in worn-out shoes, and running on hard surfaces. You know you have a plantar injury when you feel pain upon stepping on the foot first thing in the morning (or after prolonged sitting or lying down), which can be so severe that walking is impossible. The pain may diminish during the day as the tissues warm up and stretch out, and the injury may even feel fine during a run, but it will recur again later until the injury heals. Sometimes early plantar problems can be nipped in the bud by replacing worn-out shoes and switching to running on flat, soft surfaces.

The best treatment for *plantar fasciitis* is to cut back or stop running, ice and massage the *plantar fascia* up to three times a day (use a frozen juice can or frozen paper cup of water rolled under the arch for 10 to 15 minutes), and stretch the calves regularly to help relieve tightness that extends down the calf into the heel area. Orthotic devices can help correct overpronation and support the arch. Rarely, a surgeon may sever the *plantar fascia* to release the tightness.

• *Shin pain.* "Shin splints" refers to pain in the front of the lower leg. In runners, most shin pain results from inflammation of the tendons on the inside or—more rarely—outside of the tibia, or shin bone. Less commonly, shin pain is caused by a stress fracture of the tibia or a condition called compartment syndrome, in which the lower-leg muscles swell and are compressed within their protective sheaths. Shin pain caused by inflammation is very common in beginning runners who increase their mileage and/or intensity too quickly, or in runners of all levels who suddenly increase their training. The problem can be worsened by excessive hill running, or running in worn-out shoes or on hard surfaces. Often, simply backing off the intensity of training for a week or two alleviates the inflammation; icing, self-massage, and taking anti-inflammatories also can help. Stretching the calves and the Achilles tendons regularly can help keep shin pain at bay, as can strengthening all the muscles in the lower leg. Try towel scrunches: Spread out a bath towel on the floor and use your toes, one foot at a time, to scrunch it up toward you. Calf raises and tracing the alphabet with your big toe on the floor also stretch and strengthen the muscles. If you run on slanted surfaces such as roads, switch directions periodically to vary your leg-length discrepancy. If pain continues—especially if it is localized and feels worse during and after running—see a sports medicine professional, who can diagnose a possible stress fracture.

• *Iliotibial band (ITB) syndrome.* The iliotibial (IT) band is a ligament that extends down the outside of the thigh and inserts below the outside of the knee. If the knee bends inward (due to bowed legs, overpronation, downhill running, running on a banked or cambered surface, or wearing worn-out shoes), the IT band is stretched against the femur (thigh bone), causing inflammation and pain. The pain typically comes on during a run and disappears soon afterward. If untreated, the pain can become sharp and severe, with swelling and redness on the outside of the knee.

Treatment of ITB syndrome should focus on stretching the IT band. The best stretch is to stand with the affected leg (say, the right) crossed in back of the left, with the left arm holding a wall or other stable object for balance. Lean against the object, push the right hip outward, and let the left knee bend slightly. You should feel a stretch in the affected area. Hold for 10 to 30 seconds. Also try icing and self-massaging the tight, tender area. Cut back on running and other activities that cause pain and tightness, such as cycling. You can reduce your risk of reinjury by continuing to regularly stretch the ITB, as well as the quadriceps, hamstrings, and calves.

• *Achilles tendonitis.* The Achilles is the strongest tendon in the body. It attaches the two main calf muscles, the soleus and gastrocnemius, to the back of the heel bone (calcanues). Running subjects the Achilles tendon to considerable stresses, making it a common injury site. Overpronation, overtraining, increasing mileage and/or intensity too quickly, running in worn-out shoes or on hard surfaces, and wearing high-heeled dress shoes (which shorten the Achilles) all predispose runners to Achilles problems. Most Achilles injuries begin as inflammation (tendonitis) caused by tiny tears in the tendon. The tears form scar tissue, which causes the Achilles to tighten, making it vulnerable to further tearing and even rupture. It's crucial to treat Achilles tendonitis before this stage because a ruptured Achilles is extremely painful and may even prevent further running—for good.

Treat Achilles tendonitis by resting, icing, taking anti-inflammatories, self-massaging the affected area, and stretching and massaging the calves. Do not stretch the Achilles itself, as that will irritate the tendon, though gentle massage can bring blood to the Achilles (which has a poor blood supply and thus tends to heal slowly), and break up scar tissue. Cross-train instead of running until you can do so without pain; this may take six weeks or longer. You can reduce the risk of reinjury by returning to running gradually, avoiding high-heeled shoes, and not making any sudden changes in your running program. Stretch your calves by standing on the balls of your feet on a step or curb, dropping your heels off the edge, and holding for 10 to 20 seconds.

• *Blister.* Blisters develop when friction causes the skin's layers to separate and fill with fluid or blood. If a blister becomes painful, it can cause a runner to change stride, increasing the risk of other injuries. If a blister pops, pain can increase and may become debilitating, and infection may occur. Runners can get blisters on their feet due to poorly fitting or improperly laced shoes, rubbing shoe seams, wet shoes, or dirty, wet, or wrinkled socks.

You can reduce the risk of blisters by wearing shoes that fit and lacing them neither too tightly nor too loosely, wearing clean, dry, synthetic-blend socks that fit without bunching or wrinkling, and putting a lubricant (such as petroleum jelly) on vulnerable areas to reduce friction. If a blister hasn't popped, leave it alone for at least 24 hours if possible. If not, lance it by poking a small hole on each side with a sterile needle or pin and squeezing out the fluid. Cover it with an antiseptic and sterile gauze. Swab a popped blister with antiseptic, cover it, and try to avoid friction or irritation while it heals.

• *Bunion.* A bunion is a bump or enlargement on the outside of the first metatarsal-phalangeal joint, or big toe. Usually a tendency toward bunions is inherited, and they occur in runners and non-runners alike. In most cases muscle and tendon imbalances around the metatarsal area cause the position of the joint to progressively shift. This causes the outside of the toe to press and rub against shoes, which is painful and may increase the bump's size and prominence over time.

Some bunions can be managed by wearing a wide shoe with a roomy toe box, and/or using a bunion shield (available in pharmacies). Wearing a custom-fitted orthotic device also helps relieve some bunions. If these measures don't work and the pain is interfering with proper running form (not to mention lifestyle), surgery is often necessary. There are several different surgical procedures used to realign the big-toe joint. (Though the surgeon also may shave off the bump, this alone will not correct the problem.) In most cases bunion surgery requires an 8 to 12-week layoff from running, though you may be able to resume nonimpact activities such as swimming and pool-running sooner. Wearing wide, roomy shoes and possibly an orthotic device can help reduce the risk of a bunion recurring.

• *Stress fracture.* A stress fracture is an incomplete bone break. In runners, most stress fractures are caused by overuse, rather than a traumatic injury. In general, running makes bones stronger as they adapt to the stresses of running by adding bone cells. However, a fracture can occur when bone regeneration can't keep pace with the forces applied. Overtraining, changing training patterns suddenly, and structural/genetic problems all can cause stress fractures. A weakening of bone mineral, which can result from nutritional and/or hormonal problems, can predispose some people—women in particular—to stress fractures. (See Chapter 11 for more information on how running affects bones.) Common sites for stress fractures in runners are the feet (metatarsal, heel, and sesamoid bones) and bones of the lower leg (tibia and fibula). Less common sites include the patella (kneecap), femur (thigh bone), hip and pubic bones, and lower spine. Stress fractures tend to cause sharp, localized pain that is worsened by running. Pressure applied to the affected area of bone may be intensely painful, and the surrounding tissue may become inflamed as well. Early diagnosis and treatment are important because the injury will not heal properly without rest. Running on a stress fracture could also cause a complete bone break.

If you suspect a stress fracture, see a sports medicine specialist, who can perform a bone scan, a special X ray, for a definitive diagnosis. (Stress fractures generally don't show up on a conventional X ray until healing is well under way.) It's unwise to run at all on a stress fracture, but some kind of cross-training is almost always possible. Most fractures take six to eight weeks to heal, after which easy running can actually improve healing by strengthening the bone and improving the blood supply to the healing area. Most doctors recommend attempting to run six to eight weeks after diagnosing the injury, and continuing if the pain is dull or absent. A sports medicine specialist can help address the underlying cause(s) of repeated stress fractures, be they nutritional, hormonal, structural, or training-related.

• *Neuroma.* A neuroma is a thickening of a nerve, usually resulting from irritation. Running can cause or contribute to a neuroma in the foot due to improper or poorly fitting shoes, structural problems, or overpronation. The most common neuroma site in runners, known as Morton's neuroma or Morton's toe, is between the third and fourth metatarsal bones. The telltale symptom is a burning or tingling feeling in the ball of your foot and around the third and fourth toes.

You may be able to treat the problem simply by wearing wider shoes with a roomier toe box or using a toe separator between the third and fourth toes. If this doesn't work, a medical professional may recommend an orthotic device or metatarsal pad to take pressure off the nerve. The next step is usually a one-time injection of anti-inflammatory drugs. As a last resort, surgery is performed to remove the nerve branch, but this is very rare.

• *Ankle sprain/strain.* A sprain is an injury to a ligament; a strain is damage to a muscle or tendon. Traumatic ankle injuries such as sprains and strains are common in sports that involve a lot of contact, side-to-side movement, and changes in speed or direction. Runners increase their risk of an ankle injury when running on uneven surfaces or abruptly changing speed or direction. Most strains and sprains suffered by runners occur when the foot lands on an uneven surface and causes the ankle to roll outward, stressing the outside of the ankle and resulting in sudden intense pain. The ankle may swell noticeably and become bruised.

You should treat a sprain or strain as soon as possible by resting, icing, compressing, and elevating the ankle (the treatment is conveniently remembered by the acronym R-I-C-E). This should relieve the pain and swelling. See a doctor to rule out the possibility of a fracture, which needs setting to heal properly. Continue to treat a sprain or strain with RICE until the swelling and pain diminish. A sports medicine professional may also recommend a soft cast to immobilize a second- or third-degree sprain, followed by stretching and/or strengthening exercises. If you get frequent ankle sprains or strains, you can wear a brace for running and other high-impact activities.

• *Arthritis.* There's a persistent myth that running causes arthritis. Studies have shown that distance running doesn't increase the

risk of osteoarthritis, the most common type of arthritis, which affects 21 million Americans. Osteoarthritis damages the cartilage
that cushions and protects the ends of bones, which causes bones
to rub together, resulting in pain, stiffness, and inflammation.
Running actually may reduce the risk of arthritis by helping to
control body weight and reducing the chance of joint injury by
strengthening the surrounding muscles. Runners who suffer
from arthritis may have to make adjustments to their running by
warming up very slowly and carefully, avoiding changes in speed,
terrain, and direction, and possibly substituting nonimpact activities (swimming, pool-running, cycling, etc.) for some of their
running.

• *Back pain/sciatica.* It's estimated that 80 percent of the population suffers from back pain at some point. In most cases running
does not cause back pain, but may aggravate it. Runners who experience chronic or intermittent back pain should stretch and
loosen the back muscles before running, stretch regularly at
other times, and do exercises to keep the back and abdominal
muscles strong. Sticking to flat, soft, and even surfaces while running can also help. Back pain that radiates down into the buttocks, through the legs, and to the feet may be sciatica, an
irritation of the sciatic nerve. Sciatica also may cause tingling,
burning, or pins-and-needles feelings. It can be caused by tight
muscles in the back, buttocks, or legs; a herniated disk; or other
structural or biomechanical problems. Downhill running and
running on hard or uneven surfaces can aggravate sciatica. Sciatica is often chronic, and runners who suffer from it learn to
manage it by limiting their running, and stretching diligently.
Maintaining good posture and supporting the back with a pillow
while sitting and lying down also help.

## QUESTION AND ANSWER

**Q.** I feel depressed about my running injury. Any suggestions?

**A.** It's normal to feel down about a running injury, but
it doesn't do you any good. Try the following to lift your spir-

its—and speed your recovery: One, put the injury in perspective and realize that compared to, say, a broken leg, it's not that big a deal. Two, recognize that virtually every runner gets injured at some point, and 99.99 percent of us make a full recovery. Three, focus on the cross-training and supplemental training activities you can do to stay fit while recovering. Four, be a good patient by resting, icing, taking anti-inflammatories, and doing physical therapy as your doctor and therapist suggest. Five, use the time you'd normally spend running to reconnect with nonrunning family members and friends, and pursue activities you may have neglected. Six, stay plugged into running in other ways, such as volunteering at races. Finally, pay attention to the progress of your injury's healing, knowing that each day brings more healing.

### Stretching: The Truth About Injury Prevention

Most runners have been told that stretching can help keep them flexible, thus reducing their risk of injury and improving their running. If runners don't stretch regularly, they usually feel guilty about it. Those who do stretch may worry that they aren't doing the right stretches, in the right ways, or at the right times. They wonder if they should stretch more—or less. In short, when it comes to stretching, most runners out there could use some guidance.

Does stretching prevent injury? No one knows for sure. Several studies have suggested that runners who stretch are no less prone to injury than those who avoid stretching. Nonetheless, I believe in stretching, mainly because it feels great and increases my enjoyment of running. I wish I made more time for stretching. Many runners are in the same boat: They don't have time to stretch, or they don't know how to stretch properly, or they are bored by stretching, or they figure they'll play the odds and avoid stretching as long as they remain injury-free.

This section looks at what we know—and don't know—about stretching for runners, and offers guidelines on stretching for health and running enhancement. It includes a set of stretches that are simple, easy to remember, and can help keep the body limber from head to toe. There are also some suggested shortcuts to flexibility for when you truly don't have time to stretch.

Most coaches and exercise scientists recommend stretching for runners as a safeguard against injury. Runners who stretch point out that it feels good and can be meditative and relaxing. It's important, however, to stretch correctly because improper stretching can actually increase the risk of injury.

### Types of Stretching

When a muscle is stretched, receptors send a message to the nerves that control the muscle, telling it to contract. This protective mechanism prevents overstretching. The stronger and more sudden the stretch, the stronger the contraction, and these strong contractions increase the risk of injury to the muscles. Exercise scientists realized this years ago, which is why ballistic stretching—bouncing motions such as old-fashioned toe-touches—is no longer recommended by most experts.

For years many experts recommended static stretching, which involves easing into a stretch gradually and holding it for 10 to 30 seconds. However, holding the stretch for such lengthy periods encourages overstretching, stimulates the contract reflex, and can be time-consuming. Therefore, many coaches and athletes prefer contract-relax stretching, in which the muscle is briefly contracted to cause it to relax before stretching. Recently, a grow-ing number of experts have started recommending contract-relax-antagonist-contract stretching, in which the antagonist (opposing) muscle is first contracted, releasing the stretched muscle to maximally relax and elongate. This type of stretching is done in a gentle, rhythmic pattern, with deep breathing to en-courage full muscle oxygenation.

### Goals of Stretching

A runner who is new to stretching may set a goal of increasing flexibility. While this seems a worthy endeavor, it has the danger of resulting in excessive or inappropriate stretching. It really doesn't matter how flexible you are compared to someone else. Rather, your goal should be to maximize your own flexibility with-out overstretching, which can result in injury. Let your com-fort level be your guide: Stretching should never hurt. If your stretching program reduces your stiffness and soreness, while running and at other times, then consider it a success and con-tinue with it.

### Eight Effective Stretches for Runners

I recommend the following eight simple, basic stretches for run-ners at all levels. This routine is a combination of static, contract-relax, and contract-relax-antagonist-contract stretches. You may want to modify them to suit your individual needs. Ideally you should stretch when your muscles are warmed up, either from the activities of the day or with at least 5 to 10 minutes of light aerobic activity, such as jogging, walking, or cycling. In the real world, stretch at whatever time works best for you.

Performing the full set of stretches will take 8 to 10 minutes. Do as many as you can; I list them in their order of importance for most runners, but you'll figure out which are most helpful to you.

• *Hamstring stretch.* Lie on your back with your lower back pressed toward the floor. Bend your right knee about 90 degrees and place your right foot on the floor. With your left leg straight (but not locked at the knee) and the foot flexed, clasp your hands behind your left knee and raise the leg off the floor, straight up, until you feel a slight stretch in the hamstring (back of thigh). Inhale and bend the leg slightly to contract the quadriceps (front of thigh) muscle. Straighten the leg to again stretch the hamstring as you exhale. Continue to inhale and bend (count two), exhale and straighten (count two) 8 to 12 times. Switch legs and repeat on the other side.

• *Quadriceps stretch.* Stand with your right side facing a stable handhold, such as a wall or railing, at about waist level. Grasp the handhold with your right hand for balance. Raise your left foot to your buttock, keeping the upper leg parallel to the floor, and clasp the foot with your left hand. Inhale and swing the leg slightly forward to contract the hamstring (count two), then exhale as you swing it backward and pull up on the foot to stretch the quadriceps muscles in the front of the thigh (count two). Repeat 8 to 12 times, then switch legs.

• *Calf stretch.* Stand facing a wall about an arm's length away. Place your hands on the wall at shoulder height, shoulder-width apart. Slide your right foot back about two feet, shifting your weight backward. Inhale and bend the right knee slightly to contract the muscles in the front of the calf, then exhale and straighten the knee to stretch the gastrocnemius muscle in the "belly" of the calf. Repeat 8 to 12 times, then switch legs and repeat the exercise on the left leg.

• *Ankle stretches.* Sit or stand, and raise your right foot a few inches off the ground. Alternately point the toe and flex the foot in a slow, continuous, rhythmic motion. Repeat on the left foot. You can also rotate each ankle slowly to the right for several turns, then slowly to the left for several turns.

• *Achilles tendon stretch.* Stand with your left foot flat on the floor, and raise your straight right leg to place your right heel on a bench or chair. Lean forward and clasp your hands around the instep of your right foot, bending your right knee slightly if necessary. Inhale and point your right toes to relax the calf muscles, then exhale, flex your right foot, and gently pull the front of the foot toward you with your hands, feeling the stretch in the

Achilles tendon. Repeat 8 to 12 times, then switch legs and repeat the exercise.

• *Hip-flexor stretch.* Lie on your back with your feet drawn up toward your buttocks, and your arms out to the sides. Inhale and let your knees fall toward your right arm, feeling the stretch in your left hip and buttock. Exhale and hold (count two), then inhale and raise your knees slowly (count two), pause, and exhale. Repeat 8 to 12 times, then repeat the exercise letting your knees fall toward the left arm.

• *Buttocks stretch.* Lie on your stomach with your right leg straight and your left knee fully bent so the leg is tucked beneath your torso. Get comfortable, then shift your weight backward so you feel a stretch in the left buttock. Breathe deeply and rhythmically, working gently to elongate the stretch; hold for up to 30 seconds. Switch legs and repeat. This stretch may look strange, but there's nothing better for a pain in the butt!

• *Lower-back stretch.* There are many stretches for the lower back. The one that works best for me is to lie on my back, pull my knees to my chest, wrap my arms around my legs, and hold, breathing deeply, for 10 to 20 seconds. Getting on all fours, then shifting my weight backward, bending my knees and lowering my torso, and holding for 10 to 30 seconds with arms out in front of my head also does the job.

## QUESTION AND ANSWER

**Q.** My doctor tells me that with my injury, I'll never run again. Help!

**A.** The vast majority of running injuries heal to the point where running is possible. If you've been told by one doctor that your injury will permanently curtail your running, seek a second opinion from a practitioner who's independent of your current doctor. The body has remarkable healing powers. Seek out other runners who have had your injury and ask about their recovery. If your injury is serious (a ruptured Achilles tendon, for example), prepare yourself for the possibility that you may have to permanently alter your performance-running goals, shifting to goals of overall fitness and health. Running paths are full of runners who can no longer race, no longer do speed workouts, and no longer train with their fast running friends. But these people still run for health, fitness, and enjoyment. It's very unlikely that your injury will prevent your ever running again.

### The Perils and Pitfalls of Overtraining

New runners, feeling the physical and mental challenges of establishing and maintaining a regular running program, may be surprised to learn that veteran runners can fall prey to doing too *much* running, rather than too little. This is known as overtraining, and it can mean running too many miles, running too intensely, running hard too often, failing to rest adequately between hard efforts, or attempting to combine running with excessive energy drains in other areas. Overtraining is surprisingly common, especially among high-level runners, due to their compulsive nature. The point at which overtraining occurs varies from runner to runner and in the same runner at different life stages (we tend to need more rest as we get older). The effects of overtraining can set in gradually, often without a runner realizing what is wrong, and it can take weeks, months, or sometimes even years to recognize, correct, and recover from the problem.

### Types of Overtraining

• *Excessive mileage.* Theories abound on the benefits vs. risks of high-mileage training. Some runners and coaches believe that the highest mileage that can be sustained without injury or burnout is optimal; others believe that mileage should be kept as low as possible. Listen to your body and get a sense of the mileage level that's best for you. If you're struggling through your supposedly "easy" aerobic-intensity runs, you may be at a point where your mileage is hindering rather than helping your running.

• *Excessive intensity.* This means running too hard during your aerobic-intensity recovery runs or speed workouts (or both). Runners may exert themselves too much if they train with a group of faster runners. If your easy days don't allow for true recovery, burnout is a likely result. Running speed workouts too intensely increases your injury risk.

• *Insufficient recovery time between hard efforts.* Runners may do hard workouts too frequently in an attempt to get in shape quickly or when running for a team with a busy race schedule. Older runners tend to need longer recovery periods than younger runners, and can become overtrained and injury-prone if they fail to adjust their training as they age.

• *Excessive cross-training and supplemental training.* Some runners put too much time and energy into cross-training and supplemental training, making it more than a way to enhance running. For noninjured runners, cross-training should serve mainly as recovery training, not as long or intense workouts. Supplemental training should be done to enhance your running, not sap energy from it. If you are injured, don't take out your frustration by attempting overly long or intense cross-training workouts. Your goal when injured should be to maintain fitness, not increase it. Ease into any new cross-training activities just as you eased into running as a beginner. (See Chapter 9 for more information and guidelines on cross-training.)

• *Excessive total life stress.* You don't have to run megamiles or cram in too many speed workouts to end up overtrained if your life outside of running is busy or stressful, either physically or mentally. A 70-hour-a-week job, caring for small children, a heavy academic load, or an emotional stress such as a divorce combined with even a moderate running program can lead to breakdown. You are the best judge of what constitutes overload, and of which activities are negotiable. In some cases, running may be the first element to go. See Chapter 10 for more on the role of running in your life.

### Recognizing Overtraining

Many runners don't recognize overtraining. If they're not seeing the results they want, they assume they are not working hard enough. There's a tendency to "just push through it." Listed below are the physical and psychological signs of overtraining. You do not have to experience all of them to be overtrained. If you notice some of the signs early, you can often correct the problem with a few days off. If you continue to train at a high level, overtraining is likely to lead to breakdown, burnout, or injury.

Listed below are physical and psychological signs of overtraining. These symptoms are wide-ranging, and each has many possible causes apart from overtraining. Still, if all or some of them occur together and you can't pinpoint other obvious causes, consider that you might be training excessively. Look at your running log. Have you made significant changes—perhaps adding speed workouts, increasing mileage, or racing more frequently? Look at the rest of your life as well for possible causes of overload.

Physical signs of overtraining:
- excessive fatigue when running, even on "easy" days
- reduced performance level
- feeling "flat" (low energy, no zip) during workouts and races
- increase in resting pulse rate (taken upon waking in the morning, while still in bed) of five or more beats per minute
- generalized lethargy
- persistent muscle soreness
- loss of appetite
- digestive disturbances (diarrhea, upset stomach)
- weight change (usually loss) beyond your normal fluctuations
- changes in sleep patterns (trouble falling asleep, nighttime or early-morning waking, awakening not refreshed, daytime sleepiness)
- clumsiness; loss of coordination
- frequent headaches
- frequent or persistent infections (colds, coughs, etc.)
- slow wound healing
- swollen lymph glands
- irregularity or absence of menstruation in women

Psychological/emotional signs of overtraining:
- loss of excitement about upcoming running goals (such as races)
- lack of interest in (or dread of) training
- overwhelming desire to stop during workouts and races
- irritability
- anxiety; inability to relax
- moodiness
- depression
- loss of humor
- poor concentration
- forgetfulness
- loss of energy and enthusiasm for daily activities
- loss of interest in sex

Exercise scientists don't fully understand exactly what causes these symptoms, though it's likely that the following are involved: hormonal changes, possible nutritional deficiencies, anemia, chemical imbalances caused by the breakdown of muscle tissue, chronic dehydration, and depletion of stored carbohydrate (glycogen). In the end, the body loses its capacity to respond to stresses it could previously handle.

## MASSAGE THERAPY FOR RUNNERS

Massage therapy is manipulation of the body's soft tissue, primarily with the hands, with the goal of positively affecting health and well-being. Massage has ancient origins in many cultures, and is thought by many to have spiritual/emotional as well as physical benefits. In our culture, "massage parlors" were once places of ill repute. Today, however, many people associate massage with the care and treatment of athletes and others afflicted by injury, soreness, and pain, and for overall health enhancement. Many runners use massage to help keep injuries at bay, and to smooth the road to recovery after injury.

There are many types of massage. Most runners will be best served by seeking out "sports" massage, which borrows from a variety of massage techniques and usually includes pressure, friction, cross-fiber kneading, vibration, and other techniques. Massage for runners is most often used to help the muscles prepare for or recover from hard effort and to aid with injury recovery. Massage helps direct blood and other body fluids toward or away from an injury site (which in theory can enhance healing) and break up scar tissue. Massage may help with pain relief by causing a release of tension when pressure is applied to certain pressure points throughout the body. In addition, massage has a proven relaxing effect.

Massage therapists must be licensed in 29 states and the District of Columbia. This requires intensive training, practice, and an exam. (See Resources for finding a qualified massage therapist in your area.) The Commission on Massage Therapy Accreditation (COMTA) accredits and approves training programs for massage therapists, and the National Certification Board for Therapeutic Massage and Bodywork provides certification to individuals. Most massage therapists are trained in anatomy, physiology, and kinesiology (movement science).

Massage therapy techniques and practices vary widely. Some therapists (and runners) believe that a massage is not effective unless it hurts; others advocate a lighter touch. Many elite runners get a massage at least weekly whether injured or not. "I believe everyone who runs should be massaged," writes nine-time New York City Marathon winner Grete Waitz in her autobiography, *World Class*. "Runners work hard, and especially at the top level massage helps to counter the constant stress and strain by providing a form of relaxation." Most people find that massage has psychological as well as physical benefits. I see it as a reward for all the hard work of training and racing.

Massage is not free, of course. Expect to pay at least $40 for a standard one-hour session in most places. You can also try self-massage, which I find extremely helpful in preventing soreness after a hard or long workout. I self-massage my lower legs and feet on a daily basis and find it helps keep soreness and stiffness at bay. My technique is to press and rub the sore areas vigorously, working in small circles and toward the heart with my fingers and thumbs. It's not a substitute for a full-body massage from a licensed professional, but it tides me over until I see my massage therapist again.

### Dealing With Overtraining

If you recognize overtraining early and take steps to correct it, it's possible to banish the problem within days. A simple first step is to take two to four days off from running and cross-training, then do an easy aerobic-intensity run and see how you feel over the next 24 hours. If your physical and mental symptoms have significantly diminished during this time, you can gradually return to training at a reduced level.

Responding to overtraining that has been going on for weeks, months, or longer, called overtraining syndrome, poses a greater challenge. In many runners this leads eventually to injury, illness, burnout, or subpar race performances. Even if the runner manages to escape these fates, dealing with overtraining syndrome can take months. In the most extreme cases the runner never again regains his or her previous form.

Perhaps the best-known runner to suffer from chronic overtraining syndrome is Alberto Salazar, a dazzlingly talented runner who was known in the early 1980s for pushing himself relentlessly in every race and training session. (He was once given last rites after collapsing at the finish line in the Falmouth Road Race.) Salazar made the 1984 U.S. Olympic marathon team and went into the race as one of the favorites, having held the marathon world record and won the 1982 Boston and New York City marathons. He performed far below expectations (16th) and was never again able to rise to his earlier standard. Salazar now admits he was brought down by his excessive zeal for hard training and his belief that more was always better.

Exercise physiologist and ultramarathon runner Tim Noakes, M.D., recommends that the overtrained runner stop running and not run again until the desire to run returns. I can't think of better advice, though the danger here for many runners is honestly identifying "desire" to run, as opposed to other motivators, including guilt, competitive goals, and social interests, to name but a few. A good guideline is to take at least four weeks off—if not completely from running, then at least from training with a competitive goal or focus. If motivation and enthusiasm fade quickly upon your return to running, then take off additional time. Don't structure your training or apply any performance pressure until you have been running with enjoyment for at least four weeks.

If you find yourself repeatedly slipping into patterns of overtraining, a sport psychologist can help you uncover the sources of your tendency to push yourself beyond what your body can reasonably handle. Like any behavior, running can become a conduit for our compulsions. In many cases these have their origins in experiences far removed from running. Getting a handle on these factors and learning to deal with them in healthier, more positive ways can greatly enhance both the pleasure we take in running and our progress toward our running goals.

CHAPTER 6

▶▶▶▶▶▶▶▶▶▶▶▶▶▶▶▶▶▶▶▶▶▶▶▶▶▶▶▶▶▶

# Running With—
# and for—Your Head

So far, we have focused primarily on what running does to and for your body. There is, however, another component to running that is at least as important—in fact, far more so, for many runners and coaches: What running does to and for your head, and what your head can do to help your running.

In this chapter, we will look first at the many ways running can help keep your mind healthy and functioning well. Then we'll examine the mental strategies involved in running to your potential.

---

**THERAPY AT 6:30 A.M.**

When I started running as a 17-year-old, my goal was to stay in shape for other sports. It wasn't long, however, before the goal of preserving my fitness between seasons became less important. Within a few weeks, the *real* reason I dragged myself out of bed every morning was the way running made me feel between the ears—in my head.

---

My running partner and I began to refer to our runs as Getting Our Head Together Time. After a run I'd come home all but bursting with energy and good cheer. I'd quickly shower, dress, eat breakfast, kiss my parents good-bye, and head off for school. My family was delighted, but mystified: Where was the sleepy, irritable young woman they were used to having around in the mornings, and who was her cheery replacement?

After running I felt better all day: more alert and productive, less absent-minded, generally on a natural high. Of course, running was not a complete cure-all for my adolescent mood swings, but it went a long way toward taming the craziness of those days.

### How Running Helps Your Head

I have been running for more than 23 years, and I've thought a lot about why I do it. I have also listened to thousands of other runners talk about the impact of running on their lives. After all that running and all that listening, as well as studying exercise science, I have come to realize that running has helped my mind as much as my body.

Countless times, I've looked to a run to lift my spirits, restore a sense of calm, help me focus, or provide a sense of well-being. I am a happier and saner person than I'd be if I did not run.

My responses to running are not unique. Ask any regular runner why she or he runs, the answer will almost certainly include some reference to the mental and emotional benefits that running can bring. Furthermore, it has been shown that running and other vigorous, repetitive physical activities can have a positive effect on mental health and well-being. Among other findings, aerobic exercise (including running):

• Elevates mood in healthy (nondepressed) people.

• Reduces symptoms of depression in mild to moderate cases. Several cross-sectional studies show that the more depressed people exercise, the better they feel. One study showed exercise to be the most effective method for reducing the depression that can result from experiencing a stressful life event. Running and other forms of exercise are often prescribed as an adjunct to medication and/or psychotherapy in the treatment of depression. (Note: Anyone suffering from or suspecting depression or any other mental-health problem should seek help from a qualified professional.)

• Is associated with higher self-reported levels of happiness, compared to levels reported by non-exercisers. One survey found that 72 percent of those who were moderately fit (running about six miles per week, or the equivalent in other activities) described themselves as "very happy." Of those who described themselves as "pretty happy" or "not so happy," only slightly more than one third were moderately fit. In one study, college students who took part in a 15-week running program reported significant increases in their quality of life, as compared to a control group of students who reported no change.

• Can reduce anxiety levels in both normal and anxious people. This has been shown both for single bouts of exercise and for ongoing exercise programs. Several studies have found that trained athletes have lower anxiety levels than those who do not exercise. Running has been used successfully to help manage severe cases of anxiety. Although other "diversional" treatments (biofeedback, meditation, etc.) seem to work equally well, the effect produced by running may be longer-lasting.

Some research has suggested that regular exercise can even fundamentally change an individual's personality. In one study, "high-fitness" subjects were shown to have higher levels of emotional stability, self-sufficiency, self-assurance, and imaginativeness than subjects who reported low levels of fitness. Other studies have shown that higher reported levels of exercise are associated with greater self-confidence, conscientiousness, and persistence. Research also links running to stress resistance, whether the stress consists of the minor irritations of daily life such as excessive noise, or a major stressor such as a death in the family or a divorce.

None of these findings surprises me. Research has so far yet to answer the "chicken or egg" question about runners and their personality tendencies: Are calm, confident, persistent, and conscientious people drawn to running, or does running bring out those qualities in people? It is probably a bit of both. For me, running is a calming, restorative, and connecting activity, almost like rocking a baby to sleep. Running appeals to the primitive biological urge to move over the ground we inhabit, to connect to it and thus call it our own.

### A Nonscientific Examination of the Mental Benefits of Running

Science can only go so far in explaining why running is so good for mental health. Listed below are some of the nonscientific ways in which running can make life a little brighter:

• *Running provides a "time out."* Like many other people, runners tend to lead overscheduled lives in which they feel pulled in too many different directions. "There never seems to be any time for me to just be *me*," is a frequently voiced complaint. Running can provide that time. During a run I'm not a writer with a pressing deadline, a parent of two demanding young children, a daughter who's been remiss about calling her parents, or a friend who promised to e-mail a valuable piece of information. I'm a woman out for a run. To me, feeling that way—for at least a few minutes every day—is vital.

• *Running connects us to nature and to our animal selves.* The late doctor and runner/philosopher George Sheehan, M.D., used to urge runners to "be a good animal." By saying that, Sheehan reminded us of the extraordinary power running has to keep us in touch with our animal beings—the part of us that, without running, can get lost for days and weeks on end (or even permanently) amidst the e-mails and faxes, manicures and must-read articles, memos and school board meetings. When we run, we work our bodies, sweat, ache, and feel physical fatigue, hunger, and thirst—as our ancestors did back in a time when their survival depended in part on their ability to walk and run long distances. Running also gives us an excuse, most of the time, to go outside, to experience heat, cold, rain, snow, changing seasons, hills, dirt, sunlight, and wind on our faces. We didn't evolve as human beings to sit at a desk in front of a computer monitor for 10 hours at a time, and running reminds us of that.

• *Running gives us a sense of achievement.* I start most days with a run. At the end of the day I may look back on projects that fizzled, lunches that got canceled, and play-dates that never showed up. But, for better or worse, that run happened. If it served no other purpose than allowing me to cross at least one item off my daily to-do list, it was a run worth doing.

• *Running raises self-esteem.* Over time, running helps most people look better, feel better, and behave better. The internal and external feedback from this transformation can create a positive spiraling cycle of gradually rising self-esteem. I remember this from my initial forays into running in high school: I enjoyed running because it made me feel strong. I could see and feel my growing muscles, and the stopwatch told me I was running progressively farther and faster with less effort. The more I did, the better I felt. Of course, as with most experiences in life, there can be too much of a good thing. Runners have to come to terms with healthy limits for their running and recognize when trying to run more miles, or at a faster pace, can be counterproductive. (See Chapter 5 for more on this phenomenon, known as overtraining.)

• *Running puts things in perspective.* Running is a demanding activity, and as such, it can offer an enlightening perspective on
other demanding aspects of life. Everyone has moments when
they feel overwhelmed—with their own feelings, with the needs
of others, with the pressures of too many tasks to accomplish in
too little time. Sometimes there's a sense of "I can't"—can't present a more positive and upbeat face, can't comfort someone
else's pain, can't meet the needs of a child, parent, or spouse,
can't do everything that needs to be done in the next 24 hours.
Running, too, is filled with such moments, especially if it is pursued at a high level. In the late stages of a race it's all too common to feel that one simply can't keep going—the effort is just
too difficult and painful. Usually, I just need to take a deep
breath, gather myself, and keep pushing, knowing that I am doing the best I can.

## THE "RUNNER'S HIGH" RECONSIDERED

When running soared in popularity during the "running boom" of the early
to mid 1970s, there was a lot of talk about a "runner's high" that supposedly
lifted the lucky runner out of the realm of pain and suffering to someplace
above it all. This misunderstanding was probably responsible for more than a
few beginners calling it quits after a block or two of huffing and puffing.

The term runner's high—probably borrowed from the drug culture—
sprung from the perception that running was so challenging that only by entering a druglike state could someone possibly carry on with it for more
than a few hundred yards. For the most part, talk of the runner's high has
gone the way of fringed bell-bottoms, but I still get the occasional question
about whether the much-touted high really exists, and if so, how to achieve
it. Usually the questioner envisions either a state of pain-free bliss, or an almost giddy "up" feeling. As one non-runner put it to me, "I imagine it's like
being on nitrous oxide at the dentist. You know you must be in pain, but it
just doesn't bother you."

That approximates a feeling I've had maybe twice in my entire running career. I recall the final 400 meters of the half-marathon in which I ran my
best-ever time by two minutes. Every fiber in my body hurt more than I'd
imagined possible. Yet at the sight of the finish line, I felt relief literally flood
through my body. The pain didn't go away, but I knew that I could survive it

and that it would be ending soon. If that's what it takes to achieve the runner's high, I'd rather have nitrous oxide! I'm much more familiar with the feeling of pain that comes from running at my physical limits.

What is much more real and common is the "runner's calm," which I've experienced countless times. It's a feeling that comes over me during easy or moderate training runs when I experience a profound, all-encompassing calm that I seldom feel away from running. This feeling is enhanced by a heightened mental and sensory awareness. I don't get this feeling on every run, and there's no telling when it will occur and how long it will last. Beginning runners probably won't experience the "runner's calm" for at least the first few months, because the challenge of getting in shape is such a distraction. Still, it's a feeling worth waiting for, and one that, if my experience is any guide, veteran runners can count on experiencing time and again.

## QUESTION AND ANSWER

**Q.** I dropped out of a race because I didn't feel good. How can I avoid dropping out in future races?

**A.** You're bound to have races in which you consider dropping out. In fact, many elite runners admit that there comes a point in *every* race when they want to quit. Yet most of the time, they manage to finish. Running has taught me that most things in life are doable. When you feel like dropping out of a race, try backing off just slightly. Often that's all it takes to feel better and regain your focus. If the urge to quit is still there, break the race into segments and focus on one at a time: to the top of the hill, to the next mile marker, to halfway, etc. Try not to think of anything beyond that. Often if we concentrate exclusively on the present, the outcome will take care of itself. When you finish, you will feel triumphant, no matter what your result. You can then embrace this feeling of accomplishment and apply it in your next tough race.

There are times when you should definitely drop out of a race and seek medical attention. If you feel feverish, faint, disoriented, confused, dizzy, have cold or clammy skin, a severe headache, vomiting, or severe diarrhea, or develop frostbite or hypothermia, stop running and get medical help as soon as possible.

### How Running Really Helps Your Mind

The reasons behind the feelings of calm and well-being offered by running are primarily caused by chemical changes in the blood. Exercise that takes place at an aerobic intensity or higher—an effort that causes heavier than normal breathing, and increases perspiration—triggers the release into the bloodstream of hormonelike substances called endorphins. Endorphins have a calming effect, which is known to last for up to several hours after completion of the activity, depending on the intensity and duration of the exercise.

Interestingly, however, endorphins have not been proven to cross the blood-brain barrier, so it can't be stated conclusively that they are responsible for the so-called endorphin effect of exercise. About 10 years ago this led some scientists to look into other possible reasons for the calming and stress-reducing effects of aerobic exercise. These scientists, while not discounting the possible endorphin effect, speculated that other indirect effects of exercise—such as the "time out" component and raised self-esteem, both discussed in the previous section of this chapter—also could be responsible. In addition, it's likely that by increasing blood flow throughout the body (including the brain), running and other aerobic exercise would increase mental alertness and acuity, thus explaining why runners and other exercisers report feeling focused and in control during workouts and competition.

Whatever the science behind running's mental benefits, they are present and real for runners at all levels. Olympic marathon gold medalist Joan Benoit Samuelson, now in her mid-forties and the mother of two teenagers, says, "If I couldn't run again, I think I would explode. Running is my drug of choice. If I don't get out every day I get anxious and irritable." Kathrine Switzer, the first woman to officially run the Boston Marathon, in 1967, and now the director of Avon Running, says she runs for "sanity and vanity."

### How Your Head Can Help Your Running

"If you think you are beaten, you are.
If you think you dare not, you don't.

If you'd like to win, but think you can't, it's almost a cinch you won't.
If you think you'll lose, you're lost, for out in the world we find
  success begins with a fellow's will; it's all in the state of mind.
Life's battles don't always go to the stronger or faster man; but
  sooner or later the man who wins is the man who thinks he can."

                                        —*Anonymous*

The connection between running and the mind works both ways. That is, just as running strengthens you mentally, your mind makes you a stronger runner. In the purest sense, the mind truly is the athlete.

Athletes in all sports trumpet "the will to win." The mental component of winning can be huge, as baseball legend Yogi Berra reminded us in his immortal declaration, "All of this game is 90 percent mental." Runners are not the only athletes who use the mind as a powerful stimulus. But in running, an activity that is so much about pure physical effort, that mental "push" plays perhaps a more important role than in most other sports. Genetics aside, there's little luck or chance involved in doing well as a runner, and runners know this. In general, the harder you work, the better you perform. And working hard takes incredible strength of mind.

Sport psychology is a relatively new and still evolving field. Among athletes there is still, sadly, a stigma associated with consulting a sport psychologist to address mental issues affecting one's performance. Though that stigma has lessened in the past 10 to 15 years, few top-level runners will talk with candor about the mental aspects of their running, much less admit to receiving counseling from a sport psychologist. There's too much fear of accusations of "head case" or worse.

Andy Palmer, Ph.D., used to be one of those athletes. Like most young, gifted runners in the 1970s and '80s, Palmer trained with a vengeance, as much as 150 miles per week, the majority of it at a six-minute per mile pace or faster. From cold, remote northwestern Maine, he was undeterred by solitude or extremes in weather. Palmer had success, notching personal best times of 29:04 for 10k, 47:52 for 10 miles, and 2:16 for the marathon. He qualified for the U.S. Olympic Marathon Trials twice, and once held the U.S. single-age 30k record for 29-year-olds. Palmer founded Maine Running Camp in 1980 and began coaching runners at all levels, both individually and in groups. The more he listened and observed, and the more he tuned in to his own running experiences, the more convinced he became that running to one's potential was at least as much a mental exercise as a physical one. Of course training the body was important, but so was training the mind, and so many runners—even very good ones—completely neglected that aspect. Palmer went back to school and got a Ph.D. in sport psychology.

Palmer believes that without mental training, all the physical training in the world won't help a runner reach his or her potential. And he is serious about the "training" aspect of mental training. He practices, and recommends, daily meditation, focused breathing, relaxation-response exercises, and other techniques for improving the many different mental aspects of running to one's potential. As far as I'm concerned, every runner can benefit from working with a trained sport psychology professional.

Most running coaches agree that at least 50 percent of their job involves working with the minds of their athletes. Palmer finds that many runners want to pay more attention to the mental side of their running. What they don't realize is that it takes a lot of work! Like anything, the novelty can be intimidating, and the effort of mental training can lessen over time. In the next section we'll talk about specific mental strategies for improving your running. To deal with specific issues that you have, however, it's best to team up with a sport psychologist. (See Resources for suggestions on finding one in your area.) In my coaching and writing, I've tried to stress the crucial importance of mental training right alongside the physical aspect. Interestingly, despite runners' protestations that they don't need or want mental training, my spoken and written comments on the topic often elicit greater interest and response than what I have to say about the purely physical aspects of running.

## QUESTION AND ANSWER

**Q.** What's it like to work with a sport psychologist?

**A.** Sport psychologists are for runners at all levels, and meet with athletes in both group and individual settings. If you run for a school team, your coach may have a sport psychologist talk to the group at the beginning of the season and be available for individual sessions by appointment. Outside of the school setting, most sport psychologists meet one-on-one with clients, either on a short-term or ongoing basis. Most clients are concerned with resolving specific issues related to training and/or competition, such as anxiety, confidence, or body image. Most sport psychology is "talk therapy," though a sport psychologist will refer you to a medical professional if drug treatment—for anxiety or depression, for example—is warranted.

## MOTIVATIONAL MANTRAS THAT WORK

What do runners tell themselves when the going gets tough in workouts and races? Here is a collection of motivational mantras from runners of a variety of fitness levels and backgrounds:

"This is just a bad patch."
—Frank Shorter, Olympic marathon gold medalist in 1972, and silver medalist in 1976

"I say, 'Fly like an eagle.' It's corny and not very original, but it works for me."
—Judy Harrigan, 52, New York, NY

"When being passed, particularly early in long races, I say, 'It's a long race. I'll see you guys later.'"
—Barbara Anderson-Tomchin, 3:06 marathoner, Woodstock, VT

"I've been here before."
—Grete Waitz, nine-time New York City Marathon champion, 1984 Olympic marathon silver medalist

"In the middle of a race I'll sometimes say, 'This doesn't really hurt.'"
—Carly Berwick, 18:00 5k runner, Brooklyn, NY

"My favorite mantras are 'Stay tough,' 'You can do it,' and 'Concentrate.'"
—Catherine Smith, 35:00 10k runner, Wayne, NJ

"This won't last forever."
—Bill Rodgers, four-time New York City Marathon and Boston Marathon winner

"I just count: One-two-three, one-two-three, one-two-three . . ."
                                    —*Joan Baldassarri, 3:20 marathon runner, Bronx, NY*

"I'm doing my best."
                    —*Tegla Loroupe, marathon world record holder, two-time New York City Marathon winner*

"*Ya begu khorosho*—that's Russian for 'I'm running well.' "
                                    —*Jennifer Latham, 2:42 marathon runner, Somers, NY*

"I think of the people I know who have real problems. Then that hill or last mile doesn't seem so difficult."
                                    —*Kathleen Coughlin, 2:57 marathon runner, New York, NY*

"During tough workouts I used to tell myself, 'Somewhere in the world, someone is training harder than I am.' "
                                    —*Tom Fleming, two-time New York City Marathon winner, Bloomfield, NJ*

"The song 'One Moment in Time': 'Give me one moment in time when I'm all that I hoped I could be . . .' "
                                    —*Marie Wickham, New York, NY*

"During workouts I sometimes say to myself—either out loud or in my head—'Nothing without hard work.' It not only reminds me that nothing of value comes without some effort, but it's in thanks to God that I have the opportunity to work hard and hopefully extend my life—which makes the hard work a little easier. During races I sometimes say the word 'easy' when I feel an asthma attack coming on. It's not just the word that helps, but also the concentration on speaking."
                                    —*Adria Gallup-Black, 41, New York, NY*

"It may not sound very poetic, but when I start to hurt, I say to myself, 'Suck it up!' It works for me."
                                    —*Susan Doyle-Lindrud, 17:00 5k runner, Basking Ridge, NJ*

### How to Use Your Mind in Training

To many runners, the running they do every day is a "no-brainer." It's true that if you have set up a sensible running program (see Chapters 1 and 3 for details on setting up programs) and committed to your goals (see "Strategies for Maintaining Motivation," below), the actual running you do from day to day should be more or less automatic. Former 5,000-meter American record holder PattiSue Plumer once said that for the most part, her daily running was "like brushing my teeth; I don't even think about it."

Still, being mindful on the run can help make training more pleasant, healthy, and productive. Here are strategies I recommend before, during, and after training runs:

• *Don't skip your run when your brain is fried.* Many people confuse mental and physical fatigue. Most of us are tired at the end of the workday, which also happens to be the time we can fit in a run. The temptation is to go home and "relax" rather than add to the fatigue by running. Actually, the more tired you are from the workday, the more essential that run probably is. A run can be one of the best antidotes to post-work fatigue—certainly better than sipping a cocktail or "relaxing" by watching the news on TV. Within minutes of heading out the door or jumping on the treadmill, the mind is clear and the problems and pressures of the workday will seem a million miles away.

• *Give it time.* I have a rule when I don't feel like running: I give it five minutes. That is, I head out the door telling myself I'll just run for five minutes, and if I still don't feel like running, I'll come home. I can count on one hand the number of times I've decided to come home at the end of those five minutes.

• *Don't succumb to boredom.* "Running is so boring!" I've been told by more than one person who's probably never done more than dash for a bus. I do admit that the activity can, on occasion, become monotonous. When I find myself glancing at my watch and wishing the run was over, I have several strategies. My favorite is to really focus on my natural surroundings. Most of my running is done on three or four different routes, and I have been doing these same basic runs for years. However, when I am truly mindful of the sights, sounds, smells, and textures that surround me during a daily run, it can feel as though I'm running that particular route for the first time. Another strategy is to think about a work-related challenge. Often the solution becomes plain as day in the clear light of a run. My third boredom-banning technique is to try and schedule some runs with other people. I usually run alone due to my erratic schedule, and finding partners who can accommodate my schedule can be a challenge. But it's always well worth it. Running is one of the greatest conversational outlets I know.

• *Practice meditation.* On some runs I do an improvised form of meditation on some runs. I pick a word, idea, or image and just center on it for a few moments. Usually that is as long as I can manage before my attention wanders and I'm back to wondering what my son is doing at school, or reminding myself to defrost the chicken for supper. I don't force these meditative moments, and often weeks will go by without having one. If I have a race coming up, I may use the time to visualize the event and plan strategies. (see the discussion of visualization, below.)

• *Focus on the run itself.* It can also be both useful and enjoyable to use your running time to simply think about running. Especially as a race draws near, I tune in to my training, assessing pace, cadence, effort level (heart rate, breathing), and any aches and pains. All these pieces of information help me formulate a race plan.

## STRATEGIES FOR MAINTAINING MOTIVATION

Sport psychologists say that issues surrounding motivation are the most common reasons they see athletes. We all want the *results* of training—the fast times, the victories—yet many of us lack the motivation to do the work to achieve those results.

There are many instances in which a runner might find him- or herself lacking in motivation. Some runners seem to have no trouble training hard, but then lose motivation when racing. Others have trouble getting out the door to run, but are generally excited and motivated to succeed when it comes time to pin on a race number. Some people are unmotivated when the weather turns cold and wet, the days grow short and dark, and out-of-shape bodies can be hidden beneath layers of concealing clothing. Sometimes lack of motivation is fleeting: You're tired from lack of sleep and you'd rather sleep in than run today, but tomorrow you bounce out of bed as usual. Other times it can last for days, weeks, or even months.

I seldom had problems with motivation early in my running career. I had found something that I was good at, I was young and generally untroubled by injury or excessive fatigue, and I was getting faster all the time. It wasn't until I was in my mid-thirties and had been running seriously for almost 10 years that I started having trouble with motivation. I was no longer getting faster, I was busy with work and volunteer activities, and I wanted to start a family. Why, I wondered, should I continue to work so hard at running?

Getting married and pregnant in quick succession temporarily solved my motivation problem, because I could no longer train. But after giving birth I confronted a whole new set of motivational issues as I attempted to regain fitness. Whew! Any woman can tell you that getting back in shape after pregnancy is a Herculean task. (For more information and advice on running during and after pregnancy, see Chapter 11.) Several years later, I am finally back to where I want to be, but it took a lot of motivation.

Regardless of the origins of your low motivation, here are some strategies for maintaining—or regaining—a motivated mind-set. I have refined many of these ideas in conversations and e-mail exchanges with sport psychologist Andy Palmer, Ph.D., director of Maine Running Camp.

- *Set goals.* It's impossible for me to do anything if I can't tell myself why I am doing it. A goal can be as simple and unpretentious as "I want to stop eating peanut butter out of the jar in front of the TV at 10 P.M.," or as lofty and long-range as "I want to win an Olympic gold medal in 2008." It doesn't matter what your goal is, as long as it is honest and comes from within. Don't set goals to please other people, as in, "I want my husband to be proud of me." Meeting your running goals may well inspire pride in others, but you have to do it for *yourself* first and foremost. Running goals that are complex or long-range should be broken down into manageable subgoals—bite-size chunks that you can set yourself up to accomplish over a reasonable period of time. For example, if your goal is to run a marathon a year from now, and you're just getting back into running after a significant layoff, you should set subgoals of completing a 5k (3.1 miles), 10k (6.2 miles), and gradually longer races over the coming months. (See Chapters 1 and 3 for more on setting up training programs.)

• *Keep records.* Maintaining a running log brings clarity and organization to your running. (See Chapter 1 for a discussion of running logs.) Another important reason for written records is to give yourself indelible proof of your running accomplishments. Often when I'm training hard and feeling like I just can't do some particularly tough workout, I'll look at my log and see that I recently did a similar workout. That reminds me that I can do it again—and probably do it even better, thanks to the fitness I've gained in the interim. I also write down my goals and look at them periodically as a reminder.

• *Use the example of others.* Running may be solitary at times, but runners often use the inspiration of others to motivate them, both in training and racing. Heroes and heroines can inspire us. I have a photograph of Grete Waitz, nine-time winner of the New York City Marathon, that I keep on my refrigerator door. It inspires me and reminds me that everyone—even Grete Waitz—lacks motivation at some point, and we all can get through those moments.

• *Try a motivational mantra.* During a hard race or even a workout, find a word or phrase that can get you through the toughest spots. For examples of motivational mantras of some top runners, see "Motivational Mantras That Work" on page 148–149.

• *Break it up.* Break the race or workout into manageable segments and just get through them one at a time. Sometimes even mile by mile isn't small enough to subdivide a grueling event. I have a friend who once divided a tough portion of the New York City Marathon into block-by-block chunks (a New York City block is equivalent to 1/20 of a mile). It worked for him—he got through that section and finished the race.

Lack of motivation that persists for more than a couple of weeks often means that you need to take a closer look at your running program and how it fits into the rest of your life. You may have overtrained or overextended your training and racing season. (See the charts in Chapter 3 that outline various suggested training cycles.) Or you may have other factors in your life that are exhausting you. Ideally, running should play an energizing and life-enhancing role in your life, not serve as an added stress.

### Racing With Your Head

It has been said that the runner who "wants it the most" will triumph on race day. I believe that although talent and training play a more significant role in success than the so-called "will to win," athletes of equal talent and training have only their minds to pit against each other in the final sprint to the tape. Here are mental strategies for racing to your potential:

• *Embrace success.* When you set your goals (for tips on goal-setting, see "Strategies for Maintaining Motivation," page 151–153), ask yourself honestly whether reaching your potential is among them. It may not be in every competitive situation, and it doesn't have to be. I run some races primarily as a way to test my fitness for another upcoming event. I don't care who beats me or whom I beat; rather, my goal is to do my best on that day and see how my training is progressing. That said, I believe that races are a good opportunity to shoot for the best possible outcome, without holding back. We often do hold back, for various reasons. Sometimes we haven't yet had enough experience in applying our competitive instincts to running. We may feel that winning, or beating other people, isn't nice or polite. In fact, it's *not* giving your all that shows a lack of respect. Would you want someone to ease up against you?

• *Go for "flow."* Psychologist Mihaly Csikszentmihalyi has popularized the term "flow" to describe total absorption in an activity. For flow to occur, the challenge of the activity must be great but within reach; the activity must have a goal; and a focus must be maintained. Running can provide an ideal outlet for the conditions of flow, and we can reach our potential by allowing flow to occur. Try to set up race situations in which you are challenged, have a goal, and can concentrate deeply. If you feel distracted, relax and allow your focus to gradually return to the task at hand. Don't force it; it will come. It takes practice, but the rewards can be substantial.

• *Make anxiety your friend.* Practically every runner gets nervous before races, from the frontrunners to those bringing up the back of the pack. Prerace nervousness is normal, and even healthy as a way of getting to what sport psychologists call an "optimal level of arousal." "The day I stop getting nervous before races is the day I retire," says U.S. 10,000-meter Olympian Brad Hauser. Still, too much anxiety can hurt performance, and even cause a runner to drop out of a race. The best way to calm nerves, say coaches and sport psychologists, is to simply execute what has been done before in practice. "I need to go into every race, even the Olympics, knowing that there's nothing special about this race because I've done it all before," Hauser says. If you're racing for the first time, don't worry about your time or place; rather, just set a simple goal, such as finishing with a smile on your face. Andy Palmer tells runners who get nervous before and during races to "suspend judgment." That is, stop caring about the result, and just focus on running.

• *Try visualization.* Physical training can get your body ready to perform on race day the same way rehearsing a play prepares actors for opening night. By the same token, mentally "rehearsing" a race by envisioning it clearly and in detail ahead of time can prepare a runner for the feelings of the race itself. For long races in particular, I like to sit down for 15 minutes or so and visualize the race mile by mile in my head. I find a quiet place, look at a course map or course description if I have one, and recall previous experiences of the race if I've done it before. I find this strategy particularly helpful in the marathon, which is always longer and more challenging than I remember from the last one or from any training run.

### DOES RUNNING MAKE YOU SMARTER?

There is ample and well-documented evidence that running can reduce stress and elevate mood. Many people also wonder whether running and other aerobic activities can affect brain function in such a way as to increase intelligence, as measured with standard IQ tests and other tools.

Unfortunately for runners, there's not yet any direct evidence of that. In fact, many runners, myself included, freely admit that when we are in heavy training, we can get so spaced-out and fuzzy-headed, especially as a big race approaches, that we feel decidedly *less* smart! (Triathlete Karen Smyers has spoken of the "mush-head syndrome" that affects her as a major race draws near.)

There is some evidence from animal studies suggesting that running and other physical activities might be associated with increases in intelligence in humans. Researchers at the Salk Institute have found that mice who were physically active produced more new brain-cell growth than inactive mice. It's been suggested that running might delay the onset and progression of some diseases that cause degeneration of the brain and nervous system.

In unrelated studies on pregnant women and follow-up studies of their children, it's been suggested that women who are active during pregnancy might endow their children with increased brainpower. James Clapp III, M.D., compared the children of women who ran and did other aerobic activities while pregnant and those who were sedentary. The women were matched for age, income level, and socioeconomic background, and both groups had normal pregnancies and delivered their babies without major complications. Clapp reported that the women who worked out aerobically three to five times a week while pregnant gave birth to children who scored higher on standard intelligence tests administered at age 5, compared to a group of children whose mothers did not exercise during pregnancy.

For what it's worth, at many colleges and universities, track and cross-country runners on scholarship have a higher graduation rate than the student body at large and athletes in other sports.

▶▶▶▶▶▶▶▶▶▶▶▶▶▶▶▶▶▶▶▶▶▶▶▶▶▶▶▶▶▶▶▶

# CHAPTER 7

# Fueling Your Body

R unners love to eat. Like most runners, I find that running makes everything taste better. Moreover, running motivates me to seek out healthy food and drink to fuel my running.

Food and drink can have an enormous effect on both our running success and the pleasure we derive from running. Fortunately, eating well as a runner is not much different from eating healthily in general. The best runners in the world eat more or less the same diet that ordinary runners do—with cultural and ethnic variations, of course. Your diet is important to your running, but of course it will not make up for poor training, genetics, and other factors.

This chapter offers the information and insights you need to make optimal nutritional choices to support your running—and enjoy your food as well. (For specific, detailed analysis of and recommendations for your diet, consult a registered dietitian; see Resources for information on finding a dietitian in your area.)

### Basic Sports Nutrition

More than 40 nutrients are essential to human health. The body manufactures several on its own (some fats in the liver, vitamin K in the intestines, and vitamin D from sunlight absorbed through the skin), but the rest must be absorbed from food sources. The 40 essential nutrients fall into the following six categories:

• *Carbohydrates.* For runners, carbohydrates ("carbs") should make up the bulk of the diet. Carbohydrates are organic compounds made up of carbon, hydrogen, and oxygen. The molecules are arranged either in short, simple chains (simple carbohydrates) or longer, more complicated chains (complex carbohydrates). The body easily breaks down both forms of carbohydrate to fuel activity. Carbohydrates provide energy for almost all the functions of the brain and nervous system, as well as most muscle activity. They are found in all fruits, vegetables, grains, nuts, beans, milk, milk products, and in small amounts in meat, fish, and poultry. Every gram of carbohydrate contains about four calories. Nutritionists recommend that a healthy adult consume at least 50 percent of calories from carbohydrate sources. For runners and other endurance athletes, a 55 to 70 percent carbohydrate diet often is a more appropriate goal. Carbohydrate is stored as glycogen in the muscles and liver, where it can fuel about 90 to 120 minutes of high-level physical activity, depending on fitness. Runners who train an hour or less per day should aim to eat about three grams of carbohydrate per pound of body weight daily. Those training more should strive for four to five grams. (See pages 164–166 for more on how to determine what and how much to eat each day.)

• *Fats.* Do you view fat as a dietary evil? Many of us do, but in fact fat is essential to health and survival. Fats are found in meat, poultry, fish, eggs, milk, all but nonfat dairy products, nuts, seeds, legumes, and in trace amounts in most plant foods. Fats serve as a concentrated source of energy, transport fat-soluble vitamins in the body, and facilitate growth and nervous-system activity. They also improve the taste of food, which leads many people in Western cultures to consume much more fat than we need. Surveys suggest that the average American consumes about 37 percent of calories as fat. The American Heart Association and other health organizations recommend a diet that is no more than 30 percent fat for healthy adults. Saturated fat in particular contributes to the buildup of cholesterol in the blood, which can increase the risk of the artery-blocking plaque that can cause heart disease. A high-fat diet also increases the risk of breast and colon cancer. A gram of fat contains more than twice as many calories (about nine) as a gram of carbohydrate (about four). Thus, eliminating even a small amount of dietary fat can make room for the addition of significantly more carbohydrate—the runner's primary fuel source.

• *Protein.* Protein generates red blood cells, builds and repairs muscle tissue, aids in the processing of enzymes and hormones, and helps maintain the immune system. Most nutritionists recommend that about 15 percent of calories come from protein. It's important to consume a variety of protein-rich foods to obtain the full complement of amino acids that are the building blocks of protein. Runners may need slightly more protein than sedentary people to optimize muscle recovery, especially after long or strenuous exercise. These increased needs, however, are not extreme, and should not lead runners to limit carbohydrate or consume large quantities of specially engineered high-protein foods (see "Special Foods and Fluids" box, page 166). Protein is plentiful in meat, poultry, fish, eggs, and nuts. It's also found in milk, dairy products, and virtually all plant foods (especially soy products, legumes, and seeds).

• *Vitamins.* Vitamins are organic compounds needed by the body in small amounts for specific metabolic reactions and normal growth and functioning. Vitamins contains no calories, so if you take them "for energy" you are buying into myths perpetuated by the multibillion-dollar vitamin industry. There are two main types of vitamins: fat soluble (vitamins A, D, and K) and water soluble (the B vitamins and vitamins C and E). Fat-soluble vitamins can be stored in the body; water-soluble vitamins are excreted in the urine if consumed in excess. There are endless theories about the vitamin needs of runners. Most scientific evidence suggests that running and other strenuous exercise does not increase the body's vitamin needs and that taking vitamins beyond recommended daily levels will not improve running performance. Moreover, megadoses of some vitamins can have unhealthy and even dangerous side effects. There is, however, some research suggesting that vitamins C and E (along with selenium, another antioxidant) can enhance muscle recovery after exercise.

• *Minerals.* Like vitamins, minerals are needed in tiny amounts to maintain body functions. The most important minerals are calcium, potassium, sodium, iron, and zinc. Calcium, found most abundantly in milk and dairy products and in smaller amounts in leafy green vegetables and some nuts and seeds, is essential for maintaining healthy bones. Runners who get frequent stress fractures may be advised to consume more calcium-rich foods and/or take supplements. Potassium and sodium (salt) are electrolytes, which help maintain the body's water balance and distribution. A generation ago, athletes were often given sodium tablets before and during exercise. This is now thought to be overkill; though it's important to maintain adequate sodium in the body, the average Westerner's diet contains too much sodium rather than too little. Some runners wind up short of potassium, which is lost through sweating. Symptoms of potassium deficiency include muscle cramping and weakness. Bananas, oranges, grapefruit, apricots, and tomatoes are all rich in potassium. Iron, which helps transport oxygen in the blood, is abundant in red meat, poultry, egg yolks, legumes, molasses, green leafy vegetables, and whole grains. Studies have shown that running causes iron loss, possibly through perspiration and the microtrauma caused by the impact of running feet against the ground. Runners who avoid red meat and other foods rich in iron may develop iron deficiency anemia. This condition, which is diagnosed by measuring iron stores, can be treated by increasing dietary iron and taking iron supplements. It can take several months to restore iron to healthy levels. Zinc helps with wound healing and immune-system function, and may contribute to recovery from hard workouts. Some runners take a zinc supplement to improve recovery and increase their resistance to infection.

• *Water.* Water is the one nutrient we can't live without for more than a few days. The human body is about 70 percent water, and water permeates every human cell. For runners, water is essential for maintaining adequate blood flow to the working muscles and keeping the body cool by sweating. On a warm day a runner can easily lose as much as three to four pounds of water per hour due to sweating. Hydrating before running, drinking fluids on the run, and rehydrating after running are all vital to running performance and overall health. You should drink enough so that you urinate at least once every four to six hours, and your urine is clear or pale yellow.

## QUESTION AND ANSWER

**Q.** I've felt unusually tired on my runs lately. Might I be anemic?

**A.** Anemia is a condition in which the blood is deficient in red blood cells, hemoglobin (an iron-containing protein in the blood), or total volume. This reduces the oxygen-carrying capacity of the blood and causes fatigue, lethargy, loss of appetite, easy bruising, and delayed healing. A runner who develops anemia will notice a drop in performance and an increase in fatigue even during easy runs. If you suspect you might be suffering from anemia, get a blood test that includes a measure of your hemoglobin and stored blood (ferritin) levels. Clinical anemia is generally defined as hemoglobin levels below 12 grams (g) per 100 milliliters (ml) of blood in women and 13 g per 100 ml in men, though stored-blood levels offer more details of the extent of the problem. Most doctors recommend treating anemia by increasing iron in the diet and/or prescribing iron supplements (pills or, in extreme cases, injections).

To prevent anemia, make sure your diet includes iron-rich foods, such as red meat, poultry, egg yolks, and dark-green leafy vegetables, or to supplement with iron following a doctor's advice (because of the risk of oversupplementation and the possible buildup of excess iron stores). Premenopausal women have higher iron needs than men (18 mg daily for women, compared to 12 mg for men) because of the blood lost during menstruation. It's unclear whether running or other high-level physical activities increase iron needs. Some doctors refer to "sports anemia" that develops in athletes during heavy training as a result of iron lost in sweat and hemoglobin excreted in urine due to the destruction of red blood cells with increased body temperature, spleen activity, and circulation rates. Recent research also suggests that runners in the early stages of training may have reduced iron levels. The levels return to normal within several months. Don't assume you're anemic without having a blood test, and never take iron supplements (which vary widely in their iron content) except under medical supervision.

## 12 RULES OF HEALTHY EATING FOR RUNNERS

I'm not a nutritionist. I have no formal training, and no professional degrees in nutrition. My qualification is that I've eaten three meals a day, more or less, for the 23 years I've been a runner. The dozen rules below are what guide me in my food choices and eating habits.

*Rule #1: Food is fuel.* The food we eat fuels every activity our bodies perform, from running to balancing a checkbook to having sex. You must eat enough food to fuel all your body's activities. If you don't, all other discussion of food and nutrition is beside the point.

*Rule #2: Eating well is not complicated.* The basic guidelines are balance and moderation. Most people know how to eat well. Many fail to do so, however, for lifestyle or emotional reasons. These factors are worth examining, because a healthy, balanced diet can enhance all aspects of life, including running.

*Rule #3: The more variety, the better.* The more different foods and types of foods you eat, the better, because human nutrition is an evolving science. We simply don't know all the benefits or all the risks of all the nutrients in all the foods we eat. Try new foods and preparation methods. Don't settle into food "ruts." Allow yourself to eat "bad" foods in moderate quantities. I follow the 80/20 rule that a nutritionist once suggested: I figure that if I eat healthily about 80 percent of the time, what I consume the other 20 percent of the time isn't going to kill me.

*Rule #4: Drink, drink, drink.* It's all but impossible for a runner to consume too many nonalcoholic, noncaffeinated beverages. Many runners don't drink enough fluids. You are fully hydrated if your urine is pale or clear. Sports drinks can also add carbohydrate calories to fuel your running.

*Rule #5: Eat colorfully.* A plateful of brightly colored foods—especially greens, oranges, reds, and yellows—is generally healthier than a meal of dull-colored or white foods. Bright foods tend to be less processed and fresher (and therefore higher in nutrients) than dull foods.

*Rule #6: Carbohydrates rule.* Do not follow any diet that obtains less than 50 percent of calories from "carbs." Dozens of well-controlled studies show that a high-carbohydrate diet is best for fueling endurance aerobic activity. Aim for 50 to 60 percent carbohydrate, no more than 30 percent fat, and 15 percent protein for overall health and optimal running performance.

*Rule #7: There's no excuse for bonking.* Do whatever it takes to maintain the body's carbohydrate (glycogen) stores before and during exercise, thus avoiding the "bonk"—a sudden and dramatic energy lapse. The challenge comes with workouts and races lasting 90 minutes or longer, such as half-marathons, marathons, and triathlons. This is the point at which glycogen stores start to run out. Sports drinks and energy bars and gels can help replace carbohydrate. Experiment in training; every digestive system is different.

*Rule #8: Seek help for disordered-eating and body-image issues.* The eating disorders anorexia and bulimia can seriously hurt your performance—not to mention your health. Eating disorders have complications ranging from anemia to osteoporosis (loss of bone mineral), and they kill an estimated 10 to 15 percent of sufferers.

*Rule #9: Supplements? Save your money.* Taking a daily multivitamin and multimineral supplement is probably good for nutritional "insurance," though of course it's not a substitute for a healthy, balanced diet with adequate calories. There is no convincing evidence that any supplement offers a physical performance benefit.

*Rule #10: Step off the scale.* There's no "ideal" runner's weight. Scientific research shows that people fed and exercised in exactly the same way end up with widely varying weights and sizes. If you run sensibly and eat healthfully, your weight will be what it is supposed to be.

*Rule #11: Watch out for quacks.* Anyone can hang out a shingle as a "nutritionist." Be wary of any practitioner who requires you to radically change the way you eat, promises dramatic results from such changes, expresses generalized mistrust of mainstream nutrition advice, or refuses to supply information about his or her education and training.

*Rule #12: Don't forget the fun.* Enjoy your food. Eat with family and friends. Share recipes. Laugh and talk at the table. Be mindful of the blessing of having enough to eat.

### Practical Considerations: What, When, and How Much to Eat

It's not necessary to perform complex calculations to eat a diet that will optimally fuel your running. A good guideline to follow is the Food Guide Pyramid recommended by the U.S. Department of Agriculture. A copy of the Pyramid appears below. The Pyramid is recommended as a general eating plan for healthy adults. With bread, cereal, rice, and pasta making up the largest portion of the diet, and fruits and vegetables comprising the second tier, following the Pyramid ensures that the diet derives 50 percent or more of calories from carbohydrates. Another healthy feature of the Pyramid is that it puts no food off-limits, but rather suggests eating oils, fats, and sweets—the top (point) of the Pyramid—sparingly.

### What's in a Serving?

The list below, adapted from the USDA guidelines accompanying the Pyramid, gives serving sizes for foods included in the various categories. No specific serving size is given for the fats, oils, and sweets group because of the recommendation to use "sparingly."

1 cup milk or yogurt
1½ ounces natural cheese
2 ounces processed cheese
2–3 ounces cooked lean meat, poultry, or fish
½ cup cooked dry beans
1 egg
2 tablespoons peanut butter
1 cup raw leafy vegetables
½ cup other vegetables, cooked or chopped raw
¾ cup vegetable or fruit juice
1 medium apple, banana, orange
½ cup chopped, cooked, or canned fruit
1 slice bread

1 ounce ready-to-eat cereal
½ cup cooked cereal, rice, or pasta

## QUESTION AND ANSWER

**Q.** How many calories does running burn?

**A.** The caloric requirements of running vary widely depending on the physical characteristics of the runner—including sex, height, weight, body-fat percentage, and resting metabolic rate—and the intensity of running. A common estimate is 100 calories per mile for an average 150-pound runner. I find this figure useful as a reminder that I need to go into long runs and long races well fueled and make sure to replenish lots and lots of calories afterward. It's useless, though, as a way to help determine how much I should eat each day. A better strategy than counting calories burned is to learn to read and respond to cues of hunger and fullness. Do not attempt to lose or gain more than one pound per week, or the change is unlikely to be permanent. Exercise can be more effective than dieting at keeping weight off permanently. However, runners still come in all shapes and sizes, and they eat and run on widely varying caloric intakes. While it may not seem fair that your running partner can eat twice as many pancakes as you after a long run and not gain an ounce, that's a reality you'll have to accept.

## SPECIAL FOODS AND FLUIDS

Visit any race expo, health food store, or running specialty shop, or peek in the pantries of many runners, and you'll find a wide range of foods specifically engineered for endurance athletes. In recent years the market has grown for drinks, powders, bars, and gels designed to fuel performance before and during running and other activities, and to enhance recovery. What exactly do these products do? Are they necessary for successful running?

Products formulated for use before and during exercise are intended primarily to prevent dehydration and depletion of carbohydrate (glycogen). Those designed for postexercise consumption are meant to help the body rehydrate, restock glycogen stores, and aid the recovery processes. Here we look at four categories of these special fluids and fuels and what they offer runners.

- *Drinks.* Numerous studies have shown that endurance exercise performance, including running, drops significantly when a runner becomes dehydrated. (See Chapter 2 for a physiological explanation of why this happens.) For years, however, a myth persisted that drinking water and other fluids during heavy exercise caused cramping, and so many runners avoided drinking, even in long races such as the marathon. These days, even short (5k and 10k) road races offer water at "aid stations" along the course. Race medical directors warn runners about the possible consequences of dehydration, including life-threatening heat stroke and heat prostration. Though this is fortunately very rare, even mild dehydration can cause running performance to suffer as the body is forced to work harder both to keep cool and perform high-level physical activity. Water replaces lost fluids, and many runners—even some of the best in the world—drink nothing but water before, during, and after running. Sports drinks contain carbohydrates (usually simple sugars), electrolytes (primarily sodium and potassium), and sometimes other substances in a palatable, easily absorbed solution intended for use before, during, and after running and other strenuous activities.

  Research has found that athletes who consume sports drinks before and during exercise perform at a high level for longer periods than those who drink plain water. The effect is present in activities lasting as little as 45 minutes, but is particularly pronounced when exercise lasts 90 minutes or longer, the point at which the body's glycogen stores become significantly depleted. Sports drinks also help maintain the balance of electrolytes. And because sports drinks taste good to most people, they may be consumed in larger quantities than plain water, further aiding in the prevention of dehydration. After-exercise sports drinks can help restore fluids and calories quickly and conveniently. They are often available at the finish of marathons and other road races.

- *Bars.* "Energy" bars have also become popular in recent years. Like sports drinks, they are designed for use before, during, and after exercise; they're also marketed to active people as snacks and meal-replacers.

Most bars are rich in easily digested carbohydrates. Most are highly processed, and flavored and sweetened for palatability, though "natural" bars made with fruit, nuts, seeds, grains, honey, and fruit juice have become increasingly popular. Many bars are vitamin- and mineral-fortified. Bars are a convenient, portable, nutritious food for runners, but they are by no means essential to a runner's diet and have no performance-enhancing effects beyond those in other healthy, nutritious foods. Some bars are promoted for their high protein content, which manufacturers claim aids recovery. Though dietary protein does indeed help muscles repair and recover from exercise, the protein in bars is not significantly different from that in an egg or a chicken breast.

• *Gels.* The latest "energy" food available to runners is a sweetened gel designed for use before and during running. Most gels come in individual one-ounce foil packets that can be carried or pinned to clothing while running and thus ingested without breaking stride. They are flavored and heavily sweetened, most consisting of about 100 calories of pure carbohydrate, often with a modest amount of caffeine. I admit to being a major fan of gels for long training runs and races. As a runner who can't eat any solid food for many hours before races, and at least two hours before even an easy training run, I always had trouble with mid-workout and midrace glycogen depletion. Gels have essentially solved my problem. I take one or two before a long run or marathon and one or two en route, about an hour apart. My physical and mental energy remain high throughout the run (remember, carbohydrate fuels brain and nervous-system functions as well as muscle activity) and I finish feeling strong. For me it's not the specific content of gels that does the trick, but their digestibility at a time when my body desperately needs carbohydrate calories.

• *Powders.* Most powders marketed to athletes are concentrated sources of protein. As discussed on pages 159, runners' protein needs are not significantly greater than the needs of nonrunners, and the increase can easily be met by adding small amounts of nonengineered protein foods, such as lean meats, fish, eggs, and dried beans to the diet. Protein powders can be useful for those runners who don't have time to prepare or eat meals or whose diet is low in standard sources of protein. Like any food, the powders should be consumed in moderation as part of a diet that's varied and nutritionally balanced.

Keep in mind that no engineered food is a "magic potion" that will make or break your diet. Use sports drinks, energy bars, gels, and powders if you like them, find them convenient, or feel they can help your running. Recognize, however, that cheaper and possibly more suitable substitutes may exist. Before the advent of gels, for instance, some runners got a mid-workout or midrace lift by sucking orange slices or hard candies or eating bananas or other foods that can be digested easily. These foods haven't changed, and are worth trying, too. Most importantly, don't try any food for the first time in competition, because you never know how it will affect your individual system. Training—not racing—is the time for experimentation.

### Getting Your Timing Right

I'm often asked about the optimal timing of eating and exercise. Running too many hours after your last meal or snack can result in weakness, light-headedness, and poor concentration, whereas running too soon after eating can lead to discomfort, gas, indigestion, and diarrhea. (This is due to the up-and-down motion of running, which agitates the digestive system; athletes in other sports, such as cycling, are fortunate to be able to eat immediately before exercise, and even *during* workouts and races.) The following guidelines can help you avoid problems.

• *Eat every three to four hours.* We feel and perform our best—in running and other activities—when we are neither too hungry nor too full. Most dietitians recommend eating modest-sized meals, with supplemental snacks to maintain energy and fuel activity between meals (though an occasional large meal is fine for social and lifestyle reasons). This is the way young children eat, and contrary to the clean-your-plate-no-snacks pattern that many of us have been conditioned to follow, it may be healthier for grown-ups as well! Eating frequently is not the same as constant, mindless snacking, which can detract from the awareness and enjoyment of food and may lead to problems with weight control. Rather, you need to tune in to and respond to hunger cues, not wait for hunger to build to the point where it precludes healthy food choices (that is, you stuff your face with anything that is close at hand and convenient—such as an entire bag of cheese puffs). Eating frequently can help with weight control because we tend to eat more thoughtfully when we're not ravenous. In addition, the act of eating itself helps maintain a high metabolic rate.

A healthy frequent-eating plan might look something like this:

| | |
|---|---|
| 7:00 A.M. | juice |
| 7:30 A.M. | stretching routine |
| 8:15 A.M. | cereal with milk |
| 10:30 A.M. | fruit |
| 1:00 P.M. | soup, half sandwich |
| 3:30 P.M. | half sandwich |
| 6:00 P.M. | run |
| 7:30 P.M. | chicken breast, rice, broccoli |
| 10:00 P.M. | yogurt, cookie |

If you have trouble eating frequently—due to social conditioning, your schedule, or other factors—try actually writing down a schedule and reminding yourself with an alarm to eat. Keep healthy foods close at hand such as fruit, sliced raw vegetables, nuts, crackers, and juice so you can eat without interrupting what you are doing. Try to be mindful of early signs of hunger—such as lapses in concentration, and thoughts about food—and respond to them before hunger builds. Similarly, tune in to feelings of fullness and stop eating when you've had enough.

- *Have a small preexercise snack within an hour before exercise.* A light, high-carbohydrate snack can top off glycogen stores and raise your energy and alertness for running or other exercise. The following choices have about 100–150 calories each and are easily digested by most people.

- instant oatmeal (1-ounce packet)
- piece of fruit (apple, orange, peach, banana, kiwi, cantaloupe slice, grapefruit, etc.)
- 8-ounce nonfat yogurt
- 3–4 low-fat crackers

- slice of bread
- half small bagel
- 6-ounce glass of orange, apple, grapefruit, cranberry, or vegetable juice
- small handful of dried fruit (raisins, berries, apricot halves, prunes)
- 1–2 small cookies
- small energy bar (1–2 ounces)

Many people find they can eat one of the foods from this list and head out for a run as soon as 10 to 20 minutes later. Experiment to see what works for you; the worst that's likely to happen is that you feel a bit queasy or gassy on the run. Don't start a run feeling hungry to the point of light-headedness; this can be not only unpleasant but also dangerous, due to poor concentration and impaired judgment.

• *Eat something within two hours after running.* Running depletes glycogen stores, and studies show that these storage areas, located primarily in the muscles and liver, are most receptive to restocking in the two hours after significant depletion. The problem is that for many people, running suppresses the appetite for an hour or so. If you aren't hungry immediately after running, have something to drink instead: sports drink, fruit or vegetable juice, milk, etc. Keep healthy foods (whole-wheat pretzels, vegetables, fruit, yogurt) close at hand so you can nibble as hunger returns.

• *Keep a food log.* Maintaining a written record of which foods and drinks work best to fuel up before running and replenish your depleted stores afterward, and of the timing of your eating and running, can help guide you to better choices and patterns. Either make your food log a part of your running log or keep it separately.

## QUESTION AND ANSWER

**Q.** A young runner I know has gotten extremely thin and seems to eat very little. Should I worry?

**A.** Most runners are aware of the dangers of excessive weight loss and the possibility of developing patterns of disordered eating and exercise. Eating disorders are clinically defined diseases that can be life-threatening. Anorexia nervosa is characterized by self-starvation and preoccupation with weight and eating, often accompanied by intense, compulsive exercise. Bulimia involves engaging in cycles of heavy eating and purging by vomiting, laxative use, exercise, and/or self-starvation. Though running will not cause an eating disorder, runners may be more susceptible to the problem because of the caloric requirements of running and the emphasis on thinness among some runners. Although the publicity surrounding eating disorders has made many parents, teachers, and coaches more aware of the problem, many cases are still overlooked or remain untreated because of ignorance or uncertainty. Many eating disorder sufferers strongly deny there is anything wrong, and are therefore unlikely to seek treatment on their own and will resist the interventions of others.

If you suspect an eating disorder in a young runner it's probably best to express your concern to someone close to him or her, such as a parent, teacher, or coach. Intervening directly can be a challenge, and might best take the form of suggesting that the person see a nutritionist or seek out more information on the Internet. (See Resources for a few of the many Web sites dealing with eating disorders.) Adults can set a healthy example for young runners by eating healthily and downplaying the importance of weight or appearance in running. (See Chapter 12 for more information on young runners.)

---

### EATING TO RUN

Do you eat to run or run to eat? Eating to run means you recognize that running is an activity that requires plenty of calories and a variety of nutrients in healthy proportions, and that you make appropriate choices each day to fuel your running accordingly. Although you eat for other reasons—because food tastes good and provides a social milieu—you understand that its primary purpose is fueling all the activities that make up your life, including running.

Running to eat, on the other hand, can imply a less healthy relationship with food. Rather than choosing foods mindfully, the run-to-eat runner often sees running as a way to negate the effects of unhealthy eating patterns or patterns they *think* are unhealthy. He or she is the runner who justifies eating a huge slice of pie by saying, "It's okay, I'll burn it off running," or who turns a planned four-mile run into eight due to guilt feelings about the size of last night's bowl of ice cream. Sure, we all think this way on occasion, but constant, daily thoughts along these lines aren't healthy. They imply that running is some sort of punishment or atonement for the "sin" of certain food choices.

It's impossible for most of us to choose every morsel we eat based on nutritional and physical performance concerns. You shouldn't have to feel guilty every time you reach for a cookie—far from it. Indeed, many runners appreciate the fact that they can relax their stringent efforts at weight control through dieting because they run. That is healthy and pleasurable. Runners, more than sedentary people, can trust hunger cues to guide them to eating a diet that's best for them.

However, if you find yourself running to "make up" for poor food choices, or allowing yourself certain foods or quantities only if you plan to "burn them off" by running, take a closer look at your lifestyle and perhaps some of the emotions behind your decisions. A nutritionist can guide you in establishing healthier patterns.

### The Importance of Staying Hydrated

Running causes a loss of fluids from the body, due to sweating and respiration. This results in a loss of blood volume, which means that your heart must work harder to pump blood to your working muscles. If two runners of equal ability run a race or workout at the same intensity, but one is fully hydrated and the other is not, the dehydrated runner will lose to the fully hydrated runner.

Performance isn't the only reason it's crucial to stay hydrated while running. Loss of fluids representing 4 to 5 percent of body weight can cause serious physical damage. In worst cases, dehydration can lead to heat stroke and even death. Although it is possible to overhydrate (see discussion on page 176), this is very rare. Here are ways to prevent dehydration:

• *Top up the tank all day long.* Many runners become dehydrated not by neglecting to drink immediately before and during their runs but by failing to drink regularly throughout the day. You've heard the recommendation to drink eight glasses of water a day; as a runner, that's the *minimum* you should aim for. A good strategy is to fill a large (64-ounce) soft drink bottle with water at the beginning of the day and aim to empty it by day's end. If you don't like water, any nonalcoholic, noncaffeinated beverage contributes to your eight-glass-a-day total; try sports drinks, juices, milk, and warm beverages such as herbal tea. The best test of proper hydration is the need to urinate at least every two to three hours, and urine that is copious, and clear or pale. (Note: Some high-potency vitamins can turn urine bright yellow or orange.) Drinking regularly also allows your body to absorb water steadily, and thus is preferable to chugging a quart of fluid just before running and feeling it slosh around in your stomach throughout the workout.

• *Don't wait for thirst to strike.* By the time you become thirsty you are already significantly dehydrated. Drink regularly whether you are thirsty or not. If you haven't had any fluids in several hours, have a glass or two beyond what it takes to merely "wet your whistle."

• *For every alcoholic or caffeinated drink, have something nonalcoholic and noncaffeinated.* Alcohol and caffeine are diuretics, meaning that they increase the output of urine. Thus, though they can relieve thirst, they ultimately lead to less fluid in your system rather than more. I recommend avoiding alcohol and caffeine for 12 to 24 hours before warm-weather racing, particularly long distances such as the half-marathon and marathon, and rehydrating first with nonalcoholic and noncaffeinated drinks afterward.

• *Weigh yourself to determine hydration status.* A simple way to determine your hydration level is to weigh yourself before a long workout or race (particularly in warm weather), then again afterward. Though you may feel fully hydrated after the workout, chances are you have not fully topped off the tank. Continue to drink until your postexercise weight equals the figure before you started. Similarly, it's a good idea to weigh yourself once a week or so during warm-weather training. Weight loss of a pound or more is probably due to dehydration. Drink until you've returned to your normal weight.

• *Don't worry about cramps.* There's a widespread myth that drinking during exercise causes stomach cramps. This is not true. During intense activity water is slower to leave the stomach and be absorbed through the digestive tract, but this does not cause cramping. Water does continue to perform vital life functions while you exercise. It's just one more reason to make sure to start your workouts having drunk plenty of water.

• *Heed dehydration's warning signs.* Dehydration can sneak up on you during a run. By the time you are no longer sweating, you are probably seriously dehydrated. Before then your skin may actually feel clammy. Other symptoms of dehydration include increased fatigue, headache, flushed face and hands, confusion, disorientation, dizziness, weakness, and nausea. If you feel any of these symptoms while running, stop, get in the shade, and have something to drink as soon as possible. Lie down, or sit with your head between your knees. As soon as possible, apply ice to your head, neck, wrists, and ankles. Seek medical attention if symptoms don't resolve within a few minutes. The main danger of dehydration is a rapid, uncontrolled rise in body temperature, known as heatstroke or heat prostration, which in rare cases result in organ damage and even death. Serious dehydration is treated by injecting fluids intravenously, packing the body in ice, and continuing medical observation.

• *Be aware of the slight risk of overhydration.* Hyponatremia (also known as water intoxication) is a very rare condition that can develop when the body becomes overhydrated, disrupting the balance of fluids and sodium. There have been reported cases of this happening during and after marathon and ultramarathon races and Ironman-distance triathlons—which take even the top competitors eight hours to finish. Symptoms include headache (which can become severe), confusion, lethargy, weakness, nausea (at times extreme), disorientation, and slurred speech. Because these are similar to symptoms of dehydration, the problem may not be recognized at first. Severe hyponatremia can cause seizures, stupor, coma, and death. The problem seems to occur most often in untrained runners (who have lower sweat rates than more experienced athletes) who are exercising for five hours or longer and drinking plain water. Drinking sports drinks—which contain sodium and thus restore fluid/sodium balance—and/or eating salty foods can help reduce the risk of hyponatermia.

# CHAPTER 8

▶▶▶▶▶▶▶▶▶▶▶▶▶▶▶▶▶▶▶▶▶▶▶▶▶▶▶▶▶▶▶▶▶▶▶

# *Races and Racing*

R aces offer runners a multitude of opportunities. For most of us, a race presents a chance to test our fitness, enjoy the companionship of other runners, and be part of a health and fitness "happening." Some people participate in races to raise money and awareness for a cause. Others tag along with friends and family members, or sign up simply out of curiosity, wondering why all these people are prancing around wearing the colorful equivalent of underwear. This chapter looks at the many different types and distances of races, and explores the motivations for racing. It offers racing strategies, along with practical considerations for racing, such as equipment, preparation, and recovery.

## Why Race?

The majority of runners who enter races have no chance of winning—so what is their motivation? The following are some of the reasons runners of a variety of backgrounds and fitness levels are drawn to racing:

• *Competition with others.* The runners at the front of the pack embrace running as a sport in which the primary object is to win. Running pits athletes against one another in a straightforward contest of physical and mental fortitude. Though there can be many different tactics and strategies involved in winning or placing well (see pages 199–205 for more on racing strategies and tactics), at the end of the day it's simply a matter of trying to get from Point A to Point B in less time than your competitors. In road races—some of which draws tens of thousands of entrants—competition exists not just on the front lines but back into the middle of the pack, where runners of a wide range of abilities compete for age-group, club, and other honors. They may win trophies, ribbons, merchandise prizes, and prestige within the running community. Competition is fierce for the very top athletes, due to the rising professionalism of the sport and the infusion of prize money in amounts that earlier generations of runners never dreamed of.

• *Competition with oneself.* Any runner, from a world-class athlete to a 5k first-timer, competes against perhaps the most significant competitor of all—himself. As noted in Chapter 3, if you train and race on a periodized program leading up to a goal race or series of races, it makes sense to treat some of the races along the way more as workouts than all-out competitive efforts. In these races, though, you are still trying to get the best performance from yourself on that day. In addition, it's also useful to have a record of your finishing time and progression of times at significant points, such as mile markers (these interim times are known as splits). Even a runner who runs primarily or exclusively for health and fitness can benefit from competition with himself or herself. Most of us have few healthy competitive outlets in life, and a running race is one of the healthiest, simplest, and most fun ways to compete. Running fast against yourself, just for the heck of it, lets you feel like a kid again—and most of us need more of that!

• *Camaraderie.* For most runners, this is a primary motivation for racing. Road races in particular are large-scale events that typically attract hundreds or thousands of runners. Races of all types offer the chance to socialize with old friends and meet new ones. For runners who do some or all of their training alone or in small groups, running in a large crowd of other runners can offer a real charge. Most road races also offer postevent refreshments, award ceremonies, and other entertainment to facilitate socializing before and after the race.

• *Health.* Racing can enhance the overall health benefits of a running program by offering opportunities to share information with other runners, meet members of local running clubs, and attend the health and fitness expos that accompany large races. Expos offer many running-related products and services, new and often health-promoting foods, and sometimes pre- or postrace massages. In addition, racing can motivate a runner to step up a running program that has become uninspiring, or to try other types of training, such as speed workouts, tempo running, cross-training, or supplemental training.

• *Family entertainment.* Increasingly, road races are designed to appeal to families, and offer accompanying children's "fun" runs or peewee runs (over short distances, with medals or ribbons for all and no designated winners) and other events and activities that cater to the preteen set. In fact, sometimes these events and activities attract more attention and participants than the "grown-up" road races. (See Chapter 12 for more on children's running.)

• *Fund-raising.* The practice of participating in races to raise money and awareness for a cause has become increasingly popular. Runners and walkers have raised hundreds of millions of dollars for research and services for cancer, heart disease, and other major diseases; to fight domestic violence, hunger, and other societal ills, and to fund innumerable local and regional charities. These events draw new runners, not to mention the financial benefit and increased visibility for the fund-raising organizations. (See Resources for contact information for some of the major running-related charity groups.)

## AGE-GROUP RACING

The past decade has seen an increase in the popularity of age-group competition in all racing genres. Runners compete against their peers in 5-year to 10-year age brackets. Most North American road races recognize age-group performances starting at 19 and under (sometimes 14 and under) and ranging up to 70 or higher.

Runners age 40 and over are known as "masters" athletes. National-record and world-best masters performances are recognized at all standard distances on the track and roads in five-year increments, and there is also single-age recognition. Thanks to the baby-boom population in North America, masters competition is currently experiencing tremendous growth. This is expected to continue as more runners enter the 40-and-over ranks and the national interest in health and fitness continues to grow.

Participants in road races are automatically scored by age group. A runner may win an age-group ribbon, medal, or trophy and not even realize it. At the highest level, masters runners compete for prize money and travel around the country and even internationally to seek the top awards and honors. Also growing in popularity is age-graded competition, whereby performances are ranked on a system that allows for comparisons among athletes of a range of ages.

Age-group and age-graded competition make running fun and interesting not only for the 40-plus crowd but for all runners who look ahead to remaining competitive into their golden years. At age 91, Abraham Weintraub finished the 2000 New York City Marathon in 7 hours, 25 minutes, to thunderous applause. He received the New York Road Runners' Runner of the Year award for the 90-plus division and got an extended standing ovation at a banquet recognizing the NYRR's outstanding athletes. (See Chapter 13 for more on running in old age.)

### Types of Races

Runners compete on all surfaces—and even on ships at sea. Listed here are the major types of races available to runners today.

• *Road races.* By far the largest proportion of runners today participate in races on paved roads. According to the Road

Running Information Center of USA Track & Field (USATF), in 2000 nearly 7.5 million Americans finished at least one road running event. Most road races are between 1 mile and 26.2 miles (marathon), though some ultramarathon races are also contested on the roads. Even runners who race primarily on other surfaces, such as track and trails, often compete on the roads occasionally because of the convenience, accessibility, and social aspects of road racing. Road races are open to all; only a handful have qualifying standards (such as the Boston Marathon) or restrict registration due to the event's popularity and safety/personnel considerations (such as the New York City Marathon and the Marine Corps Marathon). The majority of road races are held on weekend mornings, and the greatest numbers take place in the spring and fall in most parts of the country, though on any given weekend there is probably one going on within an hour's drive in most urban and suburban areas. A road race may be a home-grown affair for just a few dozen participants, started behind a line drawn in chalk across a road by a volunteer shouting "Go" and clicking a stopwatch. Or it may be an event attracting tens of thousands, closing down city streets for hours, with a budget of millions of dollars and a director whose efforts constitute a year-round full-time job.

Today, the majority of road races in the United States are accurately measured and certified. They offer mile markers (sometimes with clocks or timers) and water stations along the way, and—increasingly—a sophisticated timing system that records each runner's starting and finishing time via a computerized chip worn on the shoe. A T-shirt commemorating the race for all entrants or finishers is another standard feature, along with free postrace refreshments. More and more road races offer musical entertainment, sometimes even along the course. Race directors generally design road-race courses to be scenic—through downtown or historic areas, parks, and the countryside. An increasing number of runners travels 100 miles or farther from their homes to race. Some courses are designed to be flat with few turns to allow for fast times, while others are purposely hilly to provide a challenge. Most races recognize the top overall and age-group finishers at a postrace awards ceremony, and many offer trophies, ribbons, and other recognition of the front-runners' accomplishments. Some races offer merchandise prizes, and a few (mostly large-scale events in big cities) give out prize money, which is considered income to the recipients and usually must be reported to the Internal Revenue Service just like any other reportable earnings. Though road racing in the U.S. is overseen by USATF and the Road Runners Club of America (RRCA), most road races are freestanding entities sponsored by local businesses, running clubs, and community organizations. Proceeds from road races generally go to covering race expenses, including permits, runner amenities, advertising, marketing, and any salaries, and with any surplus earmarked to support local charities and community-service organizations.

• *Marathon races.* Though most marathon (26.2-mile) races are contested on the road, the category deserves separate mention because of the unique characteristics of marathons. The standard marathon distance is 26.2 miles; anything longer is referred to as an ultramarathon. The popularity of marathon racing has grown steadily since 1976, according to records maintained by the Road Running Information Center for participation in the United States.

## U.S. MARATHON GROWTH

| YEAR | Estimated # of Finishers |
|------|--------------------------|
| 1976 | 25,000 |
| 1980 | 120,000 |
| 1990 | 260,000 |
| 1995 | 347,000 |
| 1996 | 396,000 |
| 1997 | 396,000 |
| 1998 | 419,000 |
| 1999 | 435,000 |
| 2000 | 451,000 |

Many runners plan their training and tune-up racing around running a quality marathon. These athletes tend to do one to three marathons per year, and treat them as peak-performance efforts. Other runners do marathons more frequently, usually with less lofty competitive aspirations. Most marathons, like shorter-distance road races, offer the standard T-shirts, mile markers, awards, and postrace refreshments and entertainment. The larger events have accompanying race expos, at which a variety of running products and services are available for sale and demonstration.

There are several compelling reasons for the popularity of marathons. Perhaps most significant is the challenge. The human body is really not designed to run 26 miles without stopping. As noted in Chapter 2, we are capable of storing enough carbohydrate (as glycogen, primarily in the muscles and liver) to fuel about 90 minutes of high-intensity activity. Training can extend that storage capacity to about two hours in most people, after which fuel sources must be replenished or the body is forced to switch to an alternate—and less efficient—fuel source. For most runners, racing a half-marathon, 25k (about 15.5 miles), or even 30k (about 18.6 miles) is relatively easy compared to preparing for and completing the 26.2-mile distance. This gives the marathon a mystique in the eyes of both participants and observers. Telling someone you've run a marathon wins instant respect and admiration. Feeling that finisher's medal around your neck, seeing your time reported in the local paper, and touching your finisher's certificate are deeply satisfying. Another reason for marathons' popularity is the festive atmosphere of the race itself. A marathon is like a parade, a journey, a wonderful carnival. A major race often includes cheering crowds throughout the route, not to mention the energy and excitement among the runners themselves. In addition, many people choose marathons as ways to visit distant cities, countries, or even continents. (There is an Antarctica Marathon, which in 2001 had to be run on the deck of a ship due to inclement weather!) Finally, there is the appeal of fund-raising for charity, which has recently become associated with marathons. Your motivation for running a marathon will help determine the type of marathon you choose—large or small, urban or rural, close at hand or thousands of miles from home. (See Resources for a listing of major marathons around the world.)

## WHY 26.2 MILES?

I'm often asked how the 26.2-mile marathon distance came to be. Though the event has its roots in ancient history, it's unlikely that the first marathon run was anything close to 26.2 miles. Legend has it that an Athenian runner named Phidippides ran 25 miles from the plains of Marathon to Athens to report on a battle victory, and after announcing, "Rejoice! We conquer!" fell over dead from the exertion. It's much more likely, however, that Phidippedes actually ran more than 150 miles from the battle site to Sparta to seek reinforcements while the battle was still in progress.

Contrary to another widely held belief, the marathon was not part of the ancient Olympic Games. However, the first modern Olympics, held in Athens in 1896, included a run of about 25 miles, dubbed a "marathon," to commemorate Phidippides' legendary run. A handful of marathons were held in the following years, including the Boston Marathon, which was first run in 1897—with 18 entrants, 15 starters, and 10 finishers.

The distance was standardized at 26 miles, 385 yards at the 1908 London Olympics. Organizers elected to lengthen the distance by more than a mile from its planned 40 kilometers (about 25 miles) so that the Princess of Wales could act as the marathon's official starter on the lawn of Windsor Castle, allowing the race to finish in the Olympic Stadium. Though marathons in the immediately ensuing years continued to vary, eventually the odd 26.2-mile distance became standard. Marathon courses today vary considerably in terms of significant factors such as hills and turns, but all certified marathon courses are 26.2 miles.

## QUESTION AND ANSWER

**Q.** When can I run my first marathon?

**A.** Increasingly, runners are drawn to running because of the allure of the marathon. At 26.2 miles, the marathon is a major physical and mental challenge, yet many runners choose it as their goal before they've even started a running program! This is unwise if your goal is to *run* the marathon. Some coaches suggest that no runner consider running a marathon until he has been running for at least a year. My recommendation is less rigid, but in keeping with that conservative advice. I suggest that no runner sign up for a marathon without first completing a 5k, 10k, and half-marathon (or a similar range of distances), all without significant walking breaks.

I offer this advice for several reasons. One, completing the shorter distances exposes you to the multiple challenges of racing—physical and mental preparation, tapering, fueling, hydration, logistics, managing anxiety, and so on. These should not be encountered for the first time in the context of the marathon's considerable challenges. Two, racing the shorter distances helps gain perspective on 26.2 miles. Races in the 15k to 20-mile range are particularly helpful in this respect. You will learn just how far 10 miles, or 13.1 miles, or 18.6 miles can be. I remember finishing my first half-marathon, in which I paced myself poorly and had to walk in the 12th mile, thinking, "How can I possibly run twice this far?" Wisely, I waited more than a year before my first marathon. There is no shame in walking portions of a marathon—or any race, for that matter. However, I believe that the goal for runners at all but ultramarathon distances should be to finish without being forced to walk. Three, attempting a marathon too soon might turn you off to all future running and racing. Wouldn't you rather run for a lifetime than quit as a result of one disastrous marathon? Finally, the marathon isn't going anywhere. Marathons exist all over the world, and they are getting better all the time in terms of variety, organization, technology, runner amenities, and other factors. The marathon will be ready whenever you are.

• *Ultramarathon races.* While relatively few runners participate in races longer than the marathon, the number of ultramarathoners is growing. Ultramarathons (commonly known as "ultras") take place on roads, track, and trails. They range in distance from 50 kilometers (about 31 miles) through 50 miles, 100k, 100 miles, and beyond, including 24-hour, 48-hour, 6-day, and transcontinental races. Competitions in which long distances are covered on foot have roots in many cultures. In the West, the sport was formalized as "pedestrian" races in 18th-century Britain, reached high levels of popularity in England and North America in the 19th century, and led to remarkable records—such as covering 500 miles in six days! Ultrarunning declined in popularity after 1900 and has been inching back since the 1960s, parallel to the growth of interest in running shorter distances, though at a much lower level of participation. Today, ultrarunning is a competitive sport with hundreds of established annual races, officially recognized national and world records and rankings, and intense rivalries at the front of the pack. Many participants, however, say that the greatest competition is with themselves, along with the vast distances covered, often over challenging terrain. For the vast majority of participants, training for ultras involves learning to take periodic walking, eating, and even sleeping breaks. Due in large part to the challenges of ultrarunning, and its status as a "fringe" sport within running, the community is very tight-knit, yet warmly receptive to newcomers, many of whom "move up" from shorter distances such as the marathon. Many find the atmosphere at ultras a welcome break from the emphasis on head-to-head competition, time, pace, and place that prevails at shorter-distance events. Ultra participants also tend to be more accepting of variations from the norm in training, equipment, and nutritional practices, making the sport a haven for free spirits. (See Resources for information and contacts for ultra races.)

• *Trail and mountain races.* Both these sports, practically unheard of as late as 1980, exploded in popularity in the late 1990s, thanks to the interest in "adventure" racing in a variety of sports. Trail and mountain racers eschew asphalt, competing instead in a more natural world in which distance and pace matter less than a willingness to meet nature on her own terms and accept her many, varied challenges. Most participants could care less about running a fast time. For many, in fact, the hillier, steeper, and rockier the trail, the better. Consider this representative description—only partly tongue-in-cheek—of the Escarpment Trail Run 30K, a mountainous trail race held in New York's Catskill Mountains: "The following physical complications have/ could occur: broken bones, tendon sprains & tears, dislocations, cuts & bruises (requiring stitches), hypothermia, hyperthermia, multiple bee stings, poison ivy, concussions, dehydration, and an occasional divorce. . . . If you have any ideas of finding some [water] along the trail, forget about it. You'll be looking for water right up to the moment you die of thirst. . . . Contestants must be prepared to deal with any of the forest's natural barriers, such as bees, slippery rocks, porcupines, black bears (not probable, but possible) and anything else that can be found in the forests of the Catskills."

Trail and mountain races offer few amenities such as mile markers, aid stations, and official timing. They cover a wide range of distances and tend to be point-to-point rather than loop courses, imparting a journeylike aspect to the events. Mountain races generally feature an assault on a summit, either as a climb to the peak, an out-and-back ascent and descent, or an "up and over" point-to-point course. Perhaps the best known in North America is the Pikes Peak mountain race in Colorado, which offers an ascent-only race and an ascent-descent marathon.

• *Adventure racing is another type of racing that continues to gain participants.* Adventure races can include running among a variety of outdoor challenges such as kayaking, rafting, mountain biking, and rock climbing. Adventure racing events include the multiday Raid Gauloises, and the shorter Xterra and Eco-Challenge Series (see Resources for contact information for these and other events).

• *Cross-country races.* Cross-country is a popular scholastic and college team sport in North America, with limited opportunities for postcollegiate runners. In Europe it's far more popular for open runners who maintain fierce intraclub rivalries. Cross-country season lasts from early fall through early spring in most areas (though the collegiate and scholastic seasons end in early December), with the World Cross Country Championships held annually in late March. Cross-country races are contested on dirt (or mud) and grass surfaces, generally run as a loop or multiple loops. The standard international distances are approximately 4k (2.5 miles) through 12k (7.5 miles), though distances are rarely exact and will vary from one course to another. To cross-country participants and fans, the sport is the purest form of running. Races tend to have large fields of up to several hundred runners. They start in open areas, with competitors sprinting toward a narrow opening onto a trail that is often wooded, and almost always hilly (so strong is the tradition of hills in cross-country that races contested in flat areas may include man-made hills!). Team tactics may predominate, with runners grouping themselves in packs to intimidate and block other runners over the typically narrow, muddy, rutted, twisting, up-and-down terrain.

• *Track races.* Those who start running in their youth may well have their first introduction to the sport on a track. A track is a safe, fun place to introduce young people to running, while at the same time making them feel like "real" runners. Adult track racers love the sport for its precise measurements and emphasis on head-to-head competition, tactics, and technique. Like other types of running, track racing has its roots in ancient times, as several ancient Greek Olympic running events were contested around an elongated oval in the Greek *stadion.* Track running today takes place both indoors and outdoors, usually on an oval track measuring between 150 meters (about 10½ laps to the mile) and 400 meters (almost precisely 4 laps to the mile). Track surfaces vary widely; today's gold standard for both indoor and outdoor tracks is a rubberized material, which is firm enough to allow for excellent toe-off and some spring, yet cushioned enough to minimize the pounding that can result in injury to distance runners, whose races include multiple laps. Other track surfaces include asphalt, grass, cinder, cement (outdoor), and wood (indoor). Runners who love track speak of it as the "great equalizer" because of its precision and uniformity. Though weather is still a factor in outdoor races, it's easier to compare track times from events run at various times and locales and thus determine superior and inferior performances. Track racing in the United States is governed by USA Track & Field. Track racing opportunities generally are fewer than opportunities to run on the road because a track can accommodate fewer runners than a road course, and the perception that track is a sport primarily for speedsters. Some communities do have active track racing programs with plenty of "all comers" meets. These events stress participation, camaraderie, and fun over competition (though there's plenty of that as well for those who choose it). See Resources for contact information for USATF-affiliated track races, or check local college and high school track offices; some allow limited numbers of non-students to enter.

## METRIC MEASUREMENTS

Though the planned conversion to the metric system in the United States in the 1970s was a dismal failure, as a runner it pays to have a passing familiarity with the way most of the rest of the world measures distance. Here is what you need to know about metric measurements to determine running distances on the track and roads.

Most tracks today are laid out in meters. A meter is approximately 39.75 inches, or slightly more than a yard. A standard outdoor track is 400 meters around, which is very close to 440-yards (¼ mile). Older tracks are likely to be 440 yards, with the 400-meter mark noted. Standard track-race distances contested in international competition include 100 meters, 200 meters (½ lap), 400 meters (1 lap), 500 meters, 800 meters (2 laps), 1000 meters (2½ laps), 1500 meters (almost 4 laps), 3,000 meters (7½ laps), 5,000 meters (12½ laps), and 10,000 meters (25 laps). In addition, scholastic and collegiate runners compete at 1600 and 3200 meters, and out of tradition the mile (very close to 1600 meters) is included in a wide variety of track meets, often as the premiere event. All these events are also run indoors, with the number of laps dependent upon the track's circumference (there is less uniformity among indoor than outdoor tracks). Meter is abbreviated "m," so you are likely to see track distances listed as 100m, 200m, and so on.

One thousand meters equals a kilometer (abbreviated "k" as in 5k, 10k, etc.), which is approximately 0.62 miles. Two of the most popular road racing distances are 5 kilometers (about 3.1 miles) and 10 kilometers (about 6.2 miles). Other racing distances include 15 kilometers (9.3 miles), 20 kilometers (12.4 miles), 25 kilometers (15.5 miles), and 30 kilometers (18.6 miles). By convention, races contested on the track are given in meters, while road and cross-country race distances are noted in kilometers. The vast majority of kilometer-distance road races in the United States include mile—rather than kilometer—markers along the route, and most runners would have no idea what their pace per kilometer is for a 5k or 10k. Similarly, splits are called out during track races for every lap, but the 1,000-meter, 2,000-meter (and so on) splits are seldom noted.

It all makes for an odd amalgam of figures, but most runners find things fairly simple once they learn a few basics. And you'll be ahead of the game when you travel to countries where the metric system is the norm.

## QUESTION AND ANSWER

**Q.** Why do I get so nervous on the starting line?

**A.** It's normal to get nervous at the start of a race, for many reasons. You're nervous because you have developed a passion for running and you care about the investment you've made in your health, fitness, and self-concept through running. Racing is also a public display of your running talent and fitness; your results will be visible to all as you cross the line. Beginning racers must also deal with the many new experiences involved with racing, from keeping track of their computer-timing chip to negotiating aid stations. For veterans, the anxiety may simply stem from knowing that the race is going to hurt at some point.

Being nervous is part of attaining what sport psychologists call an "optimal level of arousal," meaning neither too relaxed nor too excited. A former world-class runner once told me she knew it was time to retire when she no longer felt nervous at the start of races. Properly managed, prerace anxiety can actually help propel you to a higher level.

You can manage prerace nervousness by trying to pinpoint just what it is that makes you nervous and taking steps to deal with it, or using positive self-talk. For example, if you are nervous about tripping and falling at the start, plan to go out conservatively to minimize the risk of a tumble. If the possibility of not meeting a certain performance standard has you worried, recognize that you are setting these goals for yourself, and therefore you can change or discard them. (If your coach is setting the standards, make sure they are realistic for you and adjust them if needed.)

Remember that everyone gets nervous at the start of races. Most cases of prerace anxiety disappear within moments of the starter's horn. If your nervousness continues during the race, or if nervousness at any time causes palpitations, nausea, diarrhea, vomiting, or other debilitating symptoms, you should take firmer steps to deal with the problem. A sport psychologist can help with this process (see Chapter 6 for more on how a sport psychologist can help you with various issues).

### Which Distances Should You Race?

The focus of any training program should be the completion of the distance at a pace that does not vary significantly from the opening miles to the finish. Most runners enjoy racing a variety of distances. I encourage those who are new to racing to try different distances. If you have serious competitive aspirations, then you can zero in on the distance or distances at which you perform your best. Even serious competitors, however, often enjoy racing at a range of distances for the variety and to improve different aspects of their racing. Listed below are the most popular racing distances and the strengths runners need to develop to perform well at them.

• *Mile/1500 meters.* Mystique and tradition define the mile. The mile and slightly shorter 1500 meters—sometimes called the Olympic mile—are among the most challenging distances because of the combination of speed and strength needed to run them well. In addition, most mile races are contested on the track (with a few on the roads, such as New York City's Fifth Avenue Mile and the Waikiki Mile near Waikiki Beach in Honolulu). Many successful mile/1500-meter runners move up from 800 meters (half mile) by adding endurance work to their training. However, 3,000-meter, 5,000-meter, and even 10,000-meter runners can also be successful milers if they are blessed with natural speed and maintain that speed by training regularly at ATP-CP intensity. Most serious competitors also include training with weights to increase their explosive muscle strength (see Chapter 9 for more on strength training).

• *3,000 meters/steeplechase/4k.* The 3,000 meters (approximately 1.8 miles) and steeplechase are contested exclusively on the track. The steeplechase (steeple, for short) is a 3,000-meter event. It involves leaping over barricades and water jumps several times during each circuit of the oval. The steeple is a challenging event demanding speed, strength, and agility. Both steeplers and 3,000-meter runners need to develop their endurance and preserve their natural speed to excel. Most include strength work as part of their training. Most steeplechase racing is done on an outdoor track; the 3,000 meters (nonsteeple) is contested regularly both indoors and outdoors. The 4k (approximately 2½ miles) is the standard international cross-country distance, contested by both men and women at the World Cross Country Championships and other international events. This event attracts a lot of mile/1500-meter and 3,000-meter runners who love cross-country but want to compete in an event that can showcase their speed as well.

• *5,000 meters/5k.* The 5k is the standard cross-country distance for high school runners, both boys and girls, and many college women. Most track racers who specialize in the 5,000 meters are serious competitors. Young runners move up to the distance from the 1500 meters/1600 meters/mile or 3,000 meters/3200 meters/2-mile as they gain experience and confidence. These runners, however, still need to include plenty of speed-focused training if they wish to succeed at 5,000 meters, which is often a tactical race with a fast and furious sprint to the finish. They may also need to work on the race's mental aspects, as 12½ laps around a 400-meter outdoor track requires intense concentration. The successful 5,000-meter competitor must learn to relax and block out distractions. Physical training should include aerobic-intensity runs of up to 10–12 miles, lactate-threshold training, and a small amount of ATP-CP-intensity training. The 5,000 meters is contested primarily outdoors, with occasional indoor events.

On the roads, the 5k is the most popular distance run. In May 2000, 49 percent of all road-race courses certified by USATF were 5ks. There were more than one million 5k road-race performances reported to the Road Running Information Center in 2000—10 times more 5ks than the RRIC received in 1987. Because of the large number of charity races and fun runs that do not report results to RRIC, the organization estimates that there were more than 2.8 million finishers in all 5ks in the United States in 2000. Many runners choose a 5k as their first race. The distance (along with a 3.5-mile and 4-mile event, both of which are contested less often but are still popular) is easy enough to complete on minimal training by someone who is young and/or in decent physical shape from other activities. A 5k is also relatively easy for a race director to stage, in that it doesn't take as much time or space as a 10k or longer race. For most runners who race 5k/4 miles seriously on the roads, the distance is at the shorter end of their focus, so it feels fast and fun. For me, running a quality 5k definitely is a challenge, but it's over so quickly that I can do it on relatively modest training. For those focusing on the event, speed training and plenty of endurance work are in order, similar to that undertaken by a 5,000-meter track specialist.

• *10,000 meters/8k/5-mile/10k/12k.* The 10,000 meters is the longest distance regularly run on the track, and is almost always contested outdoors. Like the 5,000 meters, a 10,000-meter (25 lap) track race is a supreme test of physical and mental fitness.

Training focuses slightly less on speed and more on endurance, including sustained lactate-threshold and race-pace efforts. Many of the most successful 10,000-meter runners have also succeeded at 5,000 meters, and they continue to use their speed in the race's final 600 to 1,000 meters, where the ability to sustain a kick to the finish line can often secure a win. The 10k (about 6.2 miles) is another popular road-racing distance, though it's declined in relative popularity since the early "running boom"—a reflection of the rising popularity of 5ks. Nineteen percent of all road-race courses currently certified by USATF are 10ks, compared to 26 percent in 1994. Still, RRIC estimates that more than one million runners finished a 10k in 1999. Racing a 10k well demands a unique combination of speed and strength. The way I see it, you can fake your way through a 5k or 4-mile race on suboptimal training because it is short enough, but not a 10k. Preparation should include aerobic-intensity runs of up to 10–15 miles, plenty of lactate-threshold training, and workouts that emphasize ATP-CP-intensity running at least once every week to two weeks. Five-mile and 8k (just a few yards short of 5 miles) road races fall in the middle, but I train for them as I would a 10k, focusing on endurance at the expense of pure speed. Five-mile/8k and 10k races are easy to find in most areas. The 8k is the standard international long-course distance for women's cross-country. For men, the standard international long-course distance is 12k (about 7.5 miles) which is considered by some to be the most challenging running event of all. Long-course racers must develop their strength without losing the speed that's needed for a fast start and may be called upon in a close sprint finish. There are also 12k road races, which require training similar to that for a 10k on the roads.

• *15k/10-mile.* 15k/10-mile races are contested almost exclusively on the roads and trails, though you can find the occasional 15k cross-country race. These distances lag far behind 5ks and 10ks in popularity. Their attraction for many veteran distance runners is that they provide an honest, accurate assessment of midrange fitness for those who race the spectrum of road-race distances from 5k to the marathon. Exercise scientists often suggest that if you can't measure your lactate threshold scientifically in a lab setting, an excellent approximation is your pace in your most recent 15k (9.3-mile) or 10-mile race. Thus, a 15k/10-mile race is a great indicator of fitness. Training should include plenty of lactate-threshold-intensity training, along with aerobic-intensity runs of between 10 and 18 miles to build endurance.

• *20k/half-marathon/25k/30k/20 mile.* Many runners are able to complete these distances without the glycogen depletion that occurs in the marathon. The training is not significantly different from 15k/10-mile training; long runs are simply lengthened up to 20 miles for those specializing in the 30k/20-mile distance. Though most runners who race these distances also do marathons, the training for non-marathoners need not focus on the long training to the extent that marathon training does. Rather, training to run a quality 20k to 20-mile race is better accomplished with some shorter runs (generally not longer than 13 miles or about two hours) at projected race pace, plus a warm-up and cooldown at aerobic-intensity pace. These training runs can be interspersed with "regular" long runs of up to 25 percent of total weekly mileage, done at aerobic-intensity pace to build aerobic endurance and muscle endurance. Races at these distances are contested primarily on the roads.

• *Marathon.* There's no way to complete a marathon—at any level—without preparing specifically for the event. Most runners hold the marathon in such high regard that they train assiduously for months, following a periodized program that builds aerobic endurance and speed. See Chapter 3 for a suggested 26-week training program that focuses on running a quality marathon. Training should also include enhancing the mental ability to work hard through extreme fatigue (see Chapter 6 for more on mental training), learning to replenish fluids on the run, and increasing stores of carbohydrate (glycogen) to allow the body to work for longer periods at a higher level (see Chapter 7 for more on proper fueling and hydration for training and racing).

• *Ultramarathon.* As noted on pages 186–187, ultramarathon race distances range from 50k (31 miles) on up, including multiday events. It is beyond the scope of this book to offer specific training

and racing advice for ultramarathons. See Resources for sources of
ultramarathon training and racing information and contacts.

## WHAT TO PACK IN YOUR RACE-DAY BAG

There are certain essential items every runner should bring along to a race
of any genre, others that are needed only at certain types of races, and
some optional items. The lists below cover all these possibilities. Always
pack your bag the night before a race that you must travel to before noon.
For races later in the day, pack at least four or five hours before, and leave
yourself time to review the contents in case something slipped your mind.

It's best to pack your gear in a duffel bag, knapsack, or other portable carrier. A few races, usually large marathons, provide bags for runners to transport their gear from the start to the finish for reclaiming. Have your bag
with you at the start, and as race time draws near, either stow your bag at
the race's baggage check or leave it with a nonracing friend from whom you
can reclaim it afterward.

Follow the Boy Scout model when packing for a race: Be prepared. It's far
better to bring along items you don't need than to forget something you
will need before, during, or after the race. Remember that the weather,
course conditions, and even the rules of play can change without notice. For
example, a warm and sunny day may suddenly turn cold, windy, and rainy, ne-
cessitating a sudden change of your planned racing outfit. Or a race may un-
expectedly be converted from a competition to a fun run, and you may then
prefer to participate in your training shoes rather than racers. If you've left
them at home, you've lost that option.

*Essential items for any race:*
  the shoes and socks you plan to race in
  your race number (a bib that gets pinned to the front of your clothing)
  safety pins for pinning on your race number
  your timing chip
  racing apparel for all reasonable weather possibilities
  warm, dry postrace clothing (tops, bottoms, shoes, and socks to keep
    warm down in and keep your feet comfortable)

*Useful items:*
watch (miles may be marked but there may not be clocks or time recorders)
course map (often essential for trail/mountain races)
an old shirt or jacket for warmth that you can throw away right before the start
petroleum jelly (to prevent chafing, protect against cold and wind, prevent dryness)
waterproof sunscreen
sunglasses
hat or visor with a brim (for sun/rain/snow protection)
lightweight cotton gloves
lightweight wool or nylon-knit hat
plastic bags for dirty/wet clothes
heart rate monitor
small amount of cash
credit card
cell phone or change for a phone call
bandanna (can be used to cover the head or neck, or as a sweat rag)
small towel
pen and paper
business cards

*Items to bring when traveling to a race:*
anything that you deem useful from the list above
plane, bus, train, boat, etc. tickets
information on local area attractions
race T-shirts from your area (to trade)

*Additional items for cross-country races:*
spikes
spike key (for inserting and removing spikes)
lots of extra clothes (courses tend to be muddy)

*Additional items for track races:*
spikes
spike key (for inserting and removing spikes)

## QUESTION AND ANSWER

**Q.** I'm often too cold at the start of a race and too warm by the finish. Any suggestions?

**A.** Dressing for comfort and optimal performance in races can pose a greater challenge than dressing properly for training. The rule of thumb is to add 20 degrees to the temperature (accounting for windchill), then dress as though heading out for a stroll in that temperature. For example, if you are racing in 40-degree weather, dress as you would to feel comfortable taking a walk on a 60-degree day. Here are some additional suggestions:

- **Choose warm, lightweight fabrics.** Today's high-tech training and racing gear offers more warmth with less weight than ever before. See Chapter 4 for specific advice on warm-yet-light fabric choices; ask salespeople at running specialty stores for the most up-to-date gear.

- **Cover head and hands.** Wearing a lightweight knit cap can keep you warmer than an extra shirt or leg covering, due to the heat loss through the head. Uncovered hands can be very uncomfortable on cold days and may result in frostbite in extreme temperatures. If your hands get too warm, simply remove your gloves or mittens and tuck them into your waistband.

- **Wear a throwaway garment on top.** Keep an old shirt with you at the start of the race and remove and toss it aside either when the gun sounds or as you warm up along the course (hand it to an aid-station volunteer to avoid littering). At the start of some major races, such as the New York City Marathon (where due to the logistics of the bridge start, some runners must wait in the starting area for close to an hour before the cannon fires), volunteers collect hundreds of bags of discarded clothing for donation to charity. At the start of one very cold New York City Marathon my husband stayed warm by wearing an old ski jacket and pants until a minute or so before the start.

- **Cover cold arms with cutoff tube socks.** Keep your arms warm by purchasing a pair of long athletic "tube" socks, cutting out the toes, and slipping the socks over your arms from shoulder to wrist. You can take them off and discard them when you warm up.

## Racing Tactics

If two runners stand on the starting line with equal physical potential, the runner who employs superior racing tactics will triumph. Even those with no world-beating aspirations can benefit from learning how to race tactically. Good tactics make racing fun and interesting by allowing your head to help your feet do the job. Specific strategies and tactics are listed below. Some are more targeted to competitive runners than those whose primary goal is to finish and enjoy the experience. You don't need to call upon all these tactics in every race, but keep them in mind, because you never know when they might be useful.

• *Know the course.* This applies primarily to road, trail/mountain, and cross-country races, which vary enormously from one locale to another. (Track races are more uniform, though the track distance, configuration, and surface are all significant.) You can acquaint yourself with a new course by running (and for a road course, biking or driving) it in advance of the event. If that's not possible, the race entry form and/or Web site usually include a course description, and you can talk to other runners who are familiar with the course. Familiarizing yourself with the course—knowing when to expect the uphills, downhills, turns, and other physical characteristics—can help you plan your race strategies, or just give you an idea of when you may have to put forth more effort. There's a definite "home-course advantage" to racing a route you know well. When I compete against out-of-town runners in Central Park, where I have raced hundreds of times, I'm able to negotiate the hills, curves, and turns much better than someone who's running the course for the very first time. Cross-country racers use their home-course advantage to race tactically as a team, perhaps charging up the toughest hills to wear out the competition, or running as a pack in areas where other teams might attempt to pass them. A word of caution: The view of a course toured by bike or car can be deceiving. I've found that, depending on my mental state, hills tend to either steepen or flatten in the time between my tour and the actual race. Check out the course solely for noting the location and specific details of hills and other elements, but don't get too caught up in trying to gauge their precise degree of difficulty.

• *Chill out at a crowded start.* Typically in road races—and also in some trail, cross-country, and track competitions—there is a lot of crowding at the start. This not only makes it hard to get a good, clean start, but can be dangerous. Some runners become agitated by crowded starts. They may either burst out in front, running a pace they can't sustain to escape the crowding, or they may freeze up, running slower than they should due to anxiety about falling or getting shoved. Either way, they will probably perform below their capabilities. It's not easy to relax in crowded starting conditions. The situation at road races has been helped a lot by the introduction of computer-chip timing, which records each runner's time beginning not when the starting gun sounds, but when he or she crosses the starting line. This eliminates the need to get a "fast" start by getting across the line as quickly as possible, even if it means pushing or shoving past other runners. However, the problem of crowding persists in large races in which there is significant crowding past the starting line, sometimes lasting several miles into the race. I have several suggestions for dealing with crowded starts: One, put safety first. It's not worth hurting yourself or someone else to shave a few seconds off your time. Pushing, shoving, and dangerous weaving should never be part of your strategy. Two, try not worry too much about your time for the first mile. If crowding is severe, consider starting your watch at the one-mile mark, or as soon as you can run freely. Three, choose smaller, less crowded races, and/or races with wide starts that are less susceptible to crowding. Four, contact race officials after the event and suggest that they consider a wave start—starting in groups based on predicted finishing times—or other crowd-reducing measures.

• *Hold back in the early stages.* This strategic point can't be overemphasized. Almost all runners make the mistake of starting at an intensity level they are unable to sustain. This happens for a variety of reasons: Overexcitement at the start and in the opening stages, overconfidence based on having rested (tapered) before the race and therefore feeling physically strong, a "pack mental-ity" that develops when a few runners at the front set a too-fast pace and everyone else follows ("They're fast, so they must know what they're doing."), wishful thinking ("This is the pace I'd *like* to run."), a flat or downhill start, and the desire to build up a "cushion" against the possibility of slowing down later. Very few runners sustain an even pace throughout races of 800 meters and longer. Fewer still run "negative splits"—the second half faster than the first, which is the technique used to achieve many world-best performances. Rather, the overwhelming majority run a slower second half than first half (timing with a computer chip, which is becoming standard at road races and usually includes split times at mile and kilometer markers and halfway, allows these runners to see just how much they fall off their opening pace). Running evenly—not to mention negative splitting—demands courage and discipline. You have to watch your rivals sprint away from you and tell yourself calmly and confidently, "I will see you later—I'm sure of it." I've coached many runners who make the mistake of going out too fast, and I've worked hard on it in my own racing. There is no trick to running evenly other than to practice. Run your workouts evenly (both within each interval and for the total workout) and you will see dramatic improvements in performance. Physiologically, this makes sense if you recall two things: One, the body can only work at its high-est intensity—that is, draw upon the ATP-CP energy-delivery system—for about two minutes at the most, and the closer to that level you work, the shorter the period you will be able to maintain the effort. Two, the higher your effort intensity, the higher per-centage of carbohydrates is needed to fuel the work, which leads to depletion of carbohydrates (the body's preferred fuel source) sooner than when working at a more manageable intensity. You will finish ahead of your competitors by conserving as much of your energy as possible early on. The longer the race distance, the more important holding back becomes.

• **Break the race into segments.** Most runners perform to the best of their abilities by focusing on the present. No matter what the total race distance, what matters most is how you are feeling and what you are doing *right now*. In longer races such as the marathon, in which the total race distance may feel over-whelming, staying focused on the present can be a confidence-preserving mental tactic. At any distance, breaking up a race can improve your performance by minimizing distractions. If you can concentrate fully on your next two minutes of running, you're likely to run those two minutes with greater strength and focus than if your mind is leaping ahead to the many more min-utes and miles beyond. I break a marathon or half-marathon into 5k segments, a 10k or 5k into miles, and a shorter race into laps or other landmarks. As I arrive at each point I mentally check it off, which boosts my confidence. Yes, this is a bit of a mental de-ception—similar to the thrill you can get from crossing an item off your to-do list even though you are still deeply immersed in a long project—but in the middle of a tough race it can work wonders!

• *Let the race unfold.* To me this is such an obvious strategy—yet one that I must constantly remind myself to follow. In every race, you must come to terms with things you cannot control. You can control your physical and mental preparation—training, hydration, fueling, sleep, lifestyle factors, etc.—and your tactics and strategies during the race. You can't control anything your competitors have done to prepare or will do as the race pro-gresses. You also can't control the weather and possible freak oc-currences en route—a bee stinging you, a dog running onto the course, discarded paper cups creating a treacherous road surface at the aid stations, or a race volunteer mistakenly directing you off the course. Your job once you cross the starting line is simple: Perform to the best of your ability. Nothing else matters. Don't worry about the outcome. If you do your job, it will take care of itself.

• *Remember, it's a race.* If maximizing your performance is among your racing goals, you must *race.* I use various strategies to maintain my competitive focus. What helps most is to con-stantly monitor my effort—particularly my breathing—so that I know I'm working as hard as I can at a pace I can sustain for the full distance. It also helps to observe and monitor the effort of other runners around me—both to get a sense of how they are faring and to remind myself that my goal is to beat them! I have stock phrases that I repeat to myself, such as, "Don't fall asleep out there," and "Take it mile by mile" (see "Motivational Mantras That Work," page 148–149). Finally, I find that certain visual cues can help me focus intently on the race experience. For example, in a track race I'll look directly at the lap-count numbers held up by race officials each time I circle the oval; in a road race I'll look at the mile clocks. During many races my thoughts do wander, despite my best efforts. I tend to just let the wandering thoughts happen because the effort to reining them in tends to make me tense. As the race progresses, my focus increases naturally.

• *Assess the competition.* Looking at and listening to the runners around you serves four key purposes as a race tactic. One, it provides information about your competitors—how they are feeling, how they are likely to fare over the ensuing miles. Two, it can increase your confidence and help you relax when you realize that other runners are struggling at least as hard as you are. Three, checking out the competition can help you focus on the fact that you are racing, not just doing a training run. Finally, it can provide a break from the inward focus—tuning in to your body's feedback—that is your primary concentration while racing.

• *Make note of your strengths and weaknesses.* You can use the experience of racing to learn what you are good at, and what needs work. For example, if you often pass other runners going uphill, it's reasonable to conclude that you are a strong hill runner. Use that strength to your advantage by attacking there. If you get passed frequently on hills, use uphill segments to maintain contact, then try and pass on the flat or downhill sections. Learning your weaknesses in competition allows you to work on them in training.

• *Don't forget the little things.* Many runners learn the hard way that lack of attention to seemingly minor matters can sometimes have disastrous effects on race day. Make sure that you've attended to important things like pinning on your race number, securing your computer timing chip on your shoe, double-knotting your shoelaces, drinking enough fluids, and putting on your watch, heart rate monitor, sunglasses, sunscreen, etc. In the excitement of racing you may neglect one or more of these important tasks, so write down a list, have a friend or teammate remind you, or even tie a string around your finger if that's what it takes to jog your memory. (See "What to Pack in Your Race-Day Bag" on page 196–197 for a list of what to bring with you to a race.)

• *Feed off the energy of other runners.* It's normal to have energy highs and lows during the course of a race. When you feel a lapse, look around for someone who seems to be feeling strong, and draw upon the energy of that runner. I've employed a few visualization techniques to accomplish this. My favorite is to mentally picture a rainbow, band of light, fishing line, or piece of string connecting me to the runner directly ahead of me, then use this linking energy to bring the two of us closer.

• *Feed off the spectators.* Often I'll try to tune in to the cheers of a particular person—my husband, my coach, a friend, a coworker. Other times I'll just let the roar of the crowd pull me along, especially in a big road race such as the New York City Marathon or Boston Marathon. Of course, there's no way that cheering throngs can literally propel you to a better performance, but your ability to relax and fully embrace others' belief in your capabilities can allow you to tap into reserves you may not have realized you had.

• *Run the tangents.* In road, trail, and cross-country races, take the shortest legal route from the start to the finish. This means looking ahead and running a straight line across the road (or whatever portion of the road is open to runners) or trail rather than hugging the curb or trail-edge. In road racing in particular, running the tangents can save you several seconds with every bend in the course—and those seconds add up over the miles.

• *Accept the challenge.* Racing to your potential is not easy.

If you are new to running, no doubt the memories of your first slow, agonizing runs are probably still fresh in your mind. If you are now racing with competitive goals, it may be a shock to realize you'll have to revisit that same challenging territory in order to see progress. If doing well matters to you, you will need to learn to neither fear nor resist the challenge of running hard. The experience is not for everyone—and it doesn't have to be for you. Just realize that it's there for you if you choose to embrace it.

• *Never give up.* We've all seen races won and lost in the final meters. "It isn't over till it's over" may be a hackneyed cliché, but it accurately captures what should be your strategy in the final stages of any running race. Race your heart out, especially in the finishing strides. Your goal should be to finish as if you could run another few steps only if you absolutely had to, but not much farther than that. If you consistently finish races with energy to burn, work on pacing your efforts more evenly.

• *Run beyond the finish line.* This strategy has practical as well as philosophical implications. On a purely practical level, running as hard as you can to a point beyond the finish line guarantees you'll be moving at top speed as you cross the line, rather than losing seconds by decelerating while the clock is still ticking. This is especially important if the exact location of the finish line is unclear. On a philosophical level, running through the line is a way of ensuring to yourself and others that you follow through—completely—on what you have started.

# WHY I RACE

"I love to challenge myself. I never get quite the same adrenaline rush from my training as I do from pinning on a number and standing on a starting line. Somehow I'm able to push myself harder and run a lot faster in races than when running on my own. It's funny, it wasn't until a couple of years ago that I realized this. For years I'd been racing at about eight-minute-per-mile pace for distances up to 10 miles, never varying too much from that. Then suddenly I found I could go faster. I don't know why I was able to ramp it up like that. Maybe it was just years of running in the bank and increased confidence. Racing is fun, no matter what kind of shape I'm in. I enjoy setting goals, and watching the clock as I approach the finish line, especially if I've met or come close to my goal. It's also very social for me and my family. My older son is 9, and he's starting to want to accompany me in races. I let him do the shorter ones, and go at his pace. It's a blast for both of us."

—*Rhonda Allen, 40, Morristown, NJ*

"I took up running as an adult about 20 years ago. Actually I'd run in college, too, but not competitively—just for the health of it. Then I started doing a few races here and there and started enjoying it. I race because it's a wonderful social event, and it helps me mentally. It's like my therapy, and it's better than any psychiatrist. I race about twice a month. Sometimes I'll get in the car by myself on a Saturday morning and head off to a race while my husband and son go fishing, but other times they come too. We do it as a family. It's a wonderful thing for the three of us to share."

—*Donna Cramond, 51, Monroe, CT*

"Of course I race for the health of it, and for the fun and camaraderie, but really, I race for the food. Seriously, there's almost always a nice spread afterward—bagels, fruit, yogurt, all kinds of different goodies, and sometimes some pretty unique stuff. Last week we did a race where they had salmon, and I do an "Outback" race every year where they serve steak at the postrace party. We did a race in Louisiana recently where we had crawfish. I also really enjoy racing in different parts of the country, and experiencing the flavor of different regions. We've done a few marathons where we travel specifically to the race, but usually we'll just find something in an area where we happen to be visiting. For example, we went to a wedding in New Orleans, and we found a race to run the day before the wedding. We usually try and connect with the local running club before we leave and find out what is going on. We've raced in southern Florida a number of times, so now we get a magazine that publishes a schedule of all the races down in that region."

—*Jim Cramond, 53, Monroe, CT*

"I race even though my best years and times are behind me. I like the competition and it gives justification for the training. Sometimes I would rather go out and do a race with other runners than slog through a 15-mile training run by myself. I've never met a distance runner I didn't like."

—Hank Berkowitz, 39, Rowayton, CT

"I race to give meaning and purpose to the training. The training can be hard, and monotonous, and sometimes lonely. Racing is exciting, always different, and social. I always get more out of myself in a race than I would in a speed workout, even if I'm not in great shape. A suboptimal result can be tough on the ego, but it tells me where I am and what I need to work on—information that I need to know."

—Ed Stickles, 34, Hawthorne, NY

"I've been running since I was 19. I began racing when I moved to New York in my thirties. I had been an athlete all my life, and racing was just an extension of that. By the time I was 40, I set my sights on masters running. By this time, I had two daughters, ages 5 and 3, and I got this inkling that when I was racing, I was doing something significant for them. Each time I lined up, and particularly each time I crossed a finish line, they would watch my face, my body, my effort. I knew they would connect that with the many mornings I trained, and that would say more to them than almost anything I could verbalize about commitment, effort, physical and mental discipline, joy at accomplishment, and perseverance. I was also telling them (and myself): This is difficult and painful, but it is what you do when you live life to the max. I wanted them to understand that athletics could be their world. I guess that worked. My older daughter, 14, is a national-caliber youth soccer player, and my younger daughter, now 11, ran a 6:41 mile at age 9.

"I ran my first race as a 50-year-old last week. I hadn't raced in about a year. I realized my reasons for racing now are different yet again. Sometimes I fear aging. I know people my age who have gotten sick or died. At the race, I embraced my friend Judy. She is living with cancer, and her husband left her and her three daughters a few years ago. Seeing her reminds me that when I run a race now, it's a chance to celebrate the fact I can. I didn't run what I would have considered fast, but I still placed second in my age group. The girls are still proud, and don't really pay attention to my time. They are both faster runners than I am.

"When I reflect upon it, I never realized that running races could mean so much, and for so long."

—Gloria Averbuch, 50, Upper Montclair, NJ

"I started running when I was in my late forties, and got into racing when I was 55. I race almost every weekend, at all distances. I belong to a running club and do the races that the club puts on, plus others. It's very social, and I must admit I love the competition. I used to think I wasn't competitive, but I've found that I'm very competitive. I have gotten faster since I retired, and that gives me a whole new level of motivation."

—*Betty Kelly, 67, Meriden, CT*

CHAPTER 9

▶▶▶▶▶▶▶▶▶▶▶▶▶▶▶▶▶▶▶▶▶▶▶▶▶▶▶▶▶▶

# Cross-Training, Supplemental Training, and Active Rest

R unners do not live by running alone. Maximizing your enjoyment of running and getting the most from yourself as a runner involve a variety of other fitness activities. Incorporating
other types of exercise into your running program will make you
a better runner by reducing your risk of injury and increasing
your enthusiasm for running. This chapter shows you how to perform better and enjoy running more fully through cross-training,
supplemental training, and active rest. (Keep in mind, though,
that if you want to improve as a runner you should keep the focus
on running, due to the law of specificity of training, which dictates that your greatest improvement in an activity will result from
doing that activity.)

### Cross-training: Success Through Diversified Fitness

Cross-training has been defined in a number of different ways. I
define cross-training for runners as a portion of training that
maintains aerobic fitness in a systematic way through activities
other than running. Running remains the primary activity and

competitive focus. Cross-training activities promote aerobic fitness while relieving the injury-promoting aspects of running—primarily the activity's pounding. Through cross-training, a runner strives to:

• strengthen muscles not used in running, such as the arms and shoulders, to improve overall fitness
• reduce injury risk due to overstressing particular muscles and joints
• increase the variety of a program to prevent monotony and boredom
• prevent overtraining

## CROSS-TRAINING OPTIONS

The activities listed below are the most popular cross-training options for runners. There is no single "best" cross-training exercise. The activities you choose should be those that fit most easily into your schedule and lifestyle, that you can master with the least difficulty, and that you most enjoy.

- *Cycling (road and stationary).* Cycling offers many attractions to runners. One, runners and cyclists often mingle, making it easy for runners to get involved in cycling through their friends. Two, from a physiological standpoint cycling provides an excellent complement to running because it primarily uses the quadriceps (front of thigh) muscles, in contrast to running, which taxes the back-of-thigh hamstrings. A runner who cross-trains by cycling can therefore develop more balanced leg strength, decreasing the risk of injury resulting from relatively strong, tight hamstring muscles and weak quads. (As detailed in Chapter 5, this imbalance can predispose runners to knee and lower leg injuries.) Three, cycling is easily accessible and not difficult to master—most people know how to ride a bike. Choosing between outdoor and indoor options depends on safety and accessibility. If budget is an issue, weigh the cost of a new bicycle and helmet against that of joining a gym or health club. Cycling outdoors offers a nature fix, a variety of workout settings, and possibly a social outlet. Stationary cycling offers a steadier and more easily measured workout (many stationary bikes are programmable to simulate hill and interval-type workouts), along with safety and protection from the elements. Four, a cycling workout is nonimpact, making it a good substitute for running during recovery from many different injuries.

  Warm up and stretch the ankle, calf, quadriceps, hamstring, and lower-back muscles before starting a cycling workout, and stretch again afterward. If you have not cycled before, limit your first few workouts to 15 to 20 minutes of pedaling at "conversation" intensity, then build up gradually. Ask an experienced cyclist to observe and advise you on proper cycling form in order to avoid injury and maximize your workout's effectiveness.

- *Swimming.* The main advantages of swimming for runners are that it's nonimpact and offers a full-body workout. In addition, as with cycling, it's usually easy for a runner to plug into the swimming community. Swimming and other water exercises are also good choices if you live in a warm climate, as they offer the option of a long or intense workout without the risk of overheating. If you don't know how to swim or haven't swum in years, take a few lessons from a qualified instructor to learn the technique necessary to swim well enough to get an effective aerobic workout. Many communities offer "masters" swim programs for adults, which are technically for people age 35 and over, but in reality exist for any fitness-minded adult. These programs offer camaraderie, along with coaching advice.

Swimming workouts are generally less physically taxing than running and other land-based workouts, for two reasons. One, the water makes the workouts nonimpact, and two, the cooling effect of the water along with the water's pressure against the body help to lower heart rate even at high exertion levels. Thus, even sessions designed to allow for muscle recovery can include intervals of hard effort, which—along with varying your strokes—helps keep swimming workouts varied and interesting. Runners new to swimming should ease into the activity with moderate 20- to 30-minute sessions and include plenty of stretching, especially of the arms, shoulders, and lower back.

• *Deep-water running.* Deep-water running is performing the leg and arm motions of running while in deep water. This is done most effectively by wearing a flotation device, usually a belt or vest, for buoyancy (without a flotation device too much energy is required to stay afloat, which can cause muscle strain and compromise running form). Studies have shown that deep-water running while wearing a flotation device closely mimics the biomechanics of land running. Thus, deep-water running can help maintain running fitness better than other cross-training activities, making this an attractive option for performance-oriented runners.

Runners at all levels should consider deep-water running as a cross-training activity for several reasons. One, it's a total-body workout—legs, arms, and trunk all get a strengthening and endurance-building benefit. Two, it's a completely nonimpact activity, making it suitable for training during virtually any running injury. Three, deep-water running is easy to learn—even for non-swimmers—and though there's a bit of a knack to maintaining good form, slight variations in form do not significantly affect the workout's aerobic and muscle-strengthening benefits. (For instruction on form, check with local running clubs and gyms/health clubs.) Four, deep-water running can be more social than swimming because your head remains above water throughout. Five, because of the activity's nonpounding nature, you can work intensely more often without the increased risk of injury inherent in hard running workouts. This adds variety to deep-water running and helps curb boredom. Runners will find less need to ease into deep-water running than other cross-training activities because the exercise so closely simulates running. Be careful, though, when shifting back from deep-water to land running, as your quadriceps and calves will have lost some strength, and running's impact forces may be a shock to muscles and joints.

- *Walking/hiking.* Some runners scoff at the idea of walking for fitness, but you can get an aerobic benefit from walking that's close to that of running, by walking vigorously or hiking uphill and pumping your arms. The main advantage of walking over running is that one foot is always in contact with the ground, which greatly reduces the activity's impact. Walking has no learning curve, it can be done virtually anytime and anywhere, and it allows runners to train in the same places they would do their running workouts. To maximize walking's aerobic, calorie-burning, and strength- and endurance-building benefits, walk briskly (try to work up to at least four miles per hour, which is one mile in 15 minutes), holding the arms at waist level and bent to about 90 degrees. Studies show that carrying handheld weights has almost no effect on strength building, though it does cause a modest increase in calorie burning. Seek out uphill courses, or walk on a treadmill with an incline setting. Walking briskly on a treadmill set to an incline of 3 to 5 percent offers fitness benefits similar to running at aerobic-intensity levels. (Note to skeptics: Anne Marie Lauck, a 1996 U.S. Olympian in the marathon, once sustained a serious hamstring injury walking on a steep incline on a treadmill.) Running shoes are fine for occasional walking, though many people find walking shoes, with a slightly lower heel and thinner, more flexible midsole, a more comfortable option. Racewalking, a competitive Olympic sport, provides a vigorous upper-body and lower-body workout. The world's best racewalkers move at a faster pace than most runners!

- *Elliptical training.* The elliptical trainer is an exercise machine that came on the market in 1995 and quickly became one of the most popular pieces of hardware in gyms and health clubs. The machine simulates a motion close to running, without any impact. The exerciser plants feet on footrests that move in an elliptical (elongated oval) pattern, and can pedal either forward or backward. The activity uses muscles throughout the lower body. Most machines have adjustable resistance, thus varying the challenge of the workout and allowing for interval sessions. The position of the footrests can usually be adjusted as well, which permits different muscles—hamstrings, glutelas, quadriceps, calves—to be targeted. With many machines the exerciser also works the upper body, either by letting go of the handrails and pumping the arms on some models, or pushing and pulling levers on other models. I know several runners who have had to cut back on running due to injury and have seen their fitness program reborn thanks to the elliptical trainer. Some say it mimics the running motion—without pounding—even more closely than deep-water running. The elliptical trainer is easy to master, but ease into the activity, limiting your first few workouts to 20 to 30 minutes of low-intensity training.

- *Nordic skiing/snowshoeing.* Nordic (cross-country) exercise consistently ranks as one of the top calorie-burners among aerobic activities because it engages all the body's major muscles and can raise the heart rate to very high levels, generally higher than through running, cycling, and water activities. Many runners in cold climates maintain fitness through the winter by Nordic skiing. Nordic ski machines make the activity possible indoors on a year-round basis. Nordic skiing is virtually nonimpact and resembles running in terms of the muscular demands on the lower body. It's relatively easy to learn, though more difficult than some cross-training activities to master to the point of offering a high-intensity aerobic, strengthening, and endurance-building workout. It's best to learn Nordic skiing technique from an experienced skier who can offer pointers on your form. Snowshoeing burns fewer calories than Nordic skiing because there's little upper-body involvement, and there is some impact as the shoes hit the snow. The activity very closely resembles running, thanks to today's small, lightweight snowshoes. With a bit of practice and attention to form, your pace and exertion level will approach those of running. (Note: With Nordic skiing, snowshoeing, and other activities performed in the cold, be careful to hydrate just as you would during warm-weather activities. These activities can work up a big sweat even in subfreezing temperatures, and you may not realize how much fluid you are losing.)

- *Rowing.* Rowing—both on the water and indoors on a rowing machine—is a total-body exercise that involves the trunk and lower-body muscles (especially hamstrings and quadriceps). Rowing is nonimpact, and provides a great aerobic and calorie-burning workout. It is not difficult to learn to row well, and the activity provides a good complement to running because of the use of so many different muscles and its nonimpact nature. Good form involves engaging the leg muscles as well as those of the arms and back. Many gyms and health clubs have rowing machines, and opportunities to row on the water exist in most areas with flat bodies of water. (Check with local high schools, colleges, alumni organizations, and sports clubs.) Ease into rowing gradually, starting with 20- to 30-minute sessions at "conversation" pace, and be careful to stretch the muscles of the back, shoulders, hamstrings, and quadriceps.

• *Stair climbing.* Most people who climb stairs for fitness do so on stair-climbing machines at a health club. The exerciser either places his feet on footrests or straps them into pedals, and uses a low- or nonimpact up-and-down motion to "climb" in place. The hands either grasp handrails or move up and down for greater upper-body involvement. Most stair-climbing machines adjust for resistance (intensity) and foot position, so the exercise targets a variety of muscle groups. Stair climbing is a great cross-training activity for runners because many of the muscle-strengthening benefits are shared (both activities work the hamstrings intensely) but the pounding of running is all but eliminated. Stair climbing up real stairs involves some pounding but less than running on a land surface (running down stairs is a high-impact activity without much aerobic benefit and therefore is not recommended). Stair climbing is not necessarily the best cross-training choice due to the impact forces, but it can help build up weak quadriceps, and can be a good substitute for running at times when running outdoors is impossible due to weather or safety considerations and a treadmill is not available. However, even very fit runners will find stair climbing tough on their quadriceps, so ease into the activity by starting with "conversation"-pace workouts of no longer than 20 to 30 minutes. There are a few stair-climbing competitions, including the annual Empire State Building Run-Up in New York City: 86 floors from the ground floor to the Observation Deck. The top finishers train exclusively by stair climbing, but most of the rest are runners.

## QUESTION AND ANSWER

**Q.** Which cross-training activities are best for someone with knee problems?

**A.** It depends on the type of knee problem. Generally, activities that involve little or no pounding against a solid surface, such as swimming, deep-water running, rowing, elliptical training, Nordic skiing, and fitness walking are better to prevent and manage knee injuries than activities such as running, high-impact aerobics, and running or walking down stairs. However, runners can suffer from a large variety of injuries to the knee, so proceed carefully with any type of exercise if you have a knee injury. For example, cycling is not a suitable cross-training activity for several different knee injuries because of the constant bending and flexing of the knee during the activity. Remember to ease into any cross-training exercise that you undertake when injured, and back off if you feel pain.

### Two Sample Cross-Training Programs

The two one-week sample programs below are for runners who wish to incorporate cross-training into their fitness program at two different levels. The first contains about 20 percent cross-training activities, the second about 40 percent. Adjust the programs in terms of activity choices, mix, and scheduling to meet your needs.

### 20 PERCENT CROSS-TRAINING PROGRAM

Day 1   Elliptical trainer: 40 minutes, aerobic intensity
Day 2   Run: 60 minutes, including 25 minutes at lactate-threshold intensity
Day 3   Run: 45 minutes, aerobic intensity
Day 4   Swim: 40 minutes, including 20 minutes of intervals
Day 5   Off
Day 6   Run: 60 minutes, including 15–20 minutes at ATP-CP intensity (or race)
Day 7   Run: 130 minutes, aerobic intensity

## 40 PERCENT CROSS-TRAINING PROGRAM

Day 1    Row: 45 minutes, aerobic intensity
Day 2    Run: 50 minutes, including 20 minutes at aerobic intensity
Day 3    Deep-water run: 45 minutes, aerobic intensity
Day 4    Off
Day 5    Stair climb: 45 minutes, aerobic intensity
Day 6    Run: 45 minutes, including 15–20 minutes at ATP-CP intensity
         (or race)
Day 7    Run: 110 minutes, aerobic intensity

Many runners first encounter cross-training when they develop an injury. Unable to run, or restricted in their running, they look for substitute activities to maintain fitness and sanity while their injury heals. As soon as possible, they return to running, and don't cross-train until they are again forced to by injury.

I understand the appeal of this pattern. After all, runners love running. Given the choice between running and any of the many cross-training activities available, I will choose running hands-down. But waiting until you are injured to cross-train is not the smartest training strategy. Rather, cross-training should become part of every runner's program before injury strikes. Here is what cross-training can do:

• *Improve overall fitness.* Running is an excellent way to promote aerobic fitness, help control weight, and improve the strength and endurance of the major muscles in the lower body. However, running does very little to improve the strength and endurance of muscles in the upper body, back, and abdominal area. Strengthening these areas can reduce the risk of back problems, help prevent osteoporosis (loss of bone mineral) in the bones attached to the muscles, and improve performance in a multitude of daily tasks. For example, having a strong lower back and abdomen can contribute to any activity that involves supporting weight, bending, twisting the trunk, reaching, or using the legs. Strong arms help with a variety of pushing, pulling, twisting, and lifting activities. These fitness gains can also improve your running. Although the arms aren't the primary means of locomotion in running, they don't just "go along for the ride." Rather, strong arms can help drive the body forward, especially in the late stages of workouts and races when the legs are fatigued. A strong back and abdominal area contributes to better posture, which allows for more efficient and comfortable running.

• *Reduce injury risk.* Studies show that the risk of injury from running increases dramatically as weekly mileage rises. There are many ways of reducing your injury risk (see Chapter 5 for more on this topic), but some runners remain prone to frequent injury despite precautions. You can deal with a tendency toward injury by running fewer miles, but this may force you to compromise your running goals. Cross-training can bridge the gap between being undertrained and constantly injured. Cross-training allows you to maintain a high level of aerobic fitness without an accompanying high injury risk. Your heart and cardiovascular system don't care whether you raise your heart rate by running, swimming, rowing, cycling, or Nordic skiing. You can replace a portion of your running with these activities when you are healthy, and up to 100 percent with them during periods of injury. There are many examples of runners who cross-trained almost completely for months and came back fitter and faster than ever. If you incorporate cross-training before injury—and thus minimize or avoid injury altogether—your running will progress more quickly and steadily than if you are constantly interrupted by injury.

• *Increase the variety of training.* Some runners wish only to run. Most, however, prefer a fitness program with some variety. Cross-training allows you to spice up a running-only program. I've tried many cross-training options, including cycling (road and stationary), swimming, deep-water running, hiking, stair climbing, elliptical training, rowing, and Nordic skiing. My current selections are deep-water running and elliptical training. I'm not going to try and convince running purists to strap on a flotation vest or climb onto a StairMaster, but my suggestion is: Don't knock something until you've tried it. I thought I'd hate the elliptical trainer (too trendy, too boring) until I tried it and found that it offered a fun, varied, and challenging workout. Having a variety of training options can come to your rescue on days when it's simply not possible to run, such as when you are stuck in a hotel at 10 P.M. and the gym has no treadmill—but there is a rowing machine.

• *Prevent overtraining and burnout.* As detailed in Chapter 5, runners can become overtrained and burned out due to excessive running. Overtraining can sneak up on you, and it's difficult to reverse. It's far better to avoid overtraining in the first place, and cross-training is one of the best strategies because it limits your running mileage. It actually helps if you are not proficient in your cross-training activities, because this ineptness can help keep your training level moderate. For example, sometimes I tend to overtrain by running too hard on my recovery days. However, if I cross-train for a couple of my recovery workouts each week, I go at an easier pace because I lack the skills and fitness to push myself to a high intensity level. Be aware, though, that you can overtrain in cross-training activities just as in running by doing too much or working too intensely. Keep careful records to help ensure that your training volume and intensity remain under control, and use cross-training workouts primarily for recovery unless you are injured.

## QUESTION AND ANSWER

**Q.** All I want to do is run. Do I really have to cross-train?

**A.** Some runners view cross-training as they would a prison sentence. "I hate cross-training," 1996 U.S. Olympian Keith Brantly once said in an interview. "My idea of cross-training is pulling weeds in my garden." Others point to the example of the Kenyans, who are the best runners in the world right now, and who almost never cross-train. Opponents of cross-training also point to the law of specificity of training, which states that the best way to improve in any activity is to perform that activity.

All these arguments have merit, yet cross-training makes sense for the vast majority of runners. In fact, your love of running is the very reason you should cross-train regularly, whether injured or not. I know that the more effort I make to cross-train consistently and intelligently, the less likely I'll lose any opportunities to run due to injury or burnout. As for the Kenyans, I'm not going to argue with their success, but keep in mind that you probably don't hear about the Kenyan runners who fall by the wayside due to injury or overtraining. Kenyans are not immune to injury, and perhaps with a cross-training program some of them would experience even greater success.

The law of specificity of training has a corollary, the law of diminishing returns. Every runner reaches a point at which the risks of overtraining, injury, and burnout override any potential improvement. Cross-training, if done intelligently, allows most runners to raise that level. Through cross-training, a runner can aim higher, and enjoy longer and more frequent productive workouts, without an accompanying increased risk of injury and overtraining.

## GENERAL CROSS-TRAINING AND SUPPLEMENTAL TRAINING GUIDELINES

How, when, and how much you cross-train will depend on your injury status, fitness level, schedule, lifestyle, and running goals. Follow these basic guidelines, and adjust the specifics of the suggested schedules to best suit you:

- *Don't get hung up on numbers.* You are probably curious to know the equivalent, in running terms, of your cross-training and supplemental training workouts. In other words, if you bike 15 miles, what does that equal in terms of a run? I've seen a number of formulas, some of them highly complex, for calculating the "running equivalent" of various cross-training activities, but I don't find them very helpful. I simply record the number of minutes spent in the activity and the approximate intensity. For example: "45 min deep-water run, moderate w/5 3-min surges." Because most of my cross-training is done as recovery workouts rather than intense efforts, these notations are seldom complicated. The main purpose of recording them is to ensure that I don't overtrain. You can note your heart rate (by taking your pulse or using a heart rate monitor), or do your workouts on a machine that records heart rate, intensity level, and caloric expenditure. Over time, you will get a sense of a workout's "running equivalent," and cross-train accordingly.

- *Ease into new activities.* Cross-training and supplemental training use muscles that may be relatively weak in runners. In addition, performing any new activity initially carries significantly greater physical demands than a familiar activity. For these reasons you should ease into any new cross-training or supplemental training activity or one you've not engaged in for several months. Cross-training workouts should be at "conversation" pace and last no longer than 20 to 30 minutes for at least the first four to five sessions. You should finish your first three or four supplemental training workouts feeling as though you could easily keep going. If you feel breathless, reduce your intensity level. Stretch muscles (especially those that don't get a heavy workout in running, such as quadriceps, abdominals, back, shoulders, arms, and wrists) after a light warm-up, and stretch again after cooling down, when muscles are warm and loose. Scale back your workouts if you experience significant soreness, and stop exercising if you feel any sharp pain.

- *Focus on your goals.* Remember that the purpose of cross-training and supplemental training ultimately is to enhance your running through injury prevention, raising your aerobic fitness level, and curbing boredom and burnout. It's possible to compromise these goals by getting carried away in these activities. That's perfectly fine, as long as it is your choice. If you happen to discover a hidden talent for rowing that leads you to an Olympic gold medal, I'm certainly not going to stand in your way. If cross-training or supplemental training start to become more than a sideshow to your running, take a step back and reevaluate your goals, making changes to your overall program if needed.

- *Remember why and how you got injured.* As discussed in Chapter 5, the vast majority of running injuries result from overuse—doing too much, too soon, or too often. The injury is very likely to recur unless you change your pattern. Replacing some of your running with cross-training and/or supplemental training can be part of the solution. The real key, though, is listening and responding to physical signs of overuse and abuse before they manifest as injury. The same rule applies to cross-training and supplemental training: Pay attention, and remember that less is often more.

### Supplemental Training

Supplemental activities serve a different purpose from cross-training activities. Whereas the purpose of cross-training is to maintain aerobic fitness while reducing injury risk, supplemental activities develop other aspects of fitness, primarily strength and flexibility.

The main supplemental activities used by runners are strength training, yoga, and stretching. I discuss strength-training and yoga here; see Chapter 5 for a discussion of stretching, including a sample stretching program for runners.

• *Strength training.* Numerous studies have shown that strength training (also known as resistance training) improves running economy and efficiency—the ability to stride smoothly, with minimal energy expenditure. Strengthening the leg muscles can increase stride length and improve toe-off and follow-through, all of which help propel your body forward while running. Developing upper-body strength can preserve good running form—especially late in workouts and races, when fatigue sets in—which can help you keep up a fast pace. A strong midsection also helps maintain form and reduce injury risk. Because strength training helps strengthen both muscle and bone mineral, and raises metabolism, aiding in weight control, the American College of Sports Medicine recommends two strength-training sessions per week for all healthy adults.

A strength-training routine for runners should work the major muscles of the upper and lower body, including back and abdominals. You can strength train using machines, free weights, or the body's own resistance (crunches, push-ups, pull-ups, etc.). Runners will benefit more from a program involving many repetitions with light weights (thus emphasizing endurance, not explosive strength), rather than few repetitions with heavy weights. Most general fitness books include a strength-training program, or a trainer at a health club can design a routine to meet your individual needs. Warm up and stretch gently before strength training, and stretch again afterward to prevent the muscles from cramping or overtightening. Start with a weight that you can work with comfortably for 12–15 repetitions, and do one or two sets. Increase the weight in the smallest possible increments as you gain strength and confidence. A total-body strength-training program, including warm-up, cool-down, and stretching, should take about 30 to 40 minutes. Aim to strength train twice per week, but not on consecutive days and not the day before races or hard workouts. It's best not to strength train at all during the week before a goal race, as the benefits of added strength do not kick in for 7 to 10 days, and the fatigue and mild soreness of a workout can adversely affect running performance right away.

• *Yoga.* Yoga is a physical and mental discipline with roots in a number of Asian cultures. The word "yoga" comes from the Sanskrit root *"yug,"* meaning "to yoke or harness." Yoga refers to the linking of the lower (individual) consciousness and the higher (universal) consciousness, and has also come to suggest a union of body and mind. There are many different types of yoga, and innumerable variations within categories depending on the background, training, and preferences of the instructor. Yoga can be a valuable supplement to running, thanks to its strengthening and flexibility-building benefits and meditative mind-body aspects. Though I am unaware of any type of yoga that is *not* of potential benefit to runners, the most popular types are of the *astanga* branch of *hatha yoga*, which involve continuous movement from one pose (posture) to the next. *Astanga* is a more physical yoga practice than other forms, and generally focuses on flexibility and strength-building. Practicing *astanga* yoga can help correct the muscle and connective-tissue tightnesses and imbalances that can plague runners.

A yoga workout has a calming, yet energizing effect, and can enhance concentration by helping to quiet the mind's "chatter." If you choose to do yoga as a supplement to your running, inform your instructor that you are a runner. He or she may suggest certain poses. Keep in mind, though, that yoga is a holistic discipline whose primary purpose isn't necessarily to make you a better runner. There are no strict guidelines on when, how often, and for how long you should do yoga as a runner, though it will probably be difficult to see benefits from engaging in the practice less often than once per week, and doing it more than three to four times weekly is probably overkill in terms of enhancing your running. (See Resources for sources of information on yoga.)

## TRIATHLONS AND OTHER MULTISPORT EVENTS

In 1972 a San Diego–based runner and cyclist named David Pain held a run-bike race to celebrate his 50th birthday. USA Triathlon, the national governing body of the sports of triathlon and duathlon, calls this "the first known multisport event in the United States."

Actually, the 1904 St. Louis Olympic Games included an event called the "triathlon," which consisted of the long jump, shot put, and 100-yard dash. The swim-bike-run sport that we now call triathlon (along with the bike-run duathlon) has its roots in running. Indeed, the majority of current participants in the triathlon, which debuted as an Olympic medal sport in Sydney in 2000, come to the sport from a running background.

The earliest triathlons, held in and around San Diego's Mission Bay in 1974, were fun, quirky training sessions and low-key competitions organized by the San Diego Track Club. The runners staged these events as breaks in their grueling marathon and 10k training programs. In 1978 U.S. Naval Officer John Collins, who'd taken part in the Mission Bay triathlons, staged the inaugural Iron Man Triathlon, combining the Waikiki Rough Water Swim, the Around-Oahu Bike Ride, and the Honolulu Marathon into one daylong event. The 15 starters were all men; 12 finished, led by Gordon Haller in 11 hours, 46 minutes, 58 seconds. By 1980 hundreds were entering the annual Ironman, which had moved to Hawaii's Big Island, standardized distances at

2.4 miles of swimming, 112 miles on the bike, and 26.2 miles of running, and brought in *ABC Wide World of Sports* for coverage. In 1982 triathletes formed a national governing body, started a national racing series, and saw the founding of two national magazines.

Triathlon was held as a demonstration event at the 1996 Atlanta Olympic Games, with competitors covering what had become known as "Olympic" distances: 0.9-mile (1.5k) swim, 24.8-mile (40k) bike, 6.2-mile (10k) run. In contrast to the Ironman, this was a race the average participant could complete in about two hours; its development had helped spur the growth of the sport among the masses and sped its way to inclusion in the Olympics and other international events. USA Triathlon today has close to 20,000 members, who compete in hundreds of sanctioned events nationwide. An estimated 50 million people worldwide watch the Hawaiian Ironman competition each year.

Runners are drawn to triathlon for a variety of reasons. Some are chronically injured, and turn to biking, swimming, and other cross-training activities to manage their maladies. When they see that they can exercise, stay fit, form social ties, and compete, all while avoiding the injuries that plagued them as runners, they shift their focus to multisport training and competition. Others take up the sport after seeing, reading, or hearing about a triathlon or duathlon. Some runners continue to run for parts of the year (usually the cooler months) and turn their attention to triathlons or duathlons during the spring and summer months, when most competitions are held.

Other multisport events exist as well, and are staged formally and informally by runners and others who relish the unique challenges of multisport training and competition, as well as the spirit of fun and adventure that often surrounds these events. There are multisport events that include running along with kayaking, canoeing, rowing, hiking, mountain-biking, snowshoeing, Nordic and downhill skiing, rock climbing, dogsledding, and more. (See Resources for information on multisport events, or search under "adventure racing" and related topics.)

If triathlons, duathlons, and other multisport events appeal to you, here are some guidelines for getting started:

- *Enter your first event for fun.* Though you may be fit as a runner, multisport competition has unique elements that should be approached cautiously by a first-timer. In particular, the mass start of a triathlon can be intimidating—even dangerous—to the uninitiated. Typically hundreds of athletes hit the water at once, resulting in a churning mass of arms and legs. An unintentional kick or swipe in the face is the rule rather than the exception. Adding to the chaos is the fact that triathlon swims usually take place in open water (a river, lake, pond, bay, or open ocean)—a far cry from the familiarity of the lap lane. The transition areas of these events (where participants transform themselves from swimmers, to bikers, to runners) are also potential disaster zones for the novice intent on recording a fast time without having first learned the ropes. The bike portion has its own set of challenges, what with equipment-failure problems added to the mix of potential human shortcomings. Forget about any time or performance goals for your first "tri" or other multisport event. Rather, just use the opportunity to have fun and get in a decent workout.

• *Pick the right event for your first outing.* Though the Olympic-distance triathlon sets the standard for international competition, there are many shorter events, and these are a better bet for the novice. Two hours (the average finishing time for an Olympic-distance triathlon) is a long time to be exercising, and if something goes wrong—from dehydration to a flat tire—you may well be on the course for a lot longer. Look for an event that's contested in a multiloop format, so that if you need help or decide to bail out, you won't be in the middle of nowhere.

• *Don't let the training intimidate you.* Although full-time professional triathletes—especially those competing at the Ironman distance—may train up to eight hours a day, the average participant needs far less training. USA Triathlon offers a 13-week training program for beginner and recreational triathletes that maxes out at less than eight hours of training per week—just over an hour per day. Keep in mind that you can perform well in the triathlon and duathlon on much lower mileage than you'd log as a runner. My observation of triathletes is that they are less likely than runners to overtrain, probably because the requirements of three different sports force them to avoid "junk" training.

• *Learn to eat during exercise.* Unlike running, cycling and swimming allow for ingestion of solid food directly before and during exercise, even at a high level. In particular, successful cyclists learn to fuel up (and hydrate) before and during workouts and races, and even long-distance swimmers master this practice to a certain degree, pausing briefly during workouts to consume easily digested foods. You need to practice this in training; see Chapter 7 for more on preexercise and midexercise fueling and hydration.

## QUESTION AND ANSWER

**Q.** I usually cross-train by biking, but it's hurting my iliotibial band. What should I do?

**A.** Biking can aggravate pain and inflammation of the iliotibial (IT) band, which runs down the outside of the thigh and inserts just below the knee, due to the repeated knee flexion and extension that occurs during the pedaling motion. For this reason, biking usually does not work as a cross-training activity for runners with IT band syndrome. You should follow the first rule of injury prevention and health promotion: If it hurts, don't do it. Cross-training activities that are less likely to aggravate a painful, inflamed IT band include swimming, walking, Nordic skiing, elliptical training, and modified pool-running with the legs straight to avoid aggravating the knee. Follow the conservative care of injury—rest, icing, stretching—outlined in Chapter 5.

### Active Rest: What, When, and How

"Active rest" sounds like a contradiction in terms—and indeed, it may be so for the very unconditioned person. However, for a runner, active rest is a valuable training component. It refers to activities performed for recovery, at a level that doesn't stress the body's muscular or aerobic systems. All of the activities that qualify as active rest can also be cross-training or supplemental-training activities. You can bike, swim, deep-water run, walk/hike, elliptical train, Nordic ski, row, and stair climb as a form of active rest *if you keep both the intensity of the workout and your mental focus on the task at a low level.* This is crucial. (For all but very elite runners who have been in the sport for years, running is too intense to count as active rest, even at a very easy pace.) Active rest works the muscles gently and rhythmically through a moderate range of motion. This promotes circulation of blood and other body fluids, which can help move lactic acid and other by-products of heavy exertion away from the muscles, and bring oxygen and nutrients to the muscles, promoting recovery. It also induces relaxation by being rhythmic and repetitive. Many runners see active rest as a reward for the challenges of running and other tough workouts.

Active rest is not the same as cross-training, the purpose of which is to enhance fitness while minimizing the stresses and injury-inducing aspects of running. Nor is it supplemental training, because it shouldn't tax any muscles or body system enough to produce a training effect. Rather, it serves the purpose of recovery and injury-risk reduction. The essence of active rest is that it is nonstressful. You can do yoga, stretching, and mild strength training as forms of active rest. I recommend maintaining an aerobic intensity level of no greater than 50 percent of maximal heart rate, and applying muscle strength at no more than half your normal levels (for example, lifting 25 pounds when you would normally lift 50 pounds). Active-rest sessions should last no longer than 30 minutes—and less if the effort starts to feel taxing.

Let your mind relax during active rest, and allow your thoughts to wander. This can be a time of meditation, free association, or a period used to focus on other things in your life, such as work or relationships. You can do these sessions alone or with others, as long as the pace is relaxing for *you*.

Active rest is best performed after taxing workouts or races—either immediately following the exercise as a cooldown, later that day, or the following morning after an afternoon or evening workout. The sessions should be planned, and they should be made up of activities you enjoy and that fit conveniently into your life. For some runners, a relaxing stroll two or three times a week is all the active rest they need and have time for. Others may want to engage in a variety of active-rest activities, as often as once a day. Many people find the beginning or the end of the day ideal times for active-rest sessions.

Here are examples of different kinds of active-rest sessions to schedule at various times. You'll certainly come up with other ways to fit them in. Don't neglect these sessions. They may feel like an indulgence, but in reality there are few elements that can enhance your running more. Schedule them regularly.

- 25 minutes of light yoga and stretching upon arising
- a 30-minute walk before breakfast
- 20 minutes of leisurely swimming after your morning run
- a 25-minute bike ride to work
- 20 minutes of easy swimming or deep-water running after strength training at lunchtime
- a 25-minute walk home from work the afternoon after a morning track workout
- 30 minutes of light elliptical training before dinner
- 20 minutes of easy rowing or Nordic skiing while watching the evening news
- 25 minutes of light strength-training and stretching before bedtime

CHAPTER 10

▶▶▶▶▶▶▶▶▶▶▶▶▶▶▶▶▶▶▶▶▶▶▶▶▶▶▶▶▶▶▶▶

# The Running Life

*F*or most runners, running is part of a full and vigorous life. We fit in running around jobs, school, family activities, community responsibilities, child-care, and volunteer work. We want running to enhance our fulfillment of these multiple roles, not detract from them. At the same time, we try to set up our lives to support our running. We may pay attention to our diet, try to get enough sleep, and seek to minimize tension in our lives so that we can relax and enjoy our running.

Still, every day has but 24 hours, and there are times when it's a challenge to fit in even token amounts of running, let alone training for fitness and competitive goals. This chapter offers solutions for time-crunched runners and suggestions for setting up a lifestyle that supports running.

▼ RUNNING AND MY DAY

A few runners at the highest competitive levels are able to put their running first, and organize the rest of their day around it. Running is a full-time job for these people, and skipping a run is like calling in sick. However, even recreational runners must somehow ensure that we run regularly, and often. For me, running is something I can count on. Meetings get canceled, the kids get sick, and the toilet overflows, but on most days, I'm still going to run. It may be a short, easy few miles or it may last two hours or longer. I may feel strong, smooth, and pulsing with energy, or I may drag through the run dead-legged. We runners learn that even our worst runs can make our day better and brighter.

Here, runners describe how running fits into their day:

*Gordon Bakoulis.* "I've always been a morning runner. When I was younger I could bound out of bed and be out the door running at a good clip five minutes later. I like to take a bit more time these days. Most mornings the alarm goes off at 6:30 (though I'm usually awake already), and my husband, Alan, and I get up. He heads out for his run about 6:45 while I do chores and check e-mail. He's back by 7:30 and then it's my turn. (We used to run together before we had children, but rarely do now.) I do a few quick stretches and head out the door to run from 20 minutes to an hour. (If I'm doing a long run I'll go later in the day after my baby-sitter arrives mid-morning.) I follow a planned training schedule, so I always know what I'll be doing on a given day.

"My attitude going into my run depends on what is scheduled for that day. If I have a hard workout scheduled—hill repeats, intervals, or a tempo run—I may be a bit nervous, though once I get started, I'm fine. My mind seldom wanders, and it's as though time stands still. A part of me knows that I'll soon be heading home to the other activities of my busy day—making breakfast for the kids, taking my older son to school, shopping, working—but for the moment I'm completely absorbed by my running. On my easy running days, I'll use the time to think ahead to the day's activities and events, to make plans, work out problems, or anticipate challenging situations. Other times I'll just space out. On my long runs, which start at a relaxed effort and get progressively more challenging, I tend to adopt a combination of the two mind-sets.

"Most days I run alone. In the past I've had morning running partners, and cherished their companionship. But I love my solo morning jaunts as well. It's the only time of the day I can be completely alone, without phone calls, deadlines, or cries of 'Mommy' to answer. My run grounds me, energizes me, centers me, and keeps me sane. I wish I could put those feelings into a pill. I'd hand it out to everyone who says they can't run because they don't have time."

**Grete Waitz,** 48, nine-time New York City Marathon winner and 1984 Olympic marathon silver medalist, now retired from competitive running and living in Oslo, Norway, and Gainesville, Florida, and working as a writer, speaker, consultant on a variety of running- and fitness-related projects.

"I run about five times a week on average, for a weekly total of approximately 40 miles, give or take a few. I don't have a training program. Rather, I run within my comfort zone, depending on how I feel, the weather, and where I am in the world. I normally run between 45 and 70 minutes. On the other days I give my legs a rest from pounding. Normally I use my NordicTrack or stationary bike, but with all the traveling I am doing I have days where I don't do any exercise at all.

"I usually run with my husband, Jack. He always runs for less time than I do (50 minutes at the most), so we run together for about four miles, and then I am on my own when he falls back and takes a shorter route home. We always run early in the morning. That is my time for exercise. I have time to do it later in the day, but I prefer early morning because there are no distractions and no traffic. I also like to start the day feeling good and energized. I have always been a morning person so I don't have to struggle to get out of bed before 5 A.M. Neither Jack nor I are late-night people.

"When I was a professional competitive runner I would get upset if a planned training session did not happen. I could skip easy morning runs if I had to, but not the afternoon sessions. When you are a professional runner you plan your life around the training, so it didn't happen often that I had to drop a session.

"Now if something comes up and I can't run, I am fine with that. The goal and purpose of my running is to stay in okay shape, so I don't mind taking a day off once in a while. I believe that if you are running without a goal of performing to the best of your ability in races, one or two days off don't mean anything."

**Veronique Sentilhes,** 34, New York City: "Because I have three children, ages 2, 5, and 8, and I work full-time, I need to manage my day carefully.

On the days that I work from home, I can usually arrange things so I have time to run in the middle of the day. I go between 1 and 2 P.M. It's a nice way to shape the day into two halves—before my run and after my run. On days I'm in the office, I try to leave work a bit early, at 5 P.M. I can be running by 5:30. My husband or our sitter watches the children. I have time to run, come home, and shower before we all have dinner together at 7:30. After a day of work, then running, I feel very open to my children. I want nothing more than to spend time with them and be open to them, because I've had my time while running. For me, running is a wonderful way to spend time outdoors, in nature, and to feel alive in my environment. I live half a block from Central Park and do all my running there. Some people think it might get boring running the same place every day, but I never find it boring. Each time I'm there I notice something different—a new tree, a new planting of flowers, a statue—that I hadn't noticed before. It's a new discovery every day."

*Lauri "Tigger" Plesco,* 35, Avondale Estates, Georgia: "Before I became a mom I would spend quite a bit of time planning when to run, depending on the time, the weather, and when and what I'd eaten. Now that I have a baby I am lucky to get out the door with my running shoes on! The planning centers on Molly, who's now 2: When is she at her best, how will the weather conditions affect her, does she have a drink, a snack, her dolly, and how can I make this as much fun as possible for both of us? Once I get all that figured out, the unexpected can happen—like a diaper explosion.

"Although my husband is wonderfully supportive, I cannot depend on him to watch Molly while I run because his work hours are unpredictable. So I invested in the single most important running item available to parents: a running stroller, including a ventilated rain cover (which also protects Molly from the wind and cold). At first I disliked pushing a jogger, but now I have grown to love running with Molly and she looks forward to "running," too. Molly's naptime, 11 A.M., is the ideal running time for both of us. The only problem is that at this hour it's very warm in Atlanta during the summer months. So in summertime I either take her running first thing in the morning or after dinner, when it's cooler.

"One day a week I run over 10 miles, and two days a week I do speedwork. I do my long runs very early on Sunday mornings, without Molly. Once my husband had to work on a Sunday and I had a 23-mile run scheduled. I got up at 2:45 A.M., nursed Molly, and set off on my own while Molly and my husband slept. On Tuesday evenings I hire a baby-sitter to watch Molly while I do a group workout at a local track. Then I get up early on Saturday mornings for my second track session, and hope the track will not be locked.

"At times I wonder whether my running is selfish—such as the few times I've had to call upon my neighbors to watch Molly. I have also worried about leaving my child for three to four hours when I do my long runs. However, over the past two years I have learned that running is not selfish—it is essential. It helps me relieve stress, it energizes me, and it gives me self-confidence. Because of these things I am a well-balanced mom and this enhances my child's well-being. Molly loves to see me race and is sad if she cannot "run" with me. I believe she will be proud of me as she grows up, and that I will offer her a good example of a healthy lifestyle. Sometimes I don't know how I manage to get out the door ... but I am always glad that I did."

*Gail Waesche Kislevitz,* 50, Ridgewood, New Jersey: "I started running when I was 16, and ran through high school, college, an early (and ongoing) marriage, graduate school, having and raising two children, and a business career that involved extensive travel. Now—still running, and working from a home that seems so empty now that the kids are in college—all those years of trying to fit in running around so many other activities seem a blur. My children grew up with a running mom and are proud of that fact. They brag to their friends about my races and medals. And through my running I have taught them what it means to strive and struggle toward a personal goal. I never gave up my running because it is such a crucial part of who I am. No matter what circumstance I found myself in as life progressed, running was always my salvation. I ran with tears staining my face the night my father died. I have long talks with my mother, gone 15 years now but by my side when I run.

"Whether I am running two miles or 20, running is my daily prayer. Now that I have the flexibility of working at home, I run in the afternoon, about 4 P.M. It breaks up my day, and makes a nice division between work time and personal time. Running is my best friend, and like a friend, it knows me better than I know myself. Running kicks me out the door when I want to stall and teaches me to realize the beauty of every day."

*Brian Fullem,* 36, Newtown, Connecticut: "There isn't a day that goes by that I don't wake up and think I'm not going to run that day. I don't have a 'streak' going, but I miss maybe 10 to 12 days of running per year unless I'm seriously injured or ill. I had a streak of about two years when I was in college. I run about 60 miles a week. I'm a sports podiatrist, so I'm around runners all day, which is very motivating. To a certain extent I'm in control of my work hours, but things can come up—you really never know. I run at all different times; it depends on my schedule. Sometimes I run at lunch, sometimes I run in the morning before work, and sometimes I run after work. I'll do what I need to do. I've run in airports, at very early and very late hours. Very rarely it just doesn't work out to run on a particular day. I'm okay with that, but it just doesn't tend to happen very often."

*Kathryn Klingenstein,* 37, New York City: "I usually run right after dropping my kids off at school, so at about 9:00 or 9:30 in the morning. I don't have a job, so that's a good time for me. Or sometimes I go in the late afternoons. I find if I don't run for four or five days I start to feel really lousy. I'm tired all the time and my legs ache. And it just makes me feel good—as though I've done something worthwhile with my time. I just started running two years ago. I'd done it a little in college and enjoyed it, though I think I did it too fast, because it always hurt and I got shinsplints. So now I run at a pace that feels comfortable and relaxing. I'm exhilarated afterward rather than wiped out. I can go about the rest of my day with more energy and focus."

*Hank Berkowitz,* 39, Rowayton, Connecticut: "I've run all but 10 days a year for 20 years now. Now that I'm a family man with a daily commute on the train, I run early in the mornings. It's the only time of day that works for me, and sometimes it's the best part of my day. I've run through airports, I've run from train stations, I've left cocktail parties early to sneak in a run between drinks and dinner (I'll stick to nonalcoholic beverages when I use this strategy!), and I've left family gatherings in between courses of meals. When I'm forced to work late, I will run from my office during my dinner break, and return to eat at my desk and keep working. And I've never regretted any of it."

## QUESTION AND ANSWER

**Q.** How can I get enough sleep when I have to get up so early to run?
**A.** Many runners find scheduling their run first thing in the morning

the best way to fit it in. I've always been a morning runner. Running first thing relaxes and energizes me. I'm used to it, and to the shifts I must make on the other end of my day—in the evenings—to accommodate my early-morning running habit.

The challenge is getting out of bed. If you run in the mornings and feel short on sleep, the best tactic is to go to bed earlier. Just do whatever it takes: Turn off the TV and computer, stop making phone calls, cut out the late-night socializing, eat dinner earlier, change your children's bedtimes. It's not always easy. If these options really don't work for you, there is also the option of running at another time of day: mid-morning, lunchtime, after work, or after dinner (just don't schedule vigorous workouts late in the day, because the revving-up effect interferes with sleep). Motivate yourself with the reminder that exercise can help improve the quality of sleep, thus allowing for greater productivity during the day.

### Making Sleep a Priority

Getting adequate sleep is vital for runners. During sleep the body truly recovers from physical activity, as muscles repair at the cellular level and metabolism slows to allow for deep relaxation. Unfortunately, sleep deprivation is at epidemic proportions in our hurry-up, get-more-done Western society. Thanks to the so-called "miracles" of modern technology—from the electric lightbulb to the fax machine to e-mail—we are a 24-hour culture. What we've lost is the ability to know when to call it a day. The average healthy adult needs seven to eight hours of sleep per night, which is one to two hours more than what most of us actually get. Are you sleep-deprived? If you need an alarm clock to wake up in the morning, the answer is probably yes.

Running increases the body's need for high-quality sleep. Yet paradoxically you may find yourself requiring less sleep once you establish a regular running program. This is because running increases the *quality* of sleep, for reasons that, while not fully understood, probably relate to the fatiguing effects of exercise. It's as though physical activity tells the body: "I need this downtime, so let me take full advantage of it." Compared to non-exercisers, active people report that they fall asleep more easily, sleep more soundly, and awaken feeling more refreshed. In short, they become more efficient sleepers. The sleep needs of elite-level runners, however, may increase dramatically. Even though they are sleeping very efficiently, world-class runners report needing 9 to 10 hours of sleep per night, plus a nap of an hour or 2 during the day!

If you have difficulty getting the quality and quantity of sleep you need, here are some suggestions:

• *Create a healthy sleep environment.* Make your bedroom a calm, relaxing place that you reserve solely for sleeping and sex. Don't work, watch TV, listen to loud music, or eat in bed. Keep lighting low and install shades or curtains that block out light and noise. Invest in a firm mattress and box spring.

• *Establish regular sleep habits.* Go to bed and wake up at about the same time each day—though contrary to what you may have heard, sleeping in an hour or so on the weekends is not harmful. If you can't fall asleep, don't fight it: Try reading or drinking warm milk. Avoid activities that stimulate you mentally or physically.

• *Don't work out hard in the evenings.* Although mild exercise, such as a walk, can calm you before bedtime, running—especially doing speed workouts—within three hours of trying to go to sleep will energize you, making sleep elusive. Instead, try scheduling your hard workouts before work, on your lunch break, or right after work.

• *Minimize caffeine, especially after noon.* You may find that eliminating caffeine except during the morning hours improves your ability to fall asleep and sleep soundly through the night. Avoid heavy evening meals, as the digestion of large quantities of food at bedtime can interfere with relaxation.

• *Fight the 24/7 tendency.* You really do not have to work all the time. Some things are more important than checking your e-mail or reading the latest corporate report—like your health.

## HOW TO SERVE THE RUNNING COMMUNITY

Running can be very self-centered. Sometimes it feels selfish to put so much time and energy into getting faster and stronger. Many runners want to "give back" to the running community in some way. Here are suggestions for how you can serve other runners. I've done some of them, though not as many as I'd like. As you get involved in your local running community, you will no doubt find or create other opportunities to serve.

- *Volunteer at a race.* The entry fee you pay to run a road, track, trail, or cross-country race usually doesn't cover all of the costs of putting on the event. Thus, the running community has a tradition of encouraging volunteer support of race production. Before the race volunteers are needed for registration, setup, elite-athlete coordination, course measuring (you must be trained and certified in this capacity) and marking, and more. The tasks assigned to volunteers during a race include late registration, crowd control, course marshaling, aid-table maintenance (handing out water and sports drinks, keeping roadways clear of paper cups, etc.), split timing, and finish-line administration (keeping runners moving across the line, removing computer chips, recognizing and assisting runners in need of medical attention, etc.) After a race, volunteers help primarily with food-and-beverage distribution, awards, and cleanup, though larger races may have a wider range of needs.

In a column in the May 2001 issue of *Running Times*, writer and race director Jim Gerweck proposed the "10 percent solution" to help increase volunteering at road races: Just as churchgoers of certain denominations are asked to tithe 10 percent of their income to the church, runners should consider putting 10 percent of the time and energy they allocate to running races into volunteering at running events. The volunteering I've done at races (not 10 percent of the time I spend running them, I'm afraid) has been fun and rewarding. I've worked at finish lines helping runners move through the chutes toward the refreshments and baggage-claim areas, and I've handed out water along the course. There's nothing like the smile of appreciation on a runner's face when you hand him or her a cup of water, or simply say "Great race!" at the finish line. It's also a wonderful way to stay involved in running when you're injured or not racing for other reasons (I did it during my pregnancies). Contact your local running club or race organization about volunteering opportunities in your area.

- *Volunteer with your running club.* Running clubs carry out practically all their tasks—from coaching to putting together social events—on a volunteer basis. Clubs welcome with open arms any runner who is also interested in serving the many needs of the club—administration, bookkeeping, secretarial work, coaching, planning social events, fundraising, publicity, newsletter writing and editing, event planning, and more. Join a club to get involved. Whether you put on a bake sale or plan the annual awards dinner, the sky is the limit for your involvement and service.

- *Coach.* USA Track & Field and the Road Runners Club of America both offer certification programs for coaching adult and youth runners; see Resources for contact information. Coaching runners is challenging, and seldom pays well, but can be richly rewarding and lots of fun. Talk to local coaches to learn about training and certification opportunities in your area. Ideally you should work with an experienced coach for a year or more to learn the ropes before taking on group or individual coaching assignments on your own.

- *Get involved with your local USATF association.* The administration of running takes place at the local level through USATF associations, which work under the national governing body—but often quite independently of it, responding to local needs and preferences—to plan and administer races and meets, train coaches, set administrative policies, and more. Local and regional representatives attend USATF's national convention, held annually in December.

- *Give to running-related organizations.* Running-club membership dues, race entry fees, and local association dues don't begin to cover all the expenses associated with running and racing, and part of the balance is made up by contributions. In addition, organizations raise funds to support the next generation of elite-level runners, most of whom are on their own once they leave a university program. For example, the Road Runners Club of America, through its Roads Scholar Program, funds scholarships that allow deserving postcollegiate runners to train without having to work full-time. USATF provides a limited number of stipends, training camp facilities, and other support to qualifying athletes. See Resources for contact information for these and other support organizations.

- *Attend local track meets and cross-country races.* Almost all high schools and colleges have track and cross-country programs. Find your local teams' schedules, and make a point of getting out to cheer on the next generation of runners. Not only will you send a message to the young runners in your area that their sport is important outside the small circle of their coaches, friends, and family, you'll also have a great time. Cross-country is an exciting sport in which team tactics play a huge role, and a track meet offers such a variety of events—from pole vault to 10,000-meter run—there's sure to be something to interest every viewer.

- *Encourage more and better coverage of running.* Write or call your local newspapers, sports publications, and radio and television stations to encourage them to provide more and better coverage of running, which receives far more attention overseas than in the United States. Contact national news organizations as well, especially at the time of the Olympics and World Track & Field Championships. I once wrote a letter to the editor that was published in *Sports Illustrated*, about their failure to mention Lynn Jennings' bronze medal in the 1992 Barcelona Olympic 10,000 meters.

## QUESTION AND ANSWER

**Q.** I've found it impossible to run ever since I became a parent. Any suggestions?

**A.** New parenthood is a time that many runners find their time and energy for running sharply diminished. Both men and women may feel overwhelmed by the demands of a baby. New mothers may be out of shape, carrying excess weight, and hesitant to run due to concerns about hurting themselves or spending time away from the baby. (See Chapter 11 for more on running during and after pregnancy.) Though having a child is a life-changing event, it does not have to make running impossible. Here are some suggestions for successful running while your children are young:

- **Use a running stroller.** A running stroller is made especially for running while pushing an infant or small child. Most models have two large, sturdy back wheels (usually inflatable) and one smaller front wheel. They are built to be shock-absorbing to ensure a smooth ride. (For more information and advice on running strollers, see Chapter 11.) A baby should be able to hold its head up before using a stroller. Do not run while pushing a conventional (nonrunning) stroller, because it's not sturdy or shock-absorbent

enough to protect your child from bumps and jostlings at high speeds.

- **Team up with other running parents.** Ask other parents if they'd be willing to watch your child(ren) while you run, then offer to return the favor. If you're nervous, start with short runs (20 minutes) and see how it goes, extending your workouts as you gain confidence.

- **Consider a treadmill.** You can run on a treadmill while your baby naps or plays in a playpen or other secure area nearby. (Warning: Never use a treadmill without putting a barrier between your child and the machine.)

- **Reclaim your identity.** Reread Chapter 1 to remind yourself of the importance of defining yourself as a runner. Not only will this inspire you to start or increase your running, but it will also remind you that running is a lifetime sport and fitness activity. You may feel disconnected from your running identity right now, but that is probably temporary.

- **Realize that you are setting a positive example.** It may seem as though parenthood and regular running will never coexist, but in the long run, you are actually running for and because of your children. Running and other health-promoting activities help ensure that you'll be around to watch your children grow up. As a runner, you are modeling a positive lifestyle for your children, as well as sending a message that "me" time is essential and healthy for everyone—even Mom and Dad. See Gloria Averbuch's "Why I Race" on page 207 for a stirring example of how running transmits this message to children.

### Running to Slow Down

Stress: We all experience it. Many of the minor stresses of life center on feeling that we have too few resources—namely time, energy, and money—to accomplish all that we wish. Running can offer an antidote to this sense of "never enough"—but only if we approach our running and integrate it into our lives with the proper mind-set. In the May/June 2001 issue of *Marathon & Beyond,* Jonathan Beverly shares the following thoughts on how running—if we allow it to—can help us counter the "never enough" messages our culture is constantly sending us:

[D]espite the promises of the 20th century to give us more time, we still find ourselves overworked and overwhelmed, struggling to keep up with the ever-increasing pace of the pack. We will never have more time, yet running teaches us that we have the ability to control our perception of time and better appreciate the time we're given. . . . Just as in running, the first lesson in mastering time is learning pace. It's not a hard equation: if we're having trouble keeping up, we need to slow down. In running we take fewer steps per minute; in life, we pursue fewer activities per day.

As discussed in Chapter 6, running is a proven means of reducing anxiety and other psychological illnesses. Yet we must modify our approach to running to allow it to work its healing wonders. If running is just one more task to cram into an already over-scheduled day, if you run without taking note of your surroundings or appreciating the movements and functions of your body, if you hurry to finish every run so you can quickly get on to the next task, then *slow down*—even stop running temporarily. Take a long, hard look at the tasks that fill each day, the responsibilities you have taken on, and the feelings that compel you to try and fit more than you can into a 24-hour day. Make lists of what is negotiable and what is not. Make choices.

It's not easy to choose to do less. Society rewards us for our accomplishments. Saying no to friends, neighbors, colleagues, and family members feels like wimping out. In the long run, of course, choosing to do less gives us more time, energy, and focus for the things we've decided really matter—whether it's running, nurturing family relationships, or simply lowering the intensity of the "never enough" messages that drive us.

I confess that I'm a card-carrying member of the Hurry-Uppers Club. I've been this way ever since I can remember. I can offer a few suggestions to counter the tendency to go, go, go—or at least manage it as healthily as possible—based on my own experiences:

• Schedule at least a couple of minutes around your running, both before and after, to ease into a relaxed mind-set. Stretch—even 30 seconds makes a difference—and breathe deeply while sitting down or lying on the floor. If you're still tense as you start running, drop your shoulders, breathe deeply, and shake out your arms.

• Use your running time to tune into the natural rhythms within and around you: Notice the seasons, become aware of your breathing and the movements of your body.

• If stress and anxiety are near-constant companions, seek help in psychotherapy. I found working with a psychotherapist to be invaluable in pinpointing the sources of the feelings of inadequacy and low self-esteem that had compelled me to define myself by my achievements, including running, and distract myself from difficult feelings by seeking refuge in constant activity. Taking this step didn't transform me overnight into a mellow Type-B person, but it did help me come to terms with and manage deep-rooted anxieties. Among other things, this led to healthier, happier running.

• Let running itself become part of the de-stressing solution, by heeding the messages it imparts to us: Pace yourself, rest regularly, and replenish when you're depleted.

### Getting the Health and Medical Care You Need

Running is one of the most health-promoting activities you can integrate into your life, yet it is not a panacea. Runners still get sick and hurt. Chapter 5 provides guidelines for dealing with various running-related illnesses and injuries. Whether your health concerns are related to running or not, you need to integrate adequate, effective, and affordable health care into your life so that you can get the attention you need.

This isn't always easy. Our managed-care health system often presents challenges to those seeking routine preventive care, as well as specialized treatments. Unemployed and self-employed people may not have access to affordable health insurance, leaving gaps in their health and medical care that could lead them to neglect to get the care and attention they need.

I encourage you to put the necessary time and energy into acquiring the care you need to maintain overall good health. If you have a choice among health-insurance plans, choose one that includes preventative care, such as regular checkups and screenings. If this is not possible, try to have the standard screening tests and procedures anyway, searching out low-cost options (try contacting your local health department). Whenever possible for a running-related problem or issue, seek out a professional who deals with runners or other athletes, who will be attentive to your needs and understanding of your priorities, and can work with you to treat and manage your problem, and prevent it from recurring.

## QUESTION AND ANSWER

**Q.** What are effective strategies for running when I travel on business?

**A.** Business travel—whether across town or halfway around the world—presents unique challenges to the runner. First, of course, is the time spent getting there in a car, bus, train, or plane that might otherwise be spent running. There's also the issue of being in unfamiliar (and possibly unsafe) surroundings, far from your neighborhood running routes and running partners, and possibly among people who don't understand or appreciate running for fitness. Add jet lag to the mix with overseas or transcontinental journeys, and it's not surprising that some runners choose to postpone their fitness fix until after they unpack their bags at home.

Veteran running business travelers, though, tend to be undeterred by these challenges, and are even able to use them to their advantage. Here are strategies for running while traveling on business, culled from some globe-trotting runners:

• **Run in the mornings.** This not only ensures that the run will get done (no meetings, cocktail receptions, or late-night dinners to interfere), it also allows you to enjoy your surroundings from a perspective few tourists see. You'll come away with a more vivid, meaningful impression of the Eiffel Tower or Big Ben in the hush of 6 A.M. than you would at the height of the midday tourist crush. Running early can also be a good way to reset an internal clock that's confused by jet lag. If you can't run before the business day begins, consider lunchtime, before dinner, or during any significant break in meetings.

- **Check out health-club facilities in advance.** If you don't plan to run outside (or want an indoor option), try to find a hotel with a treadmill and other fitness equipment, or access to a nearby facility. Large hotels have greatly improved their fitness facilities in recent years, but call or visit the hotel's Web site in advance to make sure.
- **Use a good map.** Find a map that's drawn to scale and includes significant landmarks. Go online, ask at the hotel's front desk, or go to the local tourism bureau at the airport. Carry your map with you while running, but try not to refer to it too often in potentially unsafe areas, because you may be targeted as a tourist and therefore an easy mark for robbery or worse. Look for green spaces or other breaks in the street grid if you wish to run in parks or along rivers, lakes, and other bodies of water.
- **Do out-and-back routes.** You'll stand less chance of getting lost if you are retracing your steps on the return journey. In addition, having a "destination" for a run can be motivating, especially if it's something fun and interesting, like the shoreline or a building of historic, cultural, or architectural interest.
- **Plug into the local running club.** If you're able, get a name and contact information of a local running organization in advance of your visit. A club can be a great source of information on local running routes, and you may be able to hook up with others for a group run, speed workout, or even a race. (Visit www.rrca.org for a list of Road Runners Club of America–affiliated clubs for domestic travel; going through the local tourism board or chamber of commerce is often your best bet when traveling overseas.)
- **Learn a bit of the local language.** Learning how to say "Hello," "Please," "Thank you," "Can you help me?" and other basic phrases is a good idea for any traveler, and it's especially helpful for a runner who might get lost or require assistance. If you feel insecure, carry a pocket phrase-book with you on your run.
- **Respect local customs and conventions.** Ask colleagues about

the local running customs, and use common sense. When in doubt, dress on the conservative side, wearing longer shorts, covering your upper body (including midriff and upper arms), and avoid flashy colors. Don't run through or around religious sites or near those engaged in prayer or meditation.

- **Secure access to drinkable water.** Assume that all tap water is unsafe, particularly in Third World countries, unless you have been absolutely assured otherwise. Make sure you have access to bottled water for drinking before, during, and after your runs.
- **Follow your instincts.** Just as you would on even the most familiar running route, stay alert and don't deliberately run into trouble.

### Putting Energy Into Rest and Recovery

Most runners will tell you they believe in the value of rest, yet very few successfully practice what they preach. Chapter 9 discusses active rest, which is designed to promote recovery by bringing oxygen and nutrients to tired tissues, and to elongate tight, sore muscles. In addition to active rest, runners must also engage in what I call "plain old rest." By that I mean simply avoiding running, other exercise, and running-related thoughts. This disengagement of the body and mind from running is, I believe, key to keeping alive your commitment to running. Though it's particularly important after a hard race or series of races, it is also vital on a day-to-day basis. Your body will tell you when you've had too much running. It will guide you toward what you need to do—or rather, not do—to maintain its physical and emotional balance. You can also enhance recovery with proper diet, sleep, relaxation exercises, and emotional support.

## HOW TO MAKE YOUR JOB RUNNER-FRIENDLY

You are lucky if your workplace supports your running lifestyle: Many of your colleagues run or do some other type of exercise, or at least look favorably upon physical activity; you're allowed time during the workday to get up from your desk, stretch, and move about, or can take breaks from an on-your-feet occupation to sit and relax, or even stretch out on the floor. Some jobs offer even better perks, such as free or subsidized health-club membership, on-site showers, or participation in corporate-team running events and other fitness activities.

If you're fortunate enough to have a runner-friendly workplace, take advantage of the opportunities that may be afforded to you. If not, or if you want to improve your situation, here are some suggestions:

- *Identify yourself as a runner at work.* Without being self-congratulatory or smug, communicate to your coworkers that running is an important, fun, health-promoting part of your life. Put up a few running photos and other memorabilia (race numbers, finisher's medals) around your workspace, and mention recent and upcoming running events and races. Your coworkers will soon see that running forms part of your identity in a positive and dynamic way, and contributes to rather than detracts from your work ethic, productivity, and value to the company.

- *Run to and/or from work, or at lunchtime.* Running to or from work, or during your lunch break, not only helps cement the role of running in your life, it can also be a practical time-saver. When and where feasible, running saves commuting time (and expenses) and is good for the environment if you'd otherwise drive your car. Running on your lunch or other break can help make you more efficient on the job by reviving your midday energy levels and causing you to work with greater concentration to make time for your run. Those who run to work or during a break will probably want to make sure shower facilities are available, though it's possible to make do with a washing up in the restroom at work.

- *Encourage your coworkers to run.* Your example may inspire some of those in your workplace to take up running. Encourage your coworkers to run with you or to take a running class or clinic. Organizing an informal group run often works well. This puts no pressure on any individual, and if you get a sizable group, others will probably want to join, too. You can also suggest running magazines, books, or Web sites that have helped you. And of course, suggest that your coworkers buy this book!

- *Stay healthy on the job.* Make sure to stay hydrated, eat regularly and healthfully as outlined in Chapter 7, and avoid excessive fatigue, long periods of immobility, and other practices that can compromise your running.

### Living a Balanced Life

We all seek a balance among the many facets of our lives—work, leisure, family life, and community responsibilities. In this chapter I've tried to illuminate the role that running can play in creating and maintaining balance in full, busy lives. Far from being "just one more thing" to fit into a life that's already full to bursting, running can impart more energy, strength, and enthusiasm for other activities, allowing us to partake in them with greater efficiency and zest.

No matter how serious your commitment to running, I believe it should always take place within the context of a life that includes other passions. Joan Benoit Samuelson, the winner of the first women's Olympic marathon in 1984, and the American marathon record holder, thrives on the balance between running and a host of other physical activities (skiing, gardening, kayaking, and hiking, to name a few), family life (she's married, with a 14-year-old daughter and a 12-year-old son), volunteer activities, hobbies (from knitting to making jam), and more. "I wouldn't want it any other way," she says. "There's something in every court, and I really believe that's been the key to my success all along. I never lost a balanced life—I'd always go out and do things, even at the height of my career, whether it was gardening, berry picking, or whatever. My parents instilled that in me, the need to have a variety of interests."

Ideally, balanced is different from—and healthier than—the scattered, unfocused activity that many of us (myself included) fall prey to when we fail to make choices or fear disappointing others. A balanced life like Samuelson's is full of activities, passions, and commitments that we have chosen and—if we're lucky—will cultivate for a lifetime. Living life with our energies balanced among a number of chosen activities allows us to focus on each task while we are doing it, giving it the attention it deserves.

Living a balanced life involves discipline, organization, and limit-setting with ourselves and others. ("I will not run more than five miles with my friend today—even though she wants me to—because I need to prepare for tonight's Town Council meeting.") At the same time, it entails flexibility and spontaneity. If you have a planned speed session at the track, and your child's teacher calls to tell you that he has a fever and is throwing up, and your spouse is out of town, you probably won't get to the track that day. By the same token, if you arrive at the airport to find your flight delayed, and you have your running gear in your carry-on bag, what's to stop you from changing, stowing your gear in a locker, and going for a run? See "Running and My Day," page 231–235, for other examples of how runners fit running into busy lives.

Throughout this book I try to incorporate the principle of balance as a guiding force for your running. Truly integrating running into your life is not something you can force. At times, running will assume a prominent role, such as when you are gearing up for an important race or stepping up to a new fitness level. At other times, it will be far less present and compelling, such as during seasons of rest and recovery, or when other important things in your life are going on. Keeping the following principles in mind can help you integrate running into the balance of your life.

• *Set goals.* Decide what you want to accomplish in your run, in your day, and in your life. Then parcel out your time and energy accordingly.

• *Slow down.* It really is more important to do a few things well than too many things in a half-baked fashion.

• *Prioritize.* Learn to postpone things that are less important to you.

• *Be flexible.* There is usually more than one way to accomplish what needs to be done.

• *Relax.* What seems like a disaster usually isn't. Ask yourself how things will appear when you look back on them in a year, a month, a week, or even a day. Of course, reality may not always live up to the ideals we set for balancing our lives, but the goal of balance is a worthy vision toward which we all can strive.

▶▶▶▶▶▶▶▶▶▶▶▶▶▶▶▶▶▶▶▶▶▶▶▶▶▶▶▶▶▶

# CHAPTER 11

# Answers for Women Runners

More women are running than ever before. According to the Road Running Information Center, the growth of women's running is outpacing that of men's running. Women's races and run/walks attract millions of women across the country. In 2000, more women than men participated in 5k races. Membership in Team in Training, a nationwide organization that coaches beginning and novice marathon runners to complete charity marathons, was 70 percent female in 2000. Long gone are the days when running was considered "unfeminine" or too demanding for the female body and mind. Today, running is more than just acceptable for women, it's encouraged as a way to stay healthy and fit, socialize, and raise money and awareness for a cause. Running presents women with a simple, convenient, and efficient way to exercise and set a positive example for their families.

When I first thought about writing this book, I knew I wanted to write a book for both male and female runners, for several reasons. First, it's clear that the vast majority of information and advice for runners—on training, racing, nutrition, injuries, psychological issues, and more—applies to both men and women. Second, having trained with, coached, and befriended runners of both genders throughout my 23 years of running, I know that men and women are in equal need of ideas about how to integrate running into their lives. Still, the temptation was there to write a "women's running" book. I'm a woman, after all, and have written extensively about running in women's, running, and health magazines. I've also coached a women's running team since 1992. I know that running raises special concerns for women—from reproductive issues, to particular injuries, to apparel, to role models, to diet and nutritional concerns.

In the end I followed through on my plan to write this book for all runners, but the concerns of women runners remain particularly pertinent to me. This chapter provides answers to the many questions asked by women runners, and also offers a social, cultural, and historical perspective on women's running.

## SAFETY ISSUES FOR WOMEN—AND MEN

On a beautiful April evening in 1989 a lone woman ran in a remote northern section of Central Park. A gang of boys and young men accosted her, dragged her into nearby woods, raped and beat her, and left her bleeding and unconscious. Found by another runner, the woman, who became known as the "Central Park Jogger," was rushed to the hospital, where her life hung in the balance for days. Miraculously, she survived, and was eventually even able to run again.

This woman's experience played out the female runner's worst nightmare: that the sense of power and freedom afforded to her by running could be threatened—indeed, destroyed—on a run. Thousands of times I had run along the very stretch of roadway on which the "Central Park Jogger" met her attackers—like her, sometimes alone, sometimes after dark. The event made me realize that my sense of safety as a runner can be a dangerous illusion.

Running can make women—and men—feel invincible. When I run, I feel protected because I'm moving swiftly and powerfully, rarely carrying anything of value, and feeling alert to my surroundings. I've come to realize, though, that these factors are no deterrent: Though I can cover a lot of ground on the run, I'm not built to sprint; though I feel strong, many men are twice my size; though my wallet, jewelry, and headset stay at home, my running shoes and apparel make me a target for theft; though I notice most sights and sounds around me, I can also easily enter a world of my own.

I take many more safety precautions now than I used to, whether running in Central Park, through a suburban neighborhood, or on a remote woodland trail. The fact is, no runner is completely protected from assault and other crimes—anywhere. I'm grateful that the New York City running community, galvanized by the "Jogger's" experience, joined forces with the New York Police Department and the Department of Parks & Recreation to improve safety for runners and others in Central Park and all New York City parks. At the same time, I'm careful not to let those improvements—better lighting, increased police protection, community safety patrols—lull me into thinking another "Jogger"-type incident couldn't happen.

The Road Runners Club of America has been on the front lines of promoting runner safety nationwide, including crime prevention, and protection from vehicular traffic on the roads. The RRCA's list of Tips for Running Safety, reprinted below, offers all runners, women in particular, guidelines for staying safe on the run.

*The RRCA's Tips for Running Safety*

1. **DON'T WEAR HEADSETS.** Use your ears to be aware of your surroundings. Wearing headphones, you lose the use of an important sense: your hearing.

2. **Always stay alert and aware of what's going on around you.** The more aware you are, the less vulnerable you are.

3. **Carry a cell phone or change for a phone call.** Know the locations of call boxes and telephones along your regular route.

4. **Trust your intuition about a person or an area.** React on your intention and avoid a person or situation if you're unsure. If something tells you a situation is not "right," it isn't.

5. **Alter or vary your running route pattern.** Run in familiar areas if possible. In unfamiliar areas, such as while traveling, contact a local RRCA club or running store. Know where open businesses or stores are located.

6. **Run with a partner.** Run with a dog.

7. **Write down or leave word of the direction of your run.** Tell friends and family of your favorite running routes.

8. **Avoid unpopulated areas, deserted streets, and overgrown trails.** Especially avoid unlit areas, especially at night. Run clear of parked cars or bushes.

9. **Carry identification or write your name, phone number, and blood type on the inside sole of your running shoe.** Include any medical information. Don't wear jewelry.

10. **Ignore verbal harassment.** Use discretion in acknowledging strangers. Look directly at others and be observant, but keep your distance and keep moving.

11. **Run against traffic so you can observe approaching automobiles.**

12. **Wear reflective material if you must run before dawn or after dark.**

13. **Practice memorizing license tags or identifying characteristics of strangers.**

**14. Carry a noisemaker and/or OC (pepper) spray.** Get training in self-defense and the use of pepper spray.

**15. CALL POLICE IMMEDIATELY** if something happens to you or someone else, or you notice anyone out of the ordinary. It is important to report incidents immediately.

The RRCA also offers the following tips on working with local law enforcement departments and your local running community on runner safety.

*RRCA Tips on Women Runners' Empowerment*

1. **Knowledge is power.** Discuss the incidents that are occurring; create a network of information-sharing.

2. **Initiate dialogue and cooperation between the police and the local running community.** Find a law enforcement person who is also a runner and who might therefore be more understanding.

3. **Arrange a meeting between police and you or your local running organization or RRCA club.** Offer a copy of these tips for reproduction and general distribution by the police.

4. **Write a safety bulletin.** Designate someone in your running group or RRCA club to write a regularly safety bulletin and distribute it among runners and law enforcement. Distribute the safety bulletin among fitness clubs, running stores, neighborhood businesses, the media, local law enforcement officers, and political representatives. Network with all the local running clubs. Encourage them to call a central contract concerning safety problems in their areas.

5. **Create a network of women runners.** Create a system whereby women can find other women to run or walk with. Organize an annual safety workshop with police participation.

6. **Always be of assistance.** Never interfere with police procedures.

7. **Emphasize to the police that runners and walkers want to be informed of problems, and are more likely to report sightings and incidents if they have descriptions of known perpetrators.**

8. **Initiate communication between the running community and the community at large.** Encourage a coalition between your running club

and the activities of local Neighborhood Watches. Arrange for your running group or club to obtain and screen the RRCA videotape *Women Running: Run Smart. Run Safe.*

**9. Practice self-help in your community.** Have police work with you to clear overgrown trails, improve lighting, and install telephones or call boxes in strategic locations. Offer to raise the money if necessary.

**10. Promote self-defense education.** Contact your local YWCA or a police officer for information on community classes and educational tapes on self-defense. Publicize classes and screenings of self-defense techniques in your community and in your club, through postings and newsletters.

**11. Be part of the solution.** Call police immediately if something happens to you or someone else, or if you notice anyone out of the ordinary.

**12. Be a vigilante for yourself and others.** Use your intuition to report things that don't "seem right" to you. Indecent exposure incidents should be reported; though they seem benign, according to law enforcement, they aren't.

Reprinted by permission of the Road Runners Club of America. For more information, contact the RRCA at 510 North Washington Street, Alexandria, VA 22314; phone: (703) 836-0558; fax: (703) 836-4430; e-mail: office@rrca.org.

## QUESTION AND ANSWER

**Q.** As a woman runner, should I have any particular nutritional concerns?

**A.** Women runners should be sure they are meeting their needs for overall calories, iron, and calcium. Consuming sufficient calories helps provide adequate fuel for running and carrying out other daily tasks. Women who are trying to control their weight are better served over the long-term by eating moderately in response to hunger cues and exercising regularly than by restricting calories. In general, iron needs are higher in premenopausal women than men and women past menopause because of the iron loss caused by menstruation.

Although the Recommended Daily Allowance (RDA) for iron is the same for women and men (15 mg), many nutrition experts suggest that women consume more iron, about 18 mg daily. Women who experience symptoms of anemia (fatigue, paleness, easy bruising, slow healing of cuts and scrapes) should have a blood test for iron and ferritin (stored iron) levels, and consult their doctor before taking iron supplements. The National Institutes of Health recommends that women up to age 24, as well as all pregnant and breast-feeding women, consume 1,500 milligrams (mg) of calcium daily; the recommendation for men under age 65, premenopausal women age 25 and over, and menopausal women taking estrogen is 1,000 mg per day. Dairy products and calcium-fortified products are considered the best sources of calcium, along with calcium supplements under a doctor's supervision. See Chapter 7 for more on the nutritional needs of runners.

### Training Guidelines for Women

Should a woman run differently from a man? In general, no. Scientific study and real-world experience have shown that women and men of similar fitness levels can run at the same level by following the same training programs. This is welcome news to women, who for years were barred from participating in distance running events at the international level because of concerns about their inability to handle the physical demands (see "Women's Running Through the Ages," page 259–265).

Coaches of top-level women runners report that women train no differently from men of similar fitness and experience levels. "When I'm working with athletes I don't look at male or female; I look at athletes," said coach Joe Vigil of Alamosa State University in Colorado, in a 1999 article in *Running Times* magazine. Tom Fleming, who has coached other top American women runners, says, "The plans, methods, and training programs are the same [for men and women]."

A few differences are worth noting. One is that top-level women tend to train at lower mileage levels than top-level men— about 20 to 25 percent less, according to studies by Michael Pollock, Ph.D., and Phil Sparling, Ph.D. The researchers aren't sure why this is so. David E. Martin, Ph.D., chair of sport science for USA Track & Field, suggests that because women have, on average, a shorter stride length than men, and run slightly slower than men, the lower mileage protects the women from overtraining. This could mean that a woman running 80 miles per week is actually getting the same conditioning effect from those 80 miles as a man who is logging 100 miles per week. If she were to attempt 100-mile weeks, injury or breakdown would be the likely result.

Though women and men of similar fitness levels should train at similar intensities, there may be less room to maneuver women's ranges when calculating. This is due to the smaller size of a woman's heart in relation to her body, which means that at maximal aerobic effort, a woman's heart rate is closer to maximum than a man's. Therefore women need to be more careful than men to control their workout efforts at lactate-threshold intensity and ATP-CP intensity in order to avoid overtraining.

These training differences are probably most important for women at the elite competitive level who are trying to avoid crossing the line into injury or overtraining. What's crucial—for women and men runners—is to pay attention to the body's feedback and train accordingly. If you feel exhausted at your current running level, cut back on your mileage, your intensity, or both.

## WOMEN'S RUNNING THROUGH THE AGES

Women, of course, have been running for as long as their male counterparts. The difference is that until very recently, they haven't received much credit for it. Women runners have lagged far behind men not only in their competitive opportunities, but also in simply having the chance to run at all. Incredible as it sounds, women could not officially take part in marathons before 1970. Until 1972 women were barred from running more than 800 meters in Olympic competition.

Women runners today have much to celebrate—millions of women running worldwide, competitive opportunities that previous generations of women could only dream of, positive role models at all levels—yet much progress still lies ahead. In many countries women runners still struggle for opportunities to run. Competitive depth in women's running is not equal to that among their male counterparts. Women's participation still lags behind that of men at marathon and longer distances, and is just getting off the ground in the steeplechase, pole vault, and other events. Still, the most significant battles are now history. The timeline below highlights significant moments in the development of women's running.

*776 B.C.:* This marks the first recorded ancient Olympic Games. They are held roughly every four years through 393 A.D. as a combined religious and sporting festival. Women are prohibited from competing or even observing the events, under penalty of death. At least one woman violates the order by sneaking into the Games to watch her son compete as a boxer, and other women are awarded victory olive wreaths in absentia as the owners of winning chariots.

*Industrial Revolution/Victorian Era:* Vigorous physical activity is discouraged among upper-class women, who are seen as delicate, even frail, and restricted by heavy, tight-fitting clothing. Running is out of the question due to its potentially damaging effects on the female reproductive system. Meanwhile, lower-class women work side by side with men in the fields and factories.

*1888:* The Amateur Athletic Union (AAU), the national governing body for track and field in the United States, is founded in New York City to further men's amateur sports in non-academic settings.

*1896:* The first modern Olympics take place in Athens, Greece. There are no women among the 260 athletes, as stipulated by the Games' founding organizer, Baron Pierre de Courbetin. Females are, however, permitted as spectators. "We feel that the Olympic Games must be reserved for the solemn and periodic exaltation of male athleticism with internationalism as a base, loyalty as a means, arts for its setting, and female applause as reward," declares the International Olympic Committee (IOC). A Greek woman named Melpomene petitions the IOC for entry into the marathon. Her request is denied, despite having the support of Greek sportswriters. Melpomene runs the marathon anyway, unofficially, completing the race alone and outside the stadium in approximately four and a half hours—an hour and a half behind the leader, but ahead of some male finishers.

*1900:* Eleven women participate in the second modern Olympics, in Paris—in golf and lawn tennis only.

*1916:* For the first time, the AAU authorizes track-and-field competitions for women.

*1921:* The first international women's track-and-field competition is staged in Monte Carlo.

*1922:* The Federation Sportive Feminine Internationale (FSFI) is formed and stages the Women's World Games (WWG) in 1924, with women from 19 countries competing, to protest the IOC's rejection of repeated petitions to include more events for women (including track and field) in the Olympics. The Women's World Games continue to be held every four years through 1936.

*1923:* The AAU stages the first major outdoor track-and-field meet for women, in Newark, New Jersey. It includes a 100-meter sprint and a 400-meter relay.

*1926:* Violet Percy of Great Britain completes a marathon in 3 hours, 40 minutes, 22 seconds.

*1928:* The International Amateur Athletics Federation (IAAF), in the face of the success of the FSFI and the WWG, convinces the IOC to make women's track and field an official part of the 1928 Amsterdam Olympics. Five events are included: 100 meters, 800 meters, 4 × 100-meter relay, high jump, and discus throw. Unfortunately, due to reports of several women collapsing after they finish the 800, the IOC again removes women's track and field from the Olympic roster. Only the threat of a boycott by the American men's track and field team leads to a reinstatement of women's sprint events; the IOC upholds a ban on all women's events longer than 200 meters.

*1932:* American phenom Mildred "Babe" Didrikson wins three Olympic medals in Los Angeles, including gold in the 80-meter hurdles. Though admired for her accomplishments, Didrikson is derided for her masculine appearance and behavior.

*1936:* After winning two gold medals at the Berlin Olympics (100 meters and 4 × 100–meter relay), American Helen Stephens terms the Games the "covered-wagon days in women's track"—a reference to the inclusion of a mere six running events for women.

*1948:* Only four running events for women are included in the 1948 London Olympics, and Francina "Fanny" Blankers-Koen enters them all (100-meter and 200-meter sprints, 400-meter relay, and 80-meter hurdles), plus the long jump. The 30-year-old "Flying Dutch Housewife" wins gold medals in every event, then returns home to her husband and two children.

*1958:* The Road Runners Club of America is formed in New York City. Among the RRCA's goals is persuading the tradition-bound AAU to officially recognize women's distance running.

*1960:* The 1960 Rome Olympics includes a women's 800-meter run for the first time in 32 years. American sprinter Wilma Rudolph's three gold medals (100 meters, 200 meters, and 4 × 100–meter relay) propels women's track and field into the American consciousness.

*1964:* Dale Greig of Great Britain completes the Isle of Wight Marathon in England in 3:27:45, a mark that is recognized as the first official women's world record for the distance. Two months later in Auckland, New Zealand, Mildred Sampson records a time of 3:19:33 in the Owairaka Marathon.

*1966:* Roberta "Bobbi" Gibb becomes the first woman to run the Boston Marathon, finishing in 3:21:40 after hiding behind some bushes and jumping into the race just past the starting line. Dressed in Bermuda shorts and a black swimsuit, Gibb is recognized—and cheered—along the course as a "girl," but allowed by officials to continue because she's not wearing a bib number.

*1967:* Registering as "K. V. Switzer," 20-year-old Syracuse University student Kathrine Switzer officially enters the Boston Marathon. Four miles into the race, officials attempt to physically remove Switzer—dressed in baggy sweats—from the course, and lose out in a scuffle with her Syracuse teammates. The mayhem is captured on film, setting in motion events that lead to the official inclusion of women in Boston five years later. Switzer finishes in about 4:20, behind Gibb, who again runs unofficially, in 3:27:17.

The women's marathon world record falls to 3:15:22 (Maureen Wilton, Canada, May 6), then 3:07:27 (Anni Pede-Erdkamp, Germany, September 16).

*1970:* The inaugural New York City Marathon, four-plus laps of Central Park, draws one female entrant, Nina Kuscsik, who fails to finish due to illness. Still, New York is heralded as the first American marathon to officially welcome women, despite the fact that the AAU has yet to sanction female marathoners.

*1971:* Beth Bonner becomes the first woman to complete a marathon in under three hours as she finishes New York in 2:55:22; Kuscsik follows in 2:56:04.

The AAU extends the maximum sanctioned distance for women's track events to 10 miles.

*1972:* The U.S. Congress passes Title IX of the Education Amendments Act, prohibiting sex discrimination in educational institutions that receive government funding. Female participation in high school and college sports increases markedly as a result.

The Boston Marathon allows women to enter officially for the first time, with Kuscsik winning the inaugural race.

The New York Road Runners Club and Johnson Wax sponsor the first women-only road race, a six-mile named "The Mini" after the miniskirt. The event attracts an astounding 78 entrants.

At the New York City Marathon the AAU attempts to enforce a rule that women start separately from men. Rather than comply, the six women starters sit down on the starting line when the gun is fired, then get up 10 minutes later and start with the men, thus voluntarily adding 10 minutes to their times.

The Munich Olympics includes a women's 1500-meter run.

*1974:* By year's end the women's marathon world record stands at 2:43:55, set by Jacqueline Hansen of Granada Hills, California.

*1975:* The first Colgate Women's Games track meet in New York City attracts 5,000 participants; the number will increase to 22,000 by 1983, making this the world's largest female sporting event.

*1978:* Atlanta hosts the first Avon International Women's Marathon, part of a series established to increase participation in and awareness of women's marathons worldwide and thereby convince the IOC to add a women's marathon to the Olympic Games.

Norwegian track star Grete Waitz, running her first-ever marathon, breaks the world record by running 2:32:30 in New York City.

*1979:* Waitz shatters her own world mark in New York, running 2:27:33 to become the first woman in the world to run a sub-2:30 marathon.

*1980:* Rosie Ruiz jumps into the Boston Marathon a mile before the finish to steal victory from rightful winner Jacqueline Gareau. Ruiz is disqualified for cheating, and the scandal causes officials to pay greater attention to the women's "race within a race" in mixed-gender running events.

*1981:* The IOC votes to include a women's marathon and 3,000-meter race in the 1984 Los Angeles Olympics.

*1983:* American marathoner Joan Benoit breaks the world record for the distance by running 2:22:43 in the Boston Marathon.

*1984:* The first women's Olympic marathon takes place in Los Angeles, with Benoit the victor in 2:24:52 and Waitz winning the silver medal. In the 3,000 meters, Maricica Puica of Romania brings home the gold.

The American College of Obstetricians and Gynecologists (ACOG) advises pregnant women not to exercise for longer than 15 minutes at a time, nor raise their heart rate over 140 beats per minute. (Many runners raise their heart rates to 160 beats per minute even while jogging.)

*1985:* Ingrid Kristiansen of Norway lowers the marathon world record to 2:21:06. Many predict the 2:20 barrier will soon be broken.

Julia Emmons becomes race director of the Peachtree 10k in Atlanta, the world's largest 10k road race both then (25,000 participants) and now (55,000).

*1986:* Henley Gabeau becomes the first female president of the Road Runners Club of America; she is appointed executive director in 1990.

*1988:* Olga Bondarenko of the Soviet Union wins the first women's Olympic 10,000 meters in 31:05 at the Seoul Olympics.

*1992:* Ethiopian Derartu Tulu wins the women's Olympic 10,000 meters, becoming the first African woman to win an Olympic gold medal. South African Elana Meyer wins the silver medal.

*1993:* Chinese women distance runners rewrite the record books, shattering the old marks at 1500, 3,000, and 10,000 meters.

*1994:* ACOG amends its 1984 guidelines for exercise during pregnancy, eliminating both the time limit on activity and the 140-beats-per-minute recommendation, and instead urging women to follow general exercise guidelines.

On July 18, at age 42, Yekaterina Podkopyeva of Russia becomes the first masters (age 40-plus) woman to break four minutes in the 1500 meters by running 3:59.78.

*1996:* The 5,000 meters replaces the 3,000 meters as an Olympic distance running event for women at the Atlanta Olympic Games. Wang Junxia of China wins the inaugural event in 14:49.

USA Track & Field's Road Running Information Center reports that women-only races grew 18 percent between 1985 and 1996.

In the Portland (Oregon) Marathon, the number of female finishers exceeds that of male finishers.

*1997:* At the famed Bay to Breakers 12k road race in San Francisco, the majority of the 57,000 entrants are women.

*1998:* At the Rotterdam Marathon, Kenyan Tegla Loroupe breaks Ingrid Kristiansen's 13-year-old marathon world record, running 2:20:47.

At the inaugural Rock 'n' Roll Marathon in San Diego, women make up more than 50 percent of the registrants.

*1999:* Loroupe breaks her own marathon world record by running 2:20:43 at the Berlin Marathon.

*2000:* An estimated 800,000 women take part in 5k running and walking events all over the United States as part of the Susan G. Komen Race for the Cure series.

*2001:* Naoko Takahoshi smashes the 2:20 barrier by running 2:19:46 in the Berlin Marathon. One week later, Catherine Ndereba runs 2:18:47 in the Chicago Marathon.

## QUESTION AND ANSWER

**Q.** My thighs rub together and chafe when I run—any suggestions?

**A.** Women runners who suffer from chafing of their inner thighs can benefit from rubbing petroleum jelly or another lubricant on the areas where the chafing occurs. This can help prevent rubbing and chafing during runs, as well as help sooth and heal raw, chafed skin afterward. Another solution is to wear longer shorts or "fitness"/biking-style shorts for running, which provide layers of fabric between the thighs, rather than traditional running shorts. In addition, many women find this style of shorts more flattering and comfortable. Women may also experience chafing from a sports bra on their chest and underarms. For more on running apparel, see Chapter 4.

### Women's Racing

Women's participation in races has increased exponentially in recent decades, outpacing the growth of the sport among men. According to USATF's Road Running Information Center, women now make up close to half of participants in road races of all distances, and *more than half* of participants at the 5k distance. The following chart details the growth of women's participation in the marathon, where women still lag behind men, but see their numbers continuing to rise:

| Year | 1980 | 1995 | 1998 | 1999 | 2000 |
|------|------|------|------|------|------|
| % female | 10.5 | 26 | 34 | 36 | 38 |

Source: Road Running Information Center. Reprinted by permission.

### Hormonal and Reproductive Issues

One of the biggest reasons women runners have had to fight so hard for full inclusion in international competition is due to concerns about how running can affect women's hormones and reproductive capacity. Much of the advice given to women runners in the past was based on inadequate or incorrect information. Fortunately, the state of knowledge has advanced considerably in recent decades, affording women greater freedom to remain active at all points during the menstrual cycle, while trying to conceive, throughout a healthy pregnancy, and while nursing their babies.

### Running and the Menstrual Cycle

Many cultures have associated menstruation with uncleanliness, and sequestered menstruating women. Even in the second half of the 20th century, women were discouraged from engaging in vigorous physical activity before and during their periods. Today, it's normal and expected for a woman to carry on with life during her period just as she always does. In addition, research has shown that physical activity during the premenstrual period can help alleviate both physical and psychological premenstrual symptoms, thanks to the relaxing and mood-lifting effects of exercise, and to perspiration, which relieves water retention (bloating).

As for a high-level activity such as running, there's no evidence that it's harmful before or during a woman's period. World records have been set and Olympic gold medals won by premenstrual and menstruating women. A few women at the very highest levels take birth control pills and other hormone supplements to manipulate the timing of menstruation so they will not get their periods during a major competition, though most women's health experts do not condone this practice.

Another area of concern for menstruating women runners is that high-level running can lead to anovulation, or suppression of the menstrual cycle, which results in amenorrhea (the absence of menstrual periods). Though it's unclear precisely why and how this happens, it's thought to relate to loss of body fat combined with the physical stress of running.

Anovulation presents several potential health problems. One, a woman who has the possibility of becoming pregnant loses an important early indicator of pregnancy—a missed period. This could result in inadequate prenatal care, and possible harm to the fetus through drinking alcohol, smoking, or exposure to other toxins. Two, a woman who is not ovulating essentially becomes temporarily infertile (though this should not be used as a method of birth control). While in most cases she regains her fertility shortly after scaling back her running and/or increasing her body fat, this may be undesirable for a woman who is trying to become pregnant or thinking about pregnancy in the near future. Three, anovulation dramatically lowers levels of the hormones estrogen and progesterone circulating in the body. One of the functions of these chemicals (estrogen, in particular) is to stimulate the replacement of bone mineral throughout the body. Bone is organic, meaning that the body constantly replaces old bone with new. If this process is slowed or halted, bones can become thin and brittle, which puts women at increased risk of stress fractures (for more on this injury, see Chapter 5), and for osteoporosis, a disease that causes bones to weaken to the point of fracturing and collapsing. Osteoporosis is a progressive disease that affects more women than men, particularly in old age. The best way for a woman to guard against it is to keep her bones as strong as possible before menopause.

There may be other factors associated with suppression of the menstrual cycle that are not yet fully understood. If you are premenopausal and your periods are irregular, infrequent (less than every 35 days), or nonexistent as a result of running—or for any other reason—you should see a doctor who specializes in women's reproductive issues, such as a gynecologist or endocrinologist (see "Amenorrhea: A Personal History," page 268–271). If the disturbances seem to be related to exercise, there are two basic treatments: One, you can scale back your physical activities to restore your cycles naturally, or two, you can take hormone supplements to artificially boost levels of estrogen and progesterone. A woman runner with irregular periods should find a doctor who can help her fully understand the health issues associated with amenorrhea, yet who appreciates her commitment to running. Beyond that, read and learn as much as you can, talk to other women in your situation, and realize you're dealing with a complex problem that may not have an easy solution.

Over the years I've talked and corresponded with many women who've experienced menstrual disturbances related to running, and have dealt with these problems in various ways. The choice of curtailing activity vs. taking hormones (another option, though one that may carry certain health risks) is complex and very personal. A woman should consider her commitment to running, at what level running causes menstrual disturbances (some women have problems when running as little as 10 miles per week), how she responds to hormone supplementation, her need for and feelings about birth control (most women who choose the hormone-supplement route are put on the Pill), her age, her pregnancy history, and her desire to have children in the future.

## AMENORRHEA: A PERSONAL HISTORY

I was one of the last among my girlfriends to get my period. When it finally came, at age 15, I was beside myself with joy. Getting my period was an irrefutable sign of growing up. For three years my period was my friend. Then, in the spring of my senior year of high school, I joined the track team, and my periods disappeared. Several months later, I had a routine physical and told my doctor, who was unconcerned. He said it was probably due to my running, and that I'd probably get a period after the end of track season. He was right, but during a summer spent traveling in Europe, my period disappeared again.

I headed off to college in the fall, and my periods did not resume. I was running for general fitness, about 25 or 30 miles per week. In the spring I went to the student health center and had some blood tests, which revealed low levels of estrogen and progesterone, but normal levels of pituitary hormones. This was good, suggesting that my amenorrhea was simply the result of low body fat and physical stress, and would reverse itself were I to gain weight and curtail my running. I also had a test to measure my bone density, which showed the thickness of the bones in my hips and lower vertebrae to be within the normal range.

This was encouraging. So was the fact that I got my period two or three times during my junior and senior years of college. I longed to menstruate regularly as a sign of normal, healthy womanhood, but I faced a dilemma in that I wasn't about to give up running as part of the bargain. Running helped me maintain my sanity, stay in touch with the natural world, and establish and solidify important friendships during college. I took running with me wherever I went—on overseas journeys, to jobs in strange cities—and relied on it as a touchstone to my true self. I read whatever material I could find on amenorrhea and other women's health issues. The consensus seemed to be that what I was doing wasn't particularly healthy, but that the biggest concern was for my bone density, and I should continue to monitor the situation with regular bone scans.

I moved to New York City after college, settled into a job, and continued running. I ran the New York City Marathon and had joined a local running team. I saw an endocrinologist, who repeated the hormone testing I'd had in college (same results) and recommended a course of the hormone therapy Provera to induce a period. It didn't work, suggesting very low and unresponsive hormone levels, so he recommended I go on the Pill.

Taking oral contraceptives was a strange experience for me. On the one hand I was determined to finally get a handle on the amenorrhea, but on the other hand, the physical and emotional side effects were awful. I felt exhausted, bloated, fuzzy-headed, and irritable for three weeks out of every month, and despite putting considerable effort into my running, was performing poorly. I tried different brands, to no avail, and after about a year I stopped taking them. I felt like myself again, and my running improved.

In the next 10 years my running reached the world-class level. I went to World Championships, Olympic Trials, and events around the globe. I read and learned more about amenorrhea—including the fact that it's common among female distance runners. What mystified me—and what doctors can't explain—is why some women runners, like me, become amenorrheic at relatively low mileage levels, while others continue to menstruate no matter how hard they train and how low their body fat.

In 1996 I was ready for a break from high-level running. I was married and wanted to have children. I'd kept tabs on my bone density, and my levels were on the low end of the normal range, suggesting an increased risk of osteoporosis later in life. I cut back on my running, from 60 miles a week to a mere 10. It was tough. I missed running with my husband and friends, missed racing, missed my runner's body.

I saw another endocrinologist, had another round of tests, and again was urged to take Provera. As directed, I took the drug for five days, after which I was supposed to see a "withdrawal bleed" if my hormone levels were sufficient to support ovulation. I wasn't expecting anything, but to my amazement I bled. I was supposed to keep taking Provera every four weeks but I decided not to. I believed that my body would do what I was asking it to if I gave it time. I expected to get a period four weeks after the withdrawal bleed, and was devastated when I didn't. Nor did I bleed the following month, nor the month after that. I was also gaining weight, and any running I did tired me more than usual. My husband bought a home pregnancy test and forced me to take it. To my amazement, it was positive. Despite never getting a "real" period, I'd ovulated and conceived. Our son was born in July 1997.

I nursed Joey for a year, during which I ran a 2:42 marathon and qualified for the U.S. Olympic Marathon Trials. We decided to have a second child. My periods had not returned, so I simply stopped running. Within a couple of months I got my period, and two or three months after that I was pregnant again. Our second son was born in September 1999. I returned to high-level running quickly after his birth, in order to participate in the U.S. Women's Olympic Marathon Trials in February 2000. Since then I've kept running at a high level. My most recent bone scan shows that over the past few years my bones have strengthened relative to my age group. Under my doctor's guidance I eat a high-calcium diet and take calcium supplements. I've had yet another round of hormone testing, showing the same low estrogen and progesterone, and normal levels of other hormones.

To be honest, I wish I got my periods regularly like other women, but if I'm to remain a runner, this seems to be my lot. I'm grateful for the information available on athletic amenorrhea, for the excellent medical care and advice I've received, and most of all, for the two beautiful, healthy children I've been able to bring into the world.

### Running Before, During, and After Pregnancy

I coach a team of women runners, and have communicated with active women around the country about issues surrounding running and pregnancy. All women want to create the best possible environment for conception, have a healthy pregnancy, give birth to a healthy, full-term baby, and raise a healthy child. Sadly, some women are led to believe that their goals and lifestyles as runners are at odds with these wishes. This is complete myth, as my own experiences and those of thousands of other healthy, active mothers can attest, and as scientific research has proven.

In order for pregnancy to occur, a woman must ovulate (produce an egg from the ovaries) and her egg must be fertilized by sperm. If fertilization does not occur, shifting hormone levels cause the uterine lining to disintegrate within about 14 days after ovulation. If pregnancy occurs, the fertilized egg (embryo) implants in the lining of the uterus. Rather than drop suddenly, hormone levels keep rising, and the uterine lining continues to thicken to nourish the growing embryo. If the pregnancy continues, the fetus will spend the next 40 weeks developing into a full-term baby. During this time it shares the mother's food and oxygen supplies and responds to her activity level, sleeping and eating patterns, and exposure to temperature changes, chemicals, and other potential hazards.

To the question "Should I exercise while pregnant?" doctors now answer a resounding "Yes" to most healthy women. The American College of Obstetricians and Gynecologists stated in 1994, "There are no data in humans to indicate that pregnant women should limit exercise intensity and lower target heart rates because of potential adverse effects." (ACOG had previously advised women to keep their heart rate under 140 beats per minute, a standard to which some doctors still hold. Many women runners reach 140 beats per minute before they even attain a jogging pace.) ACOG recommends moderate exercise for all healthy pregnant women, under their doctor's guidance.

James Clapp III, M.D., an OB/Gyn who has conducted some of the most extensive research on exercise during pregnancy, writes in *Exercising Through Your Pregnancy* that a healthy woman who *doesn't* exercise moderately while pregnant is shortchanging her own health and well-being and possibly those of her baby. According to Clapp's research, babies born to active women are *more* likely than babies born to sedentary women to be full-term and of normal birth weight. In addition, active women are more likely to have uncomplicated deliveries with shorter labors, and to recover more quickly after childbirth than their sedentary counterparts. Other research shows that active pregnant women lower their risk of gestational diabetes, pregnancy-induced hypertension, and excessive weight gain.

Women runners should keep in mind the following guidelines for health and fitness before, during, and after pregnancy.

• *Talk to your doctor.* Make clear to your doctor that fitness is important to you and you'd like to continue to exercise while pregnant. Tell the truth about what kind of exercise and how much you are doing, even if your doctor doesn't seem to approve. Respect your doctor's opinions but don't hesitate to ask challenging questions (some doctors give conservative advice out of habit, ignorance, or to protect themselves against possible legal action).

• *Avoid exercise under certain conditions.* According to ACOG, pregnant women should not exercise vigorously if they suffer from pregnancy-induced hypertension, incompetent cervix, persistent second- or third-trimester bleeding, or intrauterine growth retardation, or have experienced preterm rupture of membranes or preterm labor during the prior or current pregnancy. Women with chronic hypertension or active thyroid, cardiac, vascular, or pulmonary disease should have a medical evaluation to determine whether exercise is appropriate, and if so, what types and intensities.

• *Listen to your body.* If running hurts, then it's probably not the best thing for you to be doing. Try walking, cycling, swimming, deep-water running, or another nonimpact activity instead. Exhaustion is a clear sign that you're overdoing it. The pregnant body is designed to protect its precious cargo from overheating, oxygen deprivation, physical trauma, and other potential dangers. If you heed and respond to signs of these possible problems, it's extremely unlikely that any harm will befall your baby.

• *Focus on health, not competition.* Health and fitness should be priorities for all pregnant women, but competition should not. Let go of your racing and high-level fitness goals, and concentrate instead on the health-promoting, sanity-saving benefits of exercise. Interestingly, the women runners I know who tried to maintain a high fitness level while pregnant and to return quickly to competition were less successful than those who scaled back, relaxed, and went back to hard training and racing only when the desire to compete returned.

• *Stay well fueled and well hydrated.* Because your baby shares your blood, oxygen, and nutrients, it's crucial that you maintain these supplies, particularly during exercise. It's a good idea to have some water and a light preexercise snack, and keep fluids with you during your workouts. Hydrate and fuel up again afterward.

• *Remember that every pregnancy is different.* Your experience with exercise during pregnancy will be different from that of every other woman—and if you are pregnant more than once, it's likely the experiences will differ from one another. I experienced no nausea at all during my first pregnancy, rarely felt more tired than usual, and ran well into my eighth month with no discomfort. During my second pregnancy I was nauseous through week 14, exhausted throughout the nine months, and was forced to switch from running to walking and swimming in my sixth month due to lower-abdominal pressure.

• *Know the signs of possible trouble.* It's crucial to pay careful and prompt attention to any kind of discomfort during exercise while pregnant. Stop exercising and seek medical attention if exercise causes pain, bleeding, dizziness, fainting, palpitations, fever, or excessive fatigue that doesn't diminish with rest.

## RUNNING AND BREAST-FEEDING

Most doctors recommend that women breast-feed their babies for 6 to 12 months if possible, for their own and their infant's health. Breast milk is formulated to contain all the nutrients a newborn baby needs for optimal health, and also contains antibodies that help boost immunity. Breast-feeding helps a new mother's uterus return to its normal size and shape, and can help a woman shed excess weight. For all these reasons, most women runners choose to breast-feed, at least initially. Once they resume running, many women have questions about combining running with nursing their babies. These concerns generally fall into the following categories:

• *Altered quality and quantity of breast milk.* Intense exercise (above the lactate threshold) can make breast milk taste sour. In one study, sedentary lactating women exercised above their lactate threshold, then produced milk with a sour taste, which caused their infants to consume less. However, subsequent studies of fit women who ran regularly for sustained periods below their lactate threshold did not experience changes in the quality or quantity of their milk, nor did their babies consume less. The question remains whether very intense exercise while breast-feeding is detrimental to babies' health. Most health experts advise lactating women to avoid nursing their babies immediately after intense exercise, when lactate levels are highest. Rather, nurse or pump before workouts—which makes for more comfortable running anyway—or wait at least an hour afterward, when lactate is largely cleared from the system. Heed your baby's reactions and preferences, and use those as a guide. I nursed my son within half an hour after completing the 2000 Olympic marathon trials, and he wasn't bothered in the least. The overall nutritional quality of breast milk should not be affected by running and other exercise as long as a woman is well nourished and adequately hydrated. Nor should milk suffer in quantity. Your pediatrician should weigh your baby at checkups to make sure he or she is gaining weight normally compared to other breast-fed infants. In addition, weigh yourself regularly, and make adjustments if you are losing more than a pound a week. You may want to lose weight more quickly, but this could cause your milk supply to diminish.

• *Effects of lactation on running fitness and performance.* Some women find they cannot regain their former running fitness while they are breast-feeding, and/or that breast-feeding makes running uncomfortable. My personal belief is that the health of your baby should supercede such concerns, even for runners at the world-class level. I've also not found breast-feeding to interfere with my pursuit of high-level running, having run in comfort for a total of two years of breast-feeding, during which I won races and qualified for and ran in the Olympic marathon trials. Still, every woman's experience is different, and if you can't breast-feed and run in comfort, or if your competitive running goals are important enough to you that you resent the energy-draining and time-consuming effects of breast-feeding, then you should wean your baby rather than harbor such resentments. In keeping with the advice of the American Academy of Pediatrics, avoid feeding a baby cow's milk (which is too rich in protein and poor in other nutrients for infants) until 12 months; use formula instead.

Most women runners are eager to resume running after childbirth. The point at which you return to running, and at what intensity, depends on your fitness level and running experience before and during pregnancy, how your delivery went (vaginal or cesarean, length of labor, any complications), whether or not you are breast-feeding, and how you're handling the care of your newborn baby.

Some doctors advise waiting six to eight weeks after childbirth before resuming running and other vigorous exercise, but often this advice has no medical basis. My suggestion is to wait until *you want to run*—a desire that comes from within and is not based on guilt or other people's expectations. If you want to try running within days of giving birth, go ahead. If you don't feel the urge until six months postpartum, that's fine, too.

Follow these guidelines when returning to running after childbirth:

• *Start slowly and increase volume and intensity gradually.* It's important to avoid stressing your joints after childbirth. Pregnancy releases a hormone called relaxin, which loosens the joints to allow for expansion of the pelvis so the baby can pass through the birth canal. After delivery this joint laxity increases a woman's susceptibility to injury. Run slowly and easily, tuning in to feedback to determine how much pounding your joints can safely handle. Taking a gradual approach to your return to running also makes sense for the same reasons it does when starting an exercise program: You'll reduce your risk of injury and overtraining, and increase your enjoyment.

• *Cross-train and train supplementally.* The pounding and intensity of running may make it inappropriate as your sole or primary form of postpartum exercise. Substitute cross-training activities, and supplement running with strength-training, to improve fitness and ensure balance in your program (see Chapter 9 for more on cross-training and supplemental training).

• *Seek out other new moms as exercise partners.* Not only will this offer companionship for workouts, but it also can be a source of information, inspiration, and advice. Many health clubs, gyms, and community centers offer exercise classes for new moms (with and without babies); if nothing is available in your area, consider simply meeting with other moms to walk or run.

• *Follow your body's advice.* As always, your body will tell you how much and what types of exercise are best for you. Listen carefully and take your exercise program one day at a time, responding to the cues you receive. I tried running four weeks after my first son was born. The first few days were fine, then a heat wave hit and running felt just awful. I backed off for a week or so, then resumed running every other day until the hot weather passed.

• *Set short-term and long-term goals.* As you gain fitness and familiarity with your postpartum body, setting some attainable goals can provide motivation and structure. Make your goals simple and action-oriented: "I will include three half-hour exercise sessions this week." Avoid performance pressure in your initial competitive efforts: "I will train to finish a 10k feeling strong," rather than targeting a specific time. Long-term, you might aim to run a marathon, or work up to an average of five hours of exercise per week. Committing to exercise rather than performance goals can be helpful in caring out the "me" time that is so important—and often neglected—for new mothers.

## QUESTION AND ANSWER

**Q.** What changes should I expect in my running as I go through menopause, and can I do anything to counteract those changes?

**A.** Women's experiences of menopause—the drop in estrogen and progesterone that leads to the cessation of the monthly menstrual cycle—vary widely. Some women experience hot flashes, mood swings, depression, irritability, sleep problems, night sweating, weight gain, fatigue, and more. According to a survey of 625 women runners of menopausal age (average age of 50.8) conducted by the Melpomene Institute for Women's Health Research, women runners reported "slower training pace," "reduced energy," and "more aches/pains" among the changes that affected them. It was not known, however, to what extent the women's complaints were due to menopause, and to what extent aging in general was responsible, and interestingly, more women (71.7 percent) attributed the changes to aging than to menopause (42.9 percent).

There is no medical evidence that running and other vigorous physical activities are dangerous or unhealthy to women during and after menopause, and indeed, running may help ease symptoms. In the same Melpomene survey, women reported that running helped reduce hot flashes, mood swings, depression, sleep problems, and night sweats, and also helped them control weight gain and raise their levels of energy and motivation.

Though you may find that you are running more slowly, or able to handle fewer miles during and after menopause, emerging medical evidence suggests that continuing to run and engage in other forms of vigorous activity is one of the healthiest decisions you can make.

## WOMEN'S RUNNING SHOES

In 1997, for the first time in history, women spent more money than men on athletic shoes, and they've continued to outspend men in this category ever since. According to a survey of the nationwide Fleet Feet chain of running specialty stores, women's running shoes make up 53 percent of total sales.

Many women ask whether they should purchase a female-specific running shoe. Almost all the major shoe companies make running shoes for women, and a handful of companies make women's shoes predominantly or exclusively. Most models today come in men's and women's versions that are truly different in ways that go beyond color and other cosmetics.

The main difference is that women's shoes are made to accommodate a foot that is proportionally wider in the forefoot and toe area and narrower in the heel than the corresponding men's model. The typical woman's foot is shaped this way, which is why many women will find a men's shoe too roomy in the heel and tight across the forefoot and in the toe box. Men's shoes also tend to be wider in general compared to women's. In addition, the male and female versions of some models have different midsole materials or constructions, upper strapping, or heel support. Finally, women's and men's shoes are sized differently, with women's models being about a size and a half larger; this means that a woman who wears size 8 women's shoes would take a 6½ in a men's model of that shoe.

Most women runners appreciate gender-specific shoe models that truly accommodate women's anatomical foot differences. Today's women's running shoes are infinitely better than pre-1990 models. Typically, these were just lighter—and often less well-made—versions of men's shoes. They may have looked the part, with their pastel colors, and names preceded by "Lady" or with the suffix "-ette," but they made no concession whatsoever to the female anatomy.

Of course, not every woman's foot is "typically" female. Women with wide feet, wide heels, and a tendency to pronate severely do better in men's models. By the same token, some male runners—those with narrow heels, for example—do better in women's shoes. The best advice to women and men is to buy the shoe that fits, meets their biomechanical needs, and that's worked for them in the past. For more information on shoe buying, see Chapter 4.

CHAPTER 12

▶▶▶▶▶▶▶▶▶▶▶▶▶▶▶▶▶▶▶▶▶▶▶▶▶▶▶▶▶▶▶▶

# Running for Children and Youth

S hould children run—for health, fitness, and/or competition?
The answer isn't obvious. On the one hand, children seem
never to stop running, and many children's games and activities
incorporate running, at least for short distances. On the other
hand, we grown-up runners know that running is a physical and
mental challenge that requires discipline, tenacity, goal-setting,
and shifting of our life's priorities—skills not evident in the average 10-year-old. Running for fitness and performance also carries
risks of injury and overtraining, and can become a platform for
compulsive tendencies. Many parents are also concerned that by
encouraging running in children we are seeking to validate our
own choices or relive our own youthful athletic history—or the
one we regret we never had. Yet we wouldn't want to unneces-
sarily discourage children from running, or prevent them from
sharing in one of our favorite activities. Clearly, children's running is a confusing issue.

There are compelling reasons to involve children in running.
It's possible for children to enjoy running from a very young age

if they are introduced to it properly, which boils down to offering children the opportunity to run in fun and playful ways, and letting them lead us—not the other way around. This chapter focuses on running for children ages 2 through 18, including health, fitness, and safety factors, the effects of running on your child's growing body, psychological and social issues, and special concerns. Whether you are a parent, grandparent, caregiver, coach, or simply interested in the next generation of runners, these topics bear close attention.

### Why Running Is Good for Children

No doubt you have heard about the concern about the unfitness of today's children and youth. Research suggests that fewer than half of all children in the United States engage in activity sufficient to benefit the cardiovascular system and promote long-term health. The Surgeon General's Report on Physical Activity and Health states that children's activity levels decline with age, with a dramatic fall reported at the onset of adolescence (particularly in girls). Nearly half of all 12- to 21-year-olds in this country do not regularly engage in physical activity; 25 percent engage in no consistent "vigorous" activity, and 14 percent report no activity at even a moderate level. Many factors are blamed for this trend, including increased television viewing and computer use in childhood, a rise in childhood obesity (which creates a vicious cycle: Overweight children tend to avoid activity, and thus grow heavier due to their sedentary lifestyle, etc.), and a lowering of physical education standards and requirements in schools.

Lack of fitness in childhood can have long-term health consequences. The main concern is the link between inactivity and obesity. Current estimates are that about one in five U.S. children is obese (defined as being 20 percent or more overweight). Obesity increases the risk of major health problems, including hyperlipidemia (high cholesterol), hypertension, type 2 diabetes, and respiratory and orthopedic problems. These effects occur even in children. In addition, obese children frequently suffer from low self-esteem and face discrimination by their peers. Obesity in childhood sets the stage for obesity in adulthood: About 50 percent of obese children age 6 and older are likely to become obese adults, compared to only 10 percent of normal-weight children.

Among obese adolescents, 70 percent are likely to become obese in adulthood.

As in adults, regular physical activity in children can help maintain a healthy body weight. Physical activity also increases cardiovascular fitness, strengthens muscles and bones, improves mental health, and enhances social ties. While there is plenty of time in adulthood to reverse the negative health consequences of an inactive childhood, evidence is strong that becoming regularly active at an early age is an excellent investment in lifelong health. Perhaps the greatest benefit is that early activity can help establish ongoing patterns of regular physical activity. In surveys of active adults, the majority report having been active as children. In one study, women who reported having had five physical education (P.E.) classes per week in elementary school were more active than women who'd had less frequent P.E. classes.

## RUNNING AND YOUR CHILD'S BODY

Children are not simply adults in miniature. As runners, children have specific physical requirements that parents and other adult supervisors should be aware of. Here is a look at the physical characteristics of children, as they apply to running:

• *Growing bones.* Bone mineral is an organic substance—that is, it's constantly renewing itself. During childhood and up through about age 19, bone growth occurs in cartilaginous areas called the epiphyseal growth plates. These are located on the ends of bones, and separate the shaft (metaphysis) from the end (epiphysis) of the bone. The cartilage that makes up these growth plates gradually hardens into mature bone during the late teenage years as the body's overall growth slows and completes. Because cartilage is much softer and weaker than bone, there is concern about children engaging in activities that pose a risk of acute trauma—such as from a football tackle—or damage due to overuse, as with distance running. Though rare, there have been cases in which an injury to the growth plates limited or even arrested growth of children's bones. In addition, during adolescence the rapid growth of bone can create tightness in children's joints when bones lengthen faster than muscle-tendon units. This tightness can result in muscle strains. Concern about growth-plate and joint damage is one of the primary reasons most children's health and medical experts recommend limiting long-distance running in children. (See page 288 for guidelines on maximum recommended training and racing distances for children at various ages.)

• *Muscles and connective tissues.* Children are vulnerable to muscle and connective tissue injuries from running for the same reason that novice adult runners are susceptible: lack of conditioning. Few children have the overall muscle strength and endurance to sustain a regular running program on an adult scale. Therefore, many experts recommend a walking/running program for any child who is running for fitness for the first time. This strategy fits the nature of most children, who are poor at pacing themselves and find continuous running for long distances at the same intensity monotonous. (See page 288 for guidelines on maximum recommended training and racing distances and training patterns and progressions for children.)

• *Heat transfer.* Children are less efficient than adults at losing heat during vigorous exercise in warm conditions. This is due to children's greater metabolic heat production per unit of body weight, combined with their greater surface-area-to-weight ratio and less-developed ability to sweat. Children also acclimatize more slowly to warm conditions than do adults. The American Academy of Pediatrics recommends the following for children exercising under warm environmental conditions: Reduce the intensity of activities lasting 15 minutes or longer; at the start of an exercise program or after traveling to a warmer climate, limit the intensity and duration of activity initially, then gradually increase it over a period of 10 to 14 days (this can be a challenge for teams that travel to warm climates for spring training); make sure children are well hydrated before exercise, and enforce periodic drinking during activity (5 ounces of cold water or flavored salted drink every 20 minutes for a child weighing 88 pounds; 9 ounces every 20 minutes for an adolescent weighing 132 pounds); dress children in lightweight, light-colored clothing limited to one layer of absorbent material, and replace sweat-soaked garments with dry clothing. Don't forget sun hats and sunscreen for children exercising on sunny days.

• *Nutritional concerns.* Parents and others who supervise children's running programs may be concerned about meeting children's caloric and nutritional needs. In addition, they may worry about the prevalence of eating disorders in young people—girls in particular—who are involved in sports such as running, in which thinness is perceived as an attribute. Young children, if left to their own devices, tend to eat enough to maintain their energy and nutritional needs no matter what their activity level. Your job as a parent or caregiver is to make nutritious, varied, and satisfying foods and drinks readily available, and set a good example with your own eating habits and attitudes. Keep in mind that many children prefer "grazing" (eating moderate amounts of food often throughout the day, rather than large meals), so it's wise to have snacks on hand at frequent intervals.

Adolescents should be counseled about the importance of eating enough to meet the energy requirements of running. Getting across the "food is fuel" message to adolescent runners can go a long way toward preventing patterns of food restriction and binge eating and/or purging that can lead to an eating disorder. If your adolescent son or daughter is a runner, or if you work with runners in that age group, make sure that information is available about nutrition and disordered eating. Watch for the warning signs of an eating disorder, including weight loss, restricted eating, excessive exercise, social withdrawal, binge eating (though this is usually done in secret), and menstrual disturbances. See Chapter 7 for more on nutritional needs of runners, and Resources for contact information for organizations that deal with eating disorders.

• *Hormonal issues.* Several studies show that athletes and dancers who begin training before their first menstrual period (known as menarche) may experience a later menarche and have an increased incidence of menstrual dysfunction—such as irregular or interrupted periods—than girls who begin training after their first periods. Experts aren't sure why these changes occur; running and other forms of intense exercise may cause a delay in menarche, or girls who start menstruating late for other reasons may be more likely to take up sports or dancing. It's known that the complex interplay of hormones that causes the menstrual cycle depends on certain levels of energy availability in the body, and that delayed menarche and menstrual abnormalities also occur in underweight women, and those with serious illness or poor nutritional status. Girls and young women who take up running after menarche may experience amenorrhea (as I did when I started running in high school). According to OB/Gyn Mona Shangold, as long as menarche has occurred by age 18, the delay is probably not harmful. However, a delay past age 18 is usually accompanied by low levels of the hormones estrogen and progesterone. As outlined in Chapter 11, one of the functions of these hormones is to maintain bone-mineral density, which is why any woman who menstruates less than once every 35 days should see her doctor. Studies have shown that adolescent girls who have a late menarche and low body weight may experience a decrease in bone-mineral density. Low bone-mineral-density levels can increase the risk of stress fractures and set the stage for a higher risk of osteoporosis later in life (see Chapter 5 for more on stress fractures, and Chapter 10 for more on osteoporosis). Hormone-replacement therapy and calcium supplementation are often recommended for delayed menarche and menstrual disturbances in girls and young women, along with scaling back an intense exercise program and increasing intake of calories and nutrients.

## QUESTION AND ANSWER

**Q.** Should I let my 12-year-old run along with me in road races?

**A.** Most road races are at least 5 kilometers (3.1 miles), which is probably too far for most 12-year-olds to race seriously. However, if your daughter is properly trained, and she is asking to race with you, it's probably okay to try a 5k or other short race together. Choose a low-key "fun run" or line up in the back of the pack to take the emphasis off time and place. Your daughter can learn from your example such things as proper pacing (if she's like most children, she'll want to start at a sprint; you can encourage her instead to maintain a "conversation" pace), fueling and hydrating before the race and drinking during it, proper race etiquette (no shoving, dodging, or weaving), and pushing through normal late-race fatigue. If she needs to stop and walk, walk with her, encouraging her to try running again if she seems up to it. Aim to finish together—with a smile. All this will make the race far from a competitive challenge for you. Make sure you're okay with that.

### Guidelines for Children's Running Programs

"How much should children run?" is perhaps a common question posed by parents and others who supervise children's physical activity. There's no one-size-fits-all answer to that question. Children's tolerance of running is set not only by their age and level of physical maturity, but also by their participation in other sports and activities, their personalities, and the culture of activity and sport that surrounds them.

The Surgeon General's Report on Health and Physical Activity recommends 30 minutes of moderate activity on most days of the week for all healthy people, including children. The National Association for Sports and Physical Education and the Year 2000 Dietary Guidelines for Americans both suggest that young people do at least 60 minutes of moderate to vigorous activity daily. That's a reasonable goal for all families—whether running is included or not.

Keep in mind that activity does not need to be continuous in order to be healthy and beneficial. This is important when working with children, who tend to exercise in spurts, interweaving intense bursts of activity with rest (which is what many team sports require). Thus, whereas an adult might get in a daily 60 minute run, bike ride, or session at the gym, a child will play freeze tag for 10 minutes, flop down on the ground for a 3-minute rest, leap up to chase a friend for another 7 minutes, sit to drink some juice for 5 minutes, hop around the yard for 6 minutes, and so on.

Advice varies widely on how to make children's exercise programs as effective as possible. The one thing most experts agree on is that the activity should be fun and noncoercive—that is, the child should *want* to do it rather than feel compelled to do it by a parent, teacher, coach, or other supervisor. Indeed, one study of the preteen and teenage exercise experience of middle-age men showed that coercion to exercise had a negative effect on physical activity in adulthood. Many adults today are turned off from running due to their memories of being forced to run laps in gym class or stadium steps in football or soccer practice. Many times these fitness activities—which coaches could so easily have made fun, interesting, and motivating—were even used as punishment for failing to meet certain performance standards, or losing competitions.

In 1988, *The Physician and Sportsmedicine,* a monthly journal targeted to physicians and other professionals specializing in sports medicine, published a set of 10 "Guidelines for Parents of Children in Sports." The guidelines were picked up in a "Dear Abby" column in 2000 and are cited on *Runner's World's* kidsrunning.com Web site. They are reprinted here to provide a helpful framework for any running program or event for children under age 18.

1. Make sure your children know that—win or lose—you love them and are not disappointed with their performance.
2. Be realistic about your child's physical ability.
3. Help your child set realistic goals.
4. Emphasize improved performance, not winning. Positively reinforce improved skills.
5. Don't relieve your own athletic past through your child.
6. Provide a safe environment for training and competition. This includes proper training methods and use of equipment.
7. Control your own emotions at games and events. Don't yell at other players, coaches, or officials.

**8.** Be a cheerleader for your child and the other children on the team.

**9.** Respect your child's coaches. Communicate openly with them. If you disagree with their approach, discuss it with them.

**10.** Be a positive role model. Enjoy sports yourself. Set your own goals. Live a healthy lifestyle.

Copyright 1990 *The Physician and Sportsmedicine.* Reprinted by permission.

## HOW FAR CAN CHILDREN SAFELY RUN?

If you are concerned about the maximum safe distance or time your child should spend running, the guidelines below may offer some help. They can be used as a general guideline when designing a children's running program.

### RECOMMENDED MAXIMUM DISTANCES FOR FUN RUNS OR RACING

| Age | Fun Run* Distance | Race Distance |
| --- | --- | --- |
| 4 and under | ⅛ mile or 200 meters | 55 yards or 50 meters |
| 5–6 | ¼ mile or 400 meters | 1/16 mile or 100 meters |
| 7–8 | ½ mile or 800 meters | ⅛ mile or 200 meters |
| 9–10 | 1 mile or 1600 meters | ¼ mile or 400 meters |
| 11–12 | 2 miles or 3200 meters | ½ mile or 800 meters |
| 13–14 | 3.1 miles or 5 kilometers | 1 mile or 1600 meters |

Reprinted by permission of kidsrunning.com, sponsored by *Runner's World.* Distances supplied by Mick Grant.

\* Fun runs are often held before or after an adult road race. They are noncompetitive events in which the outcome is finishing, not a winning time or place. Children often participate with their parents or another adult who lets the child set the pace.

The figures above apply to fun runs held on the road and races held on a track, though some children's races are held on a road or field using track distances, and some fun runs are held on a track or field. Occasionally you may want to move a child up a category to see how he/she does with the greater distance. Children who are involved in running between ages 15 and 18 usually compete for a school team, where they are under the guidance of a coach. (See page 289 for information on coaches' qualification standards.)

They will run cross-country races of up to 5k (3.1 miles) and track races of up to 2 miles. Note that 5k and 10k running is not even mentioned for children up to age 14. Also note the 4-and-under category includes toddlers, who will not be "racing" at all, but more likely holding a parent's hand, or even being scooped up and carried.

## QUESTION AND ANSWER

**Q.** How are high school track and cross-country coaches trained?

**A.** Training standards for scholastic running coaches vary widely. To find out the standards in your area, contact your school district, your state department of education, or the American Sport Education Program (www.asep.com). Minimal standards should include training in CPR and other emergency procedures. Ideally, a coach should have a background in teaching children, and training in physical education, anatomy, kinesiology (movement science), and/or exercise physiology. In addition, a coach should work with a qualified trainer who can help diagnose, treat, and rehabilitate injuries in young athletes. If you are concerned about the quality of your child's coaching at school, work with school administrators and staff to make improvements, perhaps by referring them to training and certification programs in your area.

Suggestions for structuring and overseeing children's running programs, compiled from parents, coaches, and children's health and fitness experts, are outlined below.

• *Put fun first.* Children will not run if they do not enjoy it. This requires a different approach to children's than adults' running. Most preschool-age children respond well to games involving animal activities, such as "run like a deer," "gallop like a horse," "hop like a bunny," and "sway like an elephant." At this age, instilling a joy in movement is more important than promoting fitness. Though children at this age will "race" if lined up together and told to "go!" most lack any real understanding of winning and losing. Participation is what matters. School-age children show a wide range of interest in and adaptability to running. Try to incorporate running into active skill-building games such as soccer, kickball, T-ball, tag, and other sports, rather than making running the sole attraction. You can set up an obstacle course or parcourse (a running circuit that includes other activities, such as calisthenics, strength-training, and flexibility exercises) for children to complete. Relay races are fun and foster team spirit. Junior high and high school running programs can be more competitive, but should still emphasize participation by as many as possible and include activities to foster togetherness and team spirit, such as group stretching and warming up, practicing team racing strategies, and team social events.

• *Set a good example.* Show your children the positive role that running plays in your life. Your child is unlikely to follow in your running footsteps if he senses that running is something you do out of guilt or obligation, rather than joy. Similarly, if you display an attitude of compulsion in training, or cutthroat competition in racing, you can expect your child to follow suit. If you have trouble managing these issues, work on adjusting your attitudes and behaviors before involving children—either your own or others'—in your running.

• *Let children lead the way.* Starting at about school age, your child may ask to run with you, or you may offer to run with her. You should take a different approach to these "runs" than to sessions you do on your own. It's unfair to expect young children to keep up with your pace or cover the distances you are used to. Keep the running you do with preteenage children separate from your training and racing. Let your child set the pace (if he or she starts out at a sprint, which is typical, encourage running together at "conversation" pace). If your child stops to walk, walk with him. Let him stand, sit, pick flowers, or pet a dog, then suggest a few more minutes of running. When your child is ready to quit, the run is over—even if you've gone no farther than the end of the driveway. When running with teenage children, continue to let them set the distance and pace—as long as they aren't running *you* ragged!—and keep the emphasis on the pleasure of each other's company.

• *Make it social.* Encourage your child to run with friends, class-mates, and teammates. Invite your child's friends and parents along when you run together, and organize social events afterward—breakfast or brunch at the local diner after a morning run, a barbeque in your backyard after a group run in the early evening. Set an example by running with your spouse and friends.

• *Outfit your child in proper running gear.* Young children who run as part of games and play do not need special running shoes and clothing, but if your child's interest continues, you should purchase running shoes, shorts, singlets, and other gear. Not only will this make running safer, healthier, and more comfortable, but it will also contribute to your child's sense that she is a "real" runner and that you value her running. Visit a running specialty store for the best shoe selection and assistance in choosing the right shoes for your child. (See Chapter 4 for more information and advice on gearing up.)

• *Take a long-term view.* Your goal as a parent, teacher, or coach should be to foster a lifelong interest in running, fitness, and health. If your child also breaks the county record in the mile and wins a track scholarship, that's all well and good—as long as he loves what he's doing and is having fun. The running ranks are filled with "recovering" running prodigies who burned out on the sport at a young age due to parental pressures. By the same token, some of the best runners in the world got a relatively late start in the sport, or did not display precocious talent in their youth (see "Did They Run As Kids?" on page 292–293). Let your child's running unfold on its own terms.

## QUESTION AND ANSWER

**Q.** My 5-year-old runs nonstop, but isn't she too young to start running for fitness?

**A.** Age 5 is a wonderful time to start your child running in an in-formal, fun-based program—perhaps at school or through a local running club—if she shows interest. At this age children adapt well to short, quick runs with frequent rest breaks, rather than sustained distance running. Encourage your child to play games that involve running, such as relay races and obstacle courses. Intersperse other activities with running, such as jumping, hopping, spinning, twirling, climbing, skipping, and galloping, to sustain your child's interest and add to the fun of her playtime. Bring your child along with you to races and enter her in the "peewee" or kids' run with other children her age (at age 5 she should run about 400 meters at the most). If your daughter wants to come with you when you go running, let her join you at the end or beginning. She's too young to be "training" at your level, but will get a lot of pleasure and pride out of running alongside you for short distances. You can add to the fun by stretching together, drinking water or a sports drink from a plastic sports bottle, and enjoying a healthy snack together after you've finished.

## DID THEY RUN AS KIDS?

The early running experiences of some of the best runners in the world are evidence that you don't need to become intensely involved in the sport early to rise to the top. In fact, a broad-based fitness program that emphasizes fun and enjoyment is probably the best platform for success in running, at any level. According to one study, children who participate in a variety of sports before puberty tend to perform more consistently, have fewer injuries, and stay in sports longer than those who specialize before puberty.

*Bill Rodgers,* four-time New York City Marathon and Boston Marathon winner: Rodgers ran cross-country in high school. Before that he participated in a variety of sports and activities, including baseball, basketball, football, ice hockey, badminton, golf, sledding, ice skating, swimming, fishing, hunting, camping, and hiking.

*Grete Waitz,* 1984 Olympic marathon silver medallist, nine-time New York City Marathon winner: Growing up in Norway in the 1950s and '60s, Waitz, who had two older brothers, joined the Vidar Sports Club in Oslo at age 12 after spending several months doing her own running "workouts" in her backyard. In addition to running (sprints of 60 to 100 meters), Waitz did the long jump, high jump, shot put, the hurdles. By age 16 she was the junior national champion at 400 and 800 meters.

*Paul Tergat,* five-time World Cross-Country Champion: Unlike many Kenyan runners, Tergat did not get his start by running many miles to and from school each day. (He lived just 400 meters from his school, and besides, his family owned a car.) A former basketball player, Tergat started running seriously in 1991, at age 22.

*Frank Shorter,* 1972 Olympic marathon gold medalist: Shorter was involved in a variety of sports and activities in junior high school and high school, including track and cross-country running. He competed in both sports at Yale University, where he also focused on skiing, academics, and singing in a school choral group. He started to shine as a runner only in his senior year, winning the national collegiate champion in the 6-mile. After graduation in 1969, he gradually moved up to racing longer distances, completing his first marathon in 1971.

*Joan Benoit Samuelson,* 1984 Olympic marathon gold medalist and American marathon record holder: Downhill skiing was Samuelson's passion as a child, and she dreamed of being a professional skier until she broke her leg in a skiing accident at age 15. She also did Nordic skiing, swimming, field hockey, basketball, rowing, canoeing, and other sports and outdoor activities growing up in Cape Elizabeth, Maine. As late as 1980, a year after setting an American record (2:35:15) at the 1979 Boston Marathon, she still did not concentrate on running year-round, giving it a lower priority during field hockey season at Bowdoin College.

*John Kagwe,* two-time winner of the New York City Marathon (1997 and '98): Growing up in Kenya, Kagwe played soccer and other sports without distinction. Seeking success, he turned to running in 1988 at age 19, first trying 200-meter and 400-meter sprints. He had little aptitude for the short distances, and so moved up to longer distances on the track and in cross-country. He ran his first marathon in 1994 at age 25.

*Khalid Khannouchi,* marathon world-record holder: Growing up in Morocco, Khannouchi ran to stay in shape for soccer. He began focusing on running in his late teens, and competed internationally for the first time in the 1993 World University Games, at age 21.

## Psychological and Social Issues

As with adults, running for children is psychological and social as well as physical. Keep the following points in mind as your child experiences running, adjusting your perspective and guidance to his age and needs.

• *Stress.* As noted throughout this chapter, fun should be the first goal of any child's running experience. All other goals—health, fitness, character development, competition—should follow from the fact that running is something your child chooses to do. That said, there may be times when your child finds running stressful, particularly if she joins a running team. This is not necessarily a bad thing. The stresses of working hard, setting and meeting goals, and learning how to win and lose are things all children should experience as they mature, and sports have traditionally provided a safe and controlled way for them to do this. As a parent, teacher, coach, or caregiver, you can help your child respond to the stresses that may accompany running by being as supportive as possible. The first time I realized that running wasn't always fun was during an 880-yard (half mile) high school track race. I'd already run the mile that day, and was tired, cold, hungry, and wanted to go home. As I lined up at the start I suddenly feared I would not be able to move when the gun fired. When I heard the shot a few seconds later, I lurched forward stiffly. Although I was in the lead, I was miserable. There were practically no spectators and most of my teammates were putting on their sweats, not even bothering to watch. I wanted to quit, and though I continued and won the race, the trauma of those moments has stuck with me. It's hard for a parent or coach to help a young runner through such moments. Listen carefully to what children say about their running, and watch them as they run. Talk to other parents and coaches. Most importantly, make sure your children know you love and value them no matter what the results of their efforts.

• *Social maturation.* Running should offer children a social outlet. If a child does all of her running alone, and seems to use running as a way of avoiding contact with others, keep an eye on the situation. You may need to intervene. It's fine if some runs are "just me" time, but encourage your child to run with you, other family members, and her friends as well. Suggest joining a running team, class, or club. Bring her along to races with you, even if she chooses not to participate. Seeing hundreds of runners having a great time running together should be a positive reinforcement.

• *Burnout.* Parents of any child who takes part in a sport at a young age—especially if he shows unusual talent and dedication—may be concerned the youngster will "burn out" from the physical and emotional stress and missed opportunities of a "normal" childhood. Although media reports suggest the risk of burnout in young athletes is high, there have been few studies on the effects on young athletes of intense, sustained training and high-level competition. The research that does exist suggests that burnout is experienced by only a small minority of young athletes, in sports across the board. Most children thrive on training and competition, even at a high level. Parents of young runners can help guard against problems by keeping their expectations realistic and their own emotional investment at a low level. The key is to support your child's running while letting her "own" her experiences and achievements.

▶▶▶▶▶▶▶▶▶▶▶▶▶▶▶▶▶▶▶▶▶▶▶▶▶▶▶▶▶▶▶▶

# CHAPTER 13

# *Running and Aging*

Running is a lifelong activity. Almost no one is ever too old to start running, and most people can continue running well into old age. Most general advice about running and the running lifestyle applies to runners age 50 and over just as it does to younger runners. Still, 50-and-over runners have particular questions and concerns about the health, fitness, and performance aspects of running, and about integrating running into their lives as the decades pass. This chapter addresses those issues, and directs senior runners to other resources that can enhance the role of running in their lives.

Statistics compiled by the Road Running Information Center of USA Track & Field show that participation in masters (age 40-plus) road racing has increased markedly over the past 15 years. The chart below shows the increase of the proportion of masters runners registering for road races in the United States.

## PROPORTION OF MASTERS (AGE 40+) RUNNERS REGISTERING IN U.S. ROAD RACES

|          | 1980 | 1995 | 1998 | 2000 |
|----------|------|------|------|------|
| Masters  | 26%  | 41%  | 40%  | 44%  |

With many members of the baby boom population now well into their fifties, and an ever-growing body of research pointing to the undeniable benefits of running and other forms of exercise, it's expected that the number of 50-plus runners will continue to grow.

Of course, the designation of 50 as a dividing point between "younger" and "older" runners is somewhat arbitrary. Many 50-year-olds have health and fitness profiles similar to people decades younger. In body, mind, and spirit they seem to have found the legendary Fountain of Youth. The reverse is also true: Plenty of 20- and 30-year-olds have grown old before their time. Still, the current perception is that "middle age" begins at more or less the half-century mark. Several significant physical signs of aging occur at approximately this time—with wide variations among individuals—including some loss of mobility and agility, an increased risk of major diseases, and the onset of menopause in women. In addition, many people's lives change markedly at about age 50, as their parents age and pass on—reminding them of their own mortality—their children gain independence and eventually leave home, and their retirement looms closer.

### A LATE BLOOMER WHO WOULDN'T STOP

The 50-and-over running ranks are heavily populated with people who came to the sport relatively late in life. Perhaps they realized that a sedentary lifestyle was making them look and feel older than they wanted, and could even lead to an early grave. Some late-blooming active women respond to changing social mores that encouraged them to move and sweat and push themselves and enjoy it—no matter that they were old, gray, and had never before been active.

These late-bloomers have found themselves reinvigorated physically, psychologically, and even spiritually by their involvement in running. Some have risen to the world-class level of the sport, performing incredible competitive feats and inspiring millions of others—runners and non-runners alike—with their achievements and commitment to a fit, healthy lifestyle.

One of the best-loved runners in the sport is a late-bloomer. Priscilla Welch was born in Great Britain in 1944 and did not exercise formally for the first 35 years of her life. In 1979 she was stationed at a remote military outpost with her husband, Dave. An overweight, out-of-shape smoker, Welch took up running—gradually at first—to combat boredom and improve her health. Dave, also a runner, encouraged her, and within a few months recognized that Welch had innate athletic talent. She began entering local road races and placing well, often topping the women's field despite being 10 to 20 years older than most of her competitors.

By 1984 Welch was seemingly at the top of her game as an international running star. She represented Great Britain in the 1984 Los Angeles Olympic Games in the marathon at age 39. Her entry into the masters (age 40-plus) running ranks was widely anticipated, and Welch did not disappoint. She won road races and set course and age-group records with practically every outing throughout 1985 and 1986. Her greatest triumph came in April 1987, when she set an age-group world record in the London Marathon, running an incredible 2:26:51 at age 42, a mark that still stands. The following November, Welch won the women's division of the New York City Marathon outright, running 2:30:17 just a few weeks before her 43rd birthday.

Welch continued to compete internationally at a high level into her late forties. Not only did she dominate running in her age division, but she was also always one of the friendliest and most personable competitive runners of the day, freely sharing advice, speaking to audiences around the world, and encouraging others to follow her example of giving up smoking and taking control of their lives. She was also a proponent of cross-training, living a balanced life with running, and taking advantage of massage and physical therapy to extend one's running career and enhance the enjoyment of running.

At age 48 Welch was diagnosed with breast cancer and underwent a single mastectomy and chemotherapy treatment. She recovered and continued to compete and travel to road races and other running events. The cancer returned several years later and Welch had a second surgery. Now 57, Welch is retired from competitive running, though she and Dave still run for health, fitness, and companionship on the roads and trails near their home in Boulder, Colorado. She continues to inspire other runners with her example of success, her triumph over cancer, and her belief that not only is it never too late to start running, but that nothing, at any age, need ever stand in the way of the pursuit of health.

### The Benefits of Running as We Get Older

Running for people over age 50 is healthy for the same reasons that it is healthy for people at any age. However, many of the health and fitness benefits of running can become even more significant later in life. Studies show the greatest gains for those who make the shift from a sedentary lifestyle to one that includes even a small amount of exercise, but the most recent evidence shows that benefits increase as activity level rises. Here is a summary of the benefits of running for the 50-plus crowd.

• *A longer life.* A number of large, well-controlled scientific studies have shown that men and women who engage in regular physical activity live longer than those who are sedentary. In a renowned

1986 study by Ralph Paffenbarger, Ph.D., of nearly 17,000 male Harvard University alumni, those who expended at least 2,000 calories per week in exercise—the equivalent of running about 20 miles—lived an average of two years longer than men who expended fewer calories in exercise. In one survey by the American Cancer Society, of more than a million people, those who were active on a regular basis had lower death rates from all causes.

• *Lowered risk of heart-related problems.* In particular, the effects of aerobic exercise on the strength of the heart and the efficiency of the circulatory system translate into a lessening of the risks of heart disease and other heart problems. (See Chapter 2 for a discussion of the positive effects of running and other aerobic exercise on the heart and cardiovascular system.) As we get older, maximum heart rate (the fastest rate at which the heart can beat to pump blood through the body) gradually declines. To compensate, the heart's chambers must expand (dilate) more to take in blood, then squeeze (contract) more forcefully to pump blood through the body. Regular exercise increases the heart's ability to dilate and contract, which eases the burden on the heart during all activities. Thus, keeping the heart and lungs strong and healthy can help improve quality of life with age because activities can be performed with less effort.

• *Stronger muscles and bones.* As discussed in Chapter 2, running makes the major muscles stronger, especially those of the lower body. This can help counteract the gradual, progressive losses of muscle strength and endurance that occur with age (which is thought to be mainly a result of lowered activity levels rather than an inevitable result of "aging"). Stronger muscles offer many health and lifestyle benefits to older people: greater mobility, enhanced ability to perform basic life tasks (walking, pushing, pulling, lifting, etc.), and resistance to fatigue from ordinary daily tasks. In addition, research shows that increasing muscle strength—especially through weight-bearing activities such as running—increases the density of the bones that those muscles support. As outlined in Chapter 11, keeping bones strong plays a major role in preventing the development and progression of osteoporosis, a bone-thinning disease that affects a disproportionate number of older women and can cause bone fractures and the collapse of vertebrae.

• *Enhanced social connections.* As an activity that lends itself easily to the companionship of others and can be performed in a group setting, running can help older people avoid isolation and strengthen their connections to both their peer group and people of all ages. The people they are most likely to meet through running will share their commitment to a healthy and active lifestyle.

• *A sharper mind.* In studies led by Robert Friedland, M.D., a neurologist at Case Western Reserve University School of Medicine and University Hospitals of Cleveland, Ohio, 193 people with Alzheimer's disease whose age averaged 73 were compared with 358 people whose age averaged 71 and who did not have Alzeimer's. (The researchers accounted for other factors that are believed to influence Alzheimer's risk, such as education, income, and gender.) The subjects who were less active were more than three times more likely to have Alzheimer's disease, compared to those who were more active. In a separate study conducted at California State University at Fullerton, elderly women who exercised three or more times per week had physical and verbal response times equal to those of inactive college-age women.

• *Reduction in symptoms of menopause.* Women's experiences of menopause vary considerably, and it is not clear whether running makes a difference in terms of symptoms. In a 1998 survey conducted by the Melpomene Institute for Women's Health Research, 625 women runners whose average age was 50.8 responded to questions about running, aging, and menopause. Of the 82 percent of respondents who had noticed signs and symptoms of menopause, the vast majority reported that running had helped reduce menopausal symptoms, which included hot flashes, mood swings, depression, sleep problems, and night sweats. The women also reported that running helped them control menopausal weight gain, and increased their energy levels and motivation. (See Chapter 11 for more on running and menopause.)

• *Reduced risk of depression and other mental illnesses.* As discussed in Chapter 6, running and other types of exercise can help lower the risk of a variety of mental illnesses, including depression. The incidence of depression increases with age, so this association may be especially pertinent to those age 50 and over.

## QUESTION AND ANSWER

**Q.** I've been running five to six days per week for years, but lately I feel tired and sore on that schedule. How can I adjust my running program?

**A.** The first rule of running—especially if you want to enjoy it for a lifetime—is to listen to your body. As outlined on pages 308–315, even the fittest, healthiest body undergoes age-related changes that can affect running performance and the impact of running on the body. Most people find they get more out of running as they age if they gradually reduce the intensity, duration, and frequency of their runs. If running five to six days per week feels excessive—even though that is what you're used to—try shifting to a four-to-five-day-a-week running schedule. On the other days do some strength training and/or flexibility work to maintain overall fitness and keep up the pattern of regular exercise. (See Chapter 9 for more on strength training and Chapter 5 for more on stretching and other flexibility exercises.) You might also try replacing at least one of your weekly runs with cross-training, such as cycling or water exercise. These alternative exercises place less impact stress on the body than running, and provide a refreshing alternative. (See Chapter 9 for more information on cross-training.) Keep an open mind as to what is the "best" overall running and fitness program for you, and realize that your program will probably continue to change over time. Your goal should be to remain healthy and fit, and to enjoy your running, not to adhere to a schedule that's set in stone.

### Starting a Running Program After Age 50

People age 50 and over who have never exercised formally, or who have been inactive for a long period of time, may be concerned about possible risks associated with vigorous exercise.

There is no denying that exercise presents a challenge to the body and mind. In particular there is an increased—though still minuscule—risk after 50 that vigorous exercise will stress the unconditioned heart in ways that could cause damage, or even trigger a life-threatening heart attack.

The fact is, most people who start exercising at any age will benefit from a sensible, moderate program that gradually increases the intensity and duration of the activity. Still, many health experts recommend that people over 50 see a doctor before starting a regular exercise program. The American Heart Association advises seeing a doctor *at any age* for a medical evaluation before beginning any physical activity if you've been sedentary for a long time, are overweight, or have a high risk of coronary heart disease or another chronic health problem. The evaluation may include an exercise stress test, which usually involves walking or jogging on a treadmill or riding a stationary bicycle. The test is performed in a doctor's office or laboratory while you are hooked up to an electrocardiograph, a machine that records the electrical activity of the heart. The information is recorded as an electrocardiogram (ECG or EKG), which can diagnose coronary artery disease. Blood pressure, heart rate, and the rhythms of the heart are also measured.

Once you have received medical clearance to exercise, it's best to start with a walk/run program, such as that outlined in Chapter 1. This program can be adjusted for people who want or need to progress more slowly than the schedule suggests, or those who want to continue to combine walking and running indefinitely, rather than shifting to a running-only program.

I also recommend that if you are starting to walk and/or run after age 50 you include strength-training activities in your exercise program because of the importance of maintaining bone and muscle strength as we age. From age 30 on, we lose about 3 to 6 percent of our total muscle mass per decade, mostly as the result of a decrease in activity levels rather than "aging" per se. Research shows that strength training can restore lost muscle mass, and that it is never too late to reap the benefits. In one study at the U.S. Department of Agriculture's Human Nutrition Research Center on Aging at Tufts University in Boston, 10 men and women whose age averaged in their nineties participated in an eight-week strength-training program working their leg muscles. Their strength increased by an average of 174 percent, and muscle area (measured by CT scan) increased by 9 percent. Two of the participants no longer needed the aid of a cane for walking after completing the program. Cross-training activities can also offer particular benefits to those age 50 and over who suffer from joint problems, as many cross-training activities are easier than running on the joints of the lower body (see Chapter 9 for more on strength training and cross-training).

## INSPIRATIONAL 50-PLUS RUNNERS

Among runners age 50 and over, hundreds of athletes are pursuing the sport at a high competitive level. They are proof that running is indeed a life-promoting, life-extending, and life-affirming activity. In the words of John Mc-Manus, the 2001 New York Road Runners Club's Runner of the Year in the age 70–74 division, "We're running for our lives." He speaks for all senior-citizen runners—and his words offer inspiration to runners of any age.

At finish lines, awards ceremonies, and honorary banquets and celebrations for runners, it is the oldest runners who receive the loudest and most sustained cheers. They inspire not only their peers, but also runners of all ages. Here are just a few of the current crop of top-flight senior runners, and the inspiring stories of how they got there.

*Abraham Weintraub.* When 91-year-old Abraham (Abe) Weintraub mounted the stage at the 2001 New York Road Runners Club's "Club Night" awards banquet as the top age 90-plus runner for 2000, he received a standing ovation from the 900 assembled guests. They were applauding not only Weintraub's incredible achievement in the 2000 New York City Marathon, which he ran in 7:25:12 to set a world age-group record, but also his indomitable spirit. Weintraub was born in Brooklyn to Russian parents and came of age in a tough immigrant world. During the Great Depression he turned his hand to any type of work he could find to feed his family. He began running at age 80 when his wife, Ruthie, was suffering from Alzheimer's disease, and carried on after her death, determined to offer an example of fitness and perseverance in her honor. After receiving his "Club Night" award, Weintraub commented, "I'm so happy when I finish a race. That's my main purpose." Weintraub runs about 40 road races each year. He has run the New York City Marathon ten times and the London Marathon five times. USA Track & Field has honored him as their Masters Long Distance Runner of the Year. He is a member of a local club, the Ash Can Runners, whose members are all 80 and older. He lives on his own and trains mostly by walking all over Manhattan, up to eight miles a day—journeys he combines with shopping at gourmet food stores.

*Toshiko D'Elia.* Toshiko (Toshi) D'Elia is one of the winningest masters runners of her generation, and at age 72 she has no plans to retire. The first woman over age 50 to break three hours in the marathon (with a 2:57:25 in 1980, when she was 50), she is currently setting world and American records in the 70-plus division on the roads and track, including a national-record 49:30 for 10,000 meters on the track in August 2000 at the Masters World Track & Field Championships. Born in Kyoto, Japan, in 1930, D'Elia credits growing up in post–World War II Japan, and the discipline required to survive, as laying the groundwork for her success as a runner decades later. She came to the United States on a Fulbright Scholarship in 1951 and settled in New Jersey with her husband, Fred. In 1971 at age 41 she took up running as a way to stay in shape for mountain climbing. She was the third female finisher in the 1976 New York City Marathon, in a time of 3:08:17. Three years later she ran the Boston Marathon in 2:58:03. In March 2000 D'Elia lost Fred, her husband of 37 years. She had kept a low competitive profile while nursing him during his last months, yet has since returned to world-class form. She finds her attitude changed from when she was younger and ran up to 90 miles a week, with many of those miles done as quickly as possible. "When I was younger I was more time-oriented—how fast can I finish? It didn't matter what shape I was in at the finish!" she says. "Now, it's more important to maintain consistency and not lose running time to injury."

*John Keston.* In October 1996, then 71-year-old John Keston set a marathon world age-group record of 3:00:58 in the Twin Cities Marathon. He set his sights on becoming the first man over 70 to break three hours in the marathon. Since then, Keston has suffered a fractured hip in a bicycle accident, a broken ankle from slipping and falling in the snow, and a major back injury—and still he believes that national and world records in running are within his grasp. Keston was born in London in 1924, survived the World War II bombings of London, lied about his age to enlist in the Royal Air Force, and ended up in Italy, where he saw his first opera. After the war he trained in music and theater, eventually finding an outlet for his talents in

North America as a performer, recording artist, actor, and music teacher. At age 50 Keston took an academic position in Minnesota, and some of his students talked him into running with them. At age 55 he won his age division in a 10k race. At 62 he ran a marathon in 2:58. He placed first in the 60-plus age group in his next marathon by running 2:53.

Keston, who lives in Oregon and became a U.S. citizen in 1995, says his primary goal these days "are to stay healthy, get fitter, and look to see if I can possibly get some records." He runs three days a week and fitness-walks the other days. "A major goal is to keep up that regimen," he says. "My race goals are based mainly on time because at my age, I'm mostly competing against myself. I am happy to win my age group, but I'm also happy just to be out there having a go at it."

*Helen Klein.* "I'm nothing extraordinary," 79-year-old Helen Klein likes to tell audiences in the inspirational speeches she gives around the country. Don't believe it! Born in 1922, Klein began running in 1978. Though she had no previous athletic experience, she yearned to test her physical limits. The fact that she was the last finisher in her first 10-mile race made no difference to Klein. She was drawn to increasingly longer races, in which she saw that patience and intelligence could count as much as athletic giftedness. She completed the Hawaii Ironman Triathlon—one of the oldest people ever to do so—several months after she learned to ride a bicycle and swim.

Ultradistance running became Klein's consuming passion, and the ultra world started to take notice. To date, she has set more than 75 world and U.S. age-group and single-age (the record for one age year) records, at distances ranging from 50k through the 6-day run. In one 16-week period in 1989 she completed four 100-mile endurance trail runs, known as the "Grand Slam" of ultrarunning, then added a fifth 100-miler. In 1995 at age 72 she was part of a team that completed the Eco Challenge, a 370-mile multi-sport race with four teammates (she was at least twice the age of all of them). Klein and her husband, Norm, are co–race directors of the Western States 100-Mile Endurance Run in California. She sees herself as proof that in order to do something, you need only put your mind to it.

*Ed Whitlock.* On May 13, 2001, Canadian Ed Whitlock set an age 70–74 world record at the Forest City Marathon in London, Ontario, Canada. Whitlock ran 3:00:24—coming tantalizingly close to breaking the three-hour barrier, which no one over 70 has ever done—and setting a world age-group record. The running world knew a fast age 70-plus marathon was in the cards for Whitlock in October 2000, when at age 69 years, 237 days he became the oldest person ever to run a sub-3:00 marathon with an incredible 2:52:47 performance. Born in England in 1931, Whitlock ran the mile in 4:31.4 as a teenager. He moved to Canada in his early twenties and gave up running for the next 20 years. At age 48 he became the 1500-meter world champion in the 45–49 age division, and ran a marathon in 2:31:23. However, his job as a mining engineer prevented Whitlock from devoting much time to running in his fifties. In 1999, at 68, he again won the 1500-meter world championship in his age group, as well as the 5,000-meter title. Whitlock, who is now retired from his job, runs an average of two hours per day.

*Bill Rodgers.* Bill Rodgers has been called the "ambassador of running," and probably has the best name recognition outside the sport (along with 1972 Olympic marathon gold medalist Frank Shorter) in the United States. Born in 1947, Rodgers had a solid but unspectacular track and cross-country running career in high school and college. He resisted the draft during the Vietnam War and spent his first few years out of college as a drifter, often unemployed, smoking, drinking, and searching for direction. In 1975 he entered the Boston Marathon as a relative unknown and won in an American-record time of 2:09:55. He won Boston a total of four times (1975, '78, '79, and '80) and also won four New York City Marathon titles, from 1976 through '79. Unlike many of his peers, Rodgers continued to run competitively in the open (under-40) division well into his late thirties. Upon turning 40 in 1987, Rodgers embarked upon a magnificent masters running career. He set U.S. age-group and single-age records throughout his forties, all while owning and managing the Bill Rodgers Running Center in Boston, and traveling around the world to lecture and promote running as a sport and fitness activity to running and non-running audiences. Since turning 50 in 1997, Rodgers has continued to race competitively, though at a lower level due to some injuries and increasing involvement in the promotional aspects of the sport. Rodgers loves to share views and experiences with runners over 50. He believes in making some concessions to age (lowering time goals, allowing for more recovery, and incorporating stretching, massage, and other recovery methods consistently), but is equally fervent in his belief that anyone can run well—and competitively, if they choose—for a lifetime.

## QUESTION AND ANSWER

**Q.** I've recently started taking medication for high blood pressure. Should I make any adjustments to my running program?

**A.** You should talk to your doctor about the side effects of any medication you are prescribed, including the effects on running and other types of exercise. Drugs prescribed for high blood pressure (hypertension) can have a variety of effects, including lowered heart rate, dehydration, dry mouth, fatigue, and impaired muscle contractions. Obviously, these effects may have an impact on your running. Almost certainly there will be no need to eliminate running, but you may have to make some adjustments, at least temporarily, to the intensity or duration of your runs, or possibly substitute other forms of exercise for some of your running.

### Adjusting Your Running Program with Age

If you started running before age 50, you have most likely already noticed gradual changes in how your body handles the challenges of running, and have made some adjustments to the duration, intensity, and frequency of your running and any other exercises you engage in regularly. Most runners find, however, that the concessions they must make are gradual and subtle, rather than sudden and dramatic. This can be a mixed blessing. On the positive side, you're unlikely to head out for a run one day and find yourself unable to run anywhere near as fast or as far as you did the day before, or to see your race times suddenly worsening by a minute per mile. However, the changes are so gradual that many runners tend not to accept them, or attribute them to something other than aging, such as lack of motivation or willpower.

As an older runner, you must realize that by continuing to push your body to achieve the same running feats as you did in your twenties, thirties, and forties, you are doing more harm than good and will eventually break down or burn out on running. Fortunately, there are ever-increasing opportunities for age-group and age-graded running, which allow you to compare your performances to those of your peers. This is a lot more realistic and enjoyable than trying to maintain the fitness levels of athletes

10, 20, and 30 years your junior. And don't worry—you'll find the competition as intense as it ever was, if you want it. I have seen battles just as fierce among age 40+ runners as those in the open category. As a new entrant in the 40-and-over division, I feel just as excited about beating my masters rivals as I ever did about winning overall titles.

The list below outlines the physical and emotional changes—positive as well as negative—that many runners experience as they age, and suggestions for accommodating them.

• *Decreased aerobic capacity.* Your maximal oxygen capacity ($VO_2$ max) is the greatest amount of oxygen, in milliliters, that you can use per kilogram of body weight (see Chapter 2 for more on the science of running). Simply stated, it is a measure of how efficiently your body uses the air you breathe. Most elite runners in their prime have $VO_2$ max measures of 60 and higher. $VO_2$ max is determined by genetics, training—and age. After age 30, $VO_2$ max decreases about 1 percent per year, all other factors remaining equal. The changes have to do mainly with loss of lung capacity and heart function, and changes in slow-twitch muscle fiber. You can increase your $VO_2$ max at any age if you go from a sedentary lifestyle to a pattern that includes regular aerobic exercise. You can also maintain a $VO_2$ max well above that of your inactive peers by keeping up with regular aerobic activity. What you lose is the capacity to increase your $VO_2$ max to the level it was when you were running at a high level 10, 20, 30, or more years ago. This is the primary reason why you will seldom see older (age 40-plus) runners beating younger runners with similar genetic potential and training patterns at distances of 1500 meters and longer.

• *Decreased anaerobic capacity.* As discussed in Chapter 2, your anaerobic capacity is your body's ability to generate energy without the use of oxygen; instead it relies on the ATP-CP energy-generating system. Your anaerobic capacity determines your potential for fast, explosive running over short distances, such as 100-meter and 200-meter sprints. This ability to generate energy declines with age, due primarily to changes at the cellular level in the body's slow-twitch fibers. To maintain your anaerobic capacity, you must continue to do short, fast repetitions as part of your training. Racing short distances at a high level is beneficial as well. Unfortunately, this type of training and racing carries a high injury risk, as discussed in the following pages. For the over-50 runner, this necessitates extra-careful attention to stretching, warming up, cooling down, and recovering thoroughly between hard workouts and races.

• *Reduced tolerance for high mileage.* Almost universally, older runners find they cannot maintain the high mileage levels of their younger days without risking injury, illness, and burnout. There seem to be many reasons for this, including reduced $VO_2$ max (and the consequent slower training pace), loss of muscle strength and endurance, and loss of flexibility. In addition, many older runners who have been in the sport a long time find that the "miles in the legs" that they have accumulated over the years simply start to catch up with them. Vulnerable areas become more vulnerable, making them more susceptible to injury and overtraining even at mileage levels that they were able to handle comfortably in the past. Injury-prone runners in particular have to be careful to keep their mileage at a level they can handle without a mishap. Finally, older runners who have not yet retired from the work world, or who continue to have many demands on their time and energy due to family duties, volunteer work, etc., need to remember that these activities drain their time and energy, leaving them less of a reserve than they may have had when they were in their twenties and thirties and had fewer professional, family, or civic and community responsibilities.

• *Need for longer recovery periods.* Even the most gifted and best-trained runners need longer recovery periods from hard efforts as they age. It's unclear exactly why this is so, and why older runners take longer to recover from injury and to rebuild fitness after layoffs from running. As I age (I turned 40 in February 2001) I find that although my performance levels in workouts and races has been holding steady for the past two to three years, I am no longer able to perform at a high level as often as I did in the past. In my best running days it was standard for me to do two hard speed workouts per week, plus a long run or race just about every weekend. I would keep up this pattern practically year-round, with just a short break after each of my two marathons, one in the spring and one in the fall. These days I find that one hard workout per week is more often the standard. I am not able to handle as many high-quality long runs without feeling exhausted, and I have to settle for fewer races being at the run-my-guts-out level I used to attain at virtually every competitive outing. Other masters runners at all fitness and competitive levels tell of similar experiences. Jane Welzel, who at age 46 is one of the top American masters runners and competes frequently across the country, has shifted from a two-hard-workouts-and-a-long-run-per-week program like mine to the same pattern spread over 10 days to two weeks. I also hear again and again from older runners that they need longer recovery periods from injury. This is most likely due to a number of changes in the muscles, bones, and connective tissues. I recommend that you respect your body's need for longer recovery periods as you get older, and not try to fight it. The result of ignoring or trying to override your body's changes and needs will be frustration as you find that you simply cannot force yourself to respond to training the way you did in your running prime. Beyond that, you risk serious and potentially permanent injury from attempting to fight your changing body.

• *Loss of flexibility.* Flexibility is the ability to move your muscles and joints through a range of motion with comfort and efficiency. As noted in Chapter 5, flexibility is beneficial to runners because it allows for full exertion without strain against tight, inflexible muscles. It also makes running more comfortable and may help with injury prevention. There is some loss of flexibility with age, due to the reduced resiliency of tissues that occurs even with consistent stretching and conscientious lifestyle habits such as good posture. Anecdotal evidence suggests that age-related loss of flexibility can be countered by performing regular exercises designed to maintain flexibility, such as stretching and yoga. When I ask older runners what is the one thing they wish they'd done more of when they were younger, "stretching" is often the answer. On pages 128–130 you'll find stretches and other exercises for runners designed to maintain flexibility, at any age. You can also enhance flexibility by varying your pace in your running—which keeps muscles and joints accustomed to moving through a full range of motion—and maintaining good posture throughout the day.

• *Loss of muscle strength.* A loss of lean body mass (muscle) with age—especially the fast-twitch muscle fibers that contribute to explosive strength—seems to be inevitable. However, you can do a great deal to counteract that loss with a strength-training program. In addition, running up hills, cross-training, and performing plyometric drills are all effective muscle strengtheners. Preserving strength as you age not only can help improve your running performances and resistance to running-related injuries, it also can help maintain your fitness for everyday tasks, from unscrewing a stubborn jar lid to picking up a child.

• *Changes in motivation.* As discussed in Chapter 6, motivation in running can be a challenge at any age. The difficulty as you age is that unless you are very new to running, chances are your performances are no longer on the upswing. The last time I set a lifetime personal record (PR) at any distance was in 1995, when I was 34. Statistics culled from the world's fastest distance runners show that most peak in their late twenties to early thirties (though ultradistance runners tend to peak later, often in their late thirties and early forties). In addition, due to all the changes described above, running after age 50 can be less enjoyable than in the past. As a result, it's a rare 50-plus runner who doesn't occasionally wonder, "Why bother?" and contemplate taking up shuffleboard instead. Though I can't yet speak from a 50-plus runner's perspective, I believe that motivation is primarily a matter of having a positive attitude. If you have trouble maintaining your commitment to running, you may be seeing the glass as half-empty rather than half-full. Yes, you've become slower, stiffer, and more injury-prone than you used to be. You can't run as many miles, it takes you longer to recover from speed workouts and races, and your muscles ache when you get out of bed in the morning. But have you taken a look around your local mall or supermarket lately, and noticed the number of people your age who are overweight, huffing and puffing their way up a short flight of stairs, or forced to sit down and rest every 20 minutes? Have friends worried out loud about ending up in nursing homes, unable to care for themselves? Of course, genetics and luck play a huge role in who ends up blessed with a long and healthy life. But in general, when you compare your average 50-plus American with those you see on the running trails and lining up at road races, you can't help but feel motivated to continue to count yourself among the latter group. As noted through-out this chapter, staying fit as you age is clearly a "use it or lose it" situation. Other strategies for maintaining motivation as you age include finding running partners among your peers, varying your routine by cross-training and supplemental training, choosing new race distances or genres, and keeping a careful training log to determine if you are indeed overdoing it. My 69-year-old father is a good example. A former marathoner, he now runs two to three miles, three to four times a week. On the other days he walks with my mother, stretches and does crunches to keep his midsection strong and supple, or does yardwork. He races three or four times a year, usually 5ks or 4-milers, in contrast to the marathons and half-marathons that filled up his race calendar 20 to 30 years ago. (For more motivational tips, see Chap-ter 6.)

• *Lowered pain tolerance.* Many older runners, particularly those who have been highly competitive in the sport, tell me they simply can't "make it hurt" in workouts and races the way they used to. I find this to be the case myself. I'm not sure why it's so, but my theory is that the body has actually learned a thing or two and is seeking to protect itself. Running can be a painful experience. Like college students who live for four years on pizza, beer, and all-nighters, young runners are able to sustain a high level of physical stress for years before their bodies start to "talk back." After age 50, your body knows that you simply should not be pushing yourself beyond a certain point where injury or breakdown is the likely outcome. "Back off!" it tells you—and you are forced to listen. My advice is to heed the messages, and take a more relaxed approach to maintaining performance standards, particularly in workouts, rather than attempting to breach the pain threshold as though you still had the body of a 20-year-old.

• *More patience.* Along with all the seemingly negative results of growing older as a runner come a few positives. One of these is greater patience, which can be a tremendous asset in distance running. As discussed in Chapter 8, one of the biggest mistakes runners make when racing—and in speed workouts—is starting out at too-fast a pace. Often this stems from a feeling of impatience—a desire to "get on with it" rather than allowing the race to unfold. It may also come from insecurity, and the false belief that building up a "cushion" of time will minimize the effects of late-race slowing. Younger runners may also lack the patience needed to progress gradually and steadily in a running program, and invite injury and burnout by attempting to build fitness too quickly. All these pitfalls tend to be avoided by runners in their later years. Most have learned through experience that running can't be rushed—neither individual training runs and races, nor the long-term process of getting fit and integrating running into one's lifestyle.

• *More experience.* Older runners often make better decisions in the sport simply as a result of their experience. Time is a runner's best teacher. After 23 years of running, I sometimes wrongly feel that I've "done it all" and have very little left to learn. How wrong I am! Every training run and race continues to teach me—either by imparting brand-new lessons (elliptical training is a wonderful cross-training alternative) or reinforcing old ones (don't run too fast on your easy days). Some lessons don't happen until years into a running program. For example, I had been running competitively for about 10 years when I started a race once with my shoelaces tied too tightly. I tried to ignore it, but the pinching was throwing off my stride, which I worried was going to cause an injury. And it was terribly distracting. After much agonizing, I finally stopped and loosened my laces, and felt so much better that I realized I should have done it miles earlier. So I learned two lessons: One, adjust your lace tension before you get to the starting lines; and two, if they're too tight, do something about it right away. Countless other lessons have cropped up—and continue to occur—throughout my running career. Younger and less experienced runners simply haven't put in the years and the miles yet to learn them all.

• *Better lifestyle habits.* Studies of the overall population show that in general, older people tend to have better health habits than younger folks. They pay more attention to diet, sleep patterns, safety issues, and having regular medical checkups and screening tests. All else being equal, these healthy habits can set them up to reap greater rewards from their running. When my husband started running in his mid-twenties, he had a high-fat diet, worked long hours, frequently went out late with friends, and drank heavily several times a month. In his early thirties he started to notice the negative effects of these habits on his running and overall well-being, and gradually modified them. I know that now that I am in my forties, I simply cannot function effectively as a runner, parent, employee, and community member unless I live a clean lifestyle—regular hours, careful attention to diet, and little or no drinking. I'm not saying you have to become a teetotaling vegetarian who's in bed by 9:30 every night in order to realize your running potential, but in my experience and that of other runners I know, living moderately certainly helps, especially as you get older. Fortunately, by age 50 most people have sown enough wild oats that living a clean life isn't really an issue.

## QUESTION AND ANSWER

**Q.** My 75-year-old husband wants to train for a marathon. Is there any reason for him not to try it?

**A.** People in their nineties complete marathons, so a healthy 75-year-old who wishes to train for and enter a marathon should not be discouraged. If your husband is starting to run for the first time, he should see a doctor for a medical evaluation and an exercise stress test; this will reveal any undiagnosed heart problems that could be dangerous (see page 303 for a complete description of this test). A marathon is an ambitious running goal for anyone, and should not be undertaken lightly. Your husband should start with a walk/run program (see the schedules presented in Chapter 1) and plan some tune-up races. A marathon can be a motivating, defining, and life-enhancing experience for runners of all ages. You might even want to train with your husband!

▶ ▶ ▶ ▶ ▶ ▶ ▶ ▶ ▶ ▶ ▶ ▶ ▶ ▶ ▶ ▶ ▶ ▶ ▶ ▶ ▶ ▶ ▶ ▶ ▶ ▶ ▶ ▶ ▶ ▶

# *Final Thoughts*

*I*ran a race today. It was a 5k in Central Park on a gorgeous early fall morning. How many times, I wondered as I was warming up, have my feet hit the asphalt of those roads, whether racing or training on my well-known loops? I lined up with the other runners, some of whom I've been competing against for close to two decades, and was struck by the sense of how familiar everything seemed—the adrenaline flow, the anticipation of a challenge, the last-minute checking of shoelaces—yet at the same time, how completely new. How would the race turn out? Would I win, or even place? Would I meet my time goal? Would disaster ensue in the form of a slip at a water station, a sudden muscle pull, or a collision with an errant spectator? Or would something miraculous take place, such as a time far faster than my recent workouts suggested? What would I see and hear along the way, and what emotions would I experience?

I realized that I couldn't answer any of those questions with certainty. And that was why I was there, number pinned to my singlet, shoes double-knotted, body poised to move forward: to find out. And that too is why I get up nearly every morning, put on running clothes and shoes, and go for a run. I run to learn about myself, what I can do and what I can't, what I want and what I don't, and how to create something that's important to me. I run to learn about the world around me, about other people and their capabilities, desires, and motivations. The knowledge I seek is simple, elemental. It strips away pretension and gets to the essence of life. At its core, it's the most real thing I know.

As it happened, today's race turned into a real barn burner. I ran within yards of three other women through the first two miles, at which point I began to slowly pull away. For the final mile, everything hurt as I strained forward, not wanting to show weakness or uncertainty by looking back, yet desperate to know if I had any kind of sizable lead so I could ease off just a little. I gave it everything in the final quarter mile and finished first in a time that bettered anything I'd done in the past five years. The main lesson was that I can do just about anything I put my mind to and that good competition brings out my best—things I've known about myself for a long time.

I hope you learn from this book—some new lessons perhaps, but also lessons about yourself and your running that you already, on some level, know. What I hope most is that running becomes for you, if it isn't already, a journey of discovery and knowledge about yourself and the world around you. If this book and the resources within it can act as any sort of road map or traveler's advisory, then it will have served its purpose.

# ACKNOWLEDGMENTS

*I* am grateful to so many people who helped make this book possible.

First, to all the "real" runners in my life: training partners past and present, who have shared much more than fitness; competitors who have inspired me with their talent and dedication to bring out the best in myself; those brave souls who have entrusted themselves to my coaching advice, especially the women of Moving Comfort New York racing team.

Second, to those pioneers, living and departed, who ran before it was commonplace or even acceptable, who broke down barriers, and who achieved amazing athletic feats without the benefits of today's scientific insights and functional equipment; and to those who recorded their stories.

Third, to anyone who has ever had the guts and passion to call himself or herself a "runner," and who has yearned to fully integrate that self-identity.

I am particularly grateful for the insights of Jack Daniels, David Martin, Tim Noakes, and Pete Pfitzinger. All are dedicated scientists who share a gift for translating technical data into language that can be understood and utilized by the layperson. As a non-scientist I have found their writings and personal communications invaluable in furthering my understanding of the science of running.

I also deeply appreciate the support of New York Road Runners of my efforts as a writer and runner, as well as that of Jonathan Beverly and the staff of *Running Times* magazine, which offers an ongoing forum for my ideas.

This project would not have gotten off the ground without the support of my longtime agent, Meredith Bernstein, who for years urged me to write "another running book" and worked closely with me to refine that vision and allow me to make it a reality.

In addition, I gratefully acknowledge the vision, unwavering enthusiasm, intelligent insight, and hard work of my editors (and fellow runners), Anika Streitfelds and Shauna Summers of Ballantine Books. I am deeply indebted to Anika, Shauna, and their colleagues for believing in this project and working side by side with me at every stage of its writing, editing, and production.

Finally, I thank my husband, Alan Ruben, for his genuine belief and interest in this book, and for taking on more than his share of childcare duties when deadlines loomed large. And I thank my children, Joey and Sammy, for making me smile and reminding me of the joys of running.

# BIBLIOGRAPHY

The following books are part of my running "library." They are not intended as an exhaustive list of books on the subject of running. Rather, they are among those on running and related topics that I have found the most useful, inspirational, and readable over the years.

## AGING:

*Running and Racing After 35* by Allan Lawrence and Mark Scheid. Boston: Little, Brown, 1990.

*Running Past 50* by Richard Benyo. Champaign, IL: Human Kinetics, 1998.

## CROSS-TRAINING/SUPPLEMENTAL TRAINING:

*Cross-Training* by Gordon Bakoulis Bloch. New York: Fireside Books, 1992.

*On the Run: Exercise and Fitness for Busy People* by Grete Waitz. Emmaus, PA: Rodale Press, 2000.

*Power Yoga* by Beryl Bender Birch. New York: Fireside Books, 1995.
*Stretching* by Bob Anderson. London: Pelham Books, 1980.
*The Whartons' Stretch Book* by Jim and Phil Wharton. New York: Times Books, 1997.


EXERCISE SCIENCE:

*Aerobics* by Kenneth H. Cooper, M.D. New York: Bantam Books, 1968.
*Exercise Physiology: Energy, Nutrition, and Human Performance* by William D. McArdle, Frank L. Katch, and Victor L. Katch. Philadelphia: Lea & Febiger, 1991.
*Lore of Running* by Tim Noakes, Ph.D. Champaign, IL: Human Kinetics, 1991.
*Periodization Training for Sports* by Tudor O. Bompa, Ph.D. Champaign, IL: Human Kinetics, 1999.


HISTORY:

*The American Marathon* by Pamela Cooper. Syracuse, NY: Syracuse University Press, 1998.
*Boston Marathon* by Tom Derderian. Champaign, IL: Human Kinetics, 1996.
*The New York City Marathon: Twenty-Five Years* by Peter Gambaccini. New York: Rizzoli, 1994.


INSPIRATION:

*The Elements of Effort* by John Jerome. New York: Breakaway Books, 1997.
*Magical Running: A Unique Path the Running Fulfillment* by Bobby McGee. Bobbysez Publishing, 2000.
*The Quotable Runner* by Mark Will-Weber. New York: Breakaway Books, 1995.
*Racing the Antelope: What Animals Can Teach Us About Running and Life* by Bernd Heinrich. New York: Cliff Street Books, 2001.
*The Runner's Guide to the Meaning of Life* by Amby Burfoot. Emmaus, PA: Rodale Press, 2000.
*The Runner's Literary Companion*, edited by Garth Battista. New York: Breakaway Books, 1994.
*Running for the Soul* by Claudia Piepenburg. San Diego: Road Runner Sports, 2000.
*Running Within* by Jerry Lynch and Warren Scott. Champaign, IL: Human Kinetics, 1999.

*World Class* by Grete Waitz and Gloria Averbuch. New York: Warner
    Books, 1986.


MARATHON:

*The Essential Marathoner* by John Hanc and Grete Waitz. New York: Lyons
    & Burford, 1996.
*First Marathons: Personal Encounters With the 26.2-Mile Monster* by Gail
    Waesche Kislevitz. New York: Breakaway Books, 1999.
*How to Train for and Run Your Best Marathon* by Gordon Bakoulis Bloch.
    New York: Fireside Books, 1993.


NUTRITION:

*Eat Smart, Play Hard: Fueling for Maximum Fitness and Peak Performance* by
    Liz Applegate, Ph.D. Emmaus, PA: Rodale Press, 2001.
*Endurance Sports Nutrition* by Suzanne Girard Eberle, M.S., R.D.
    Champaign, IL: Human Kinetics, 2000.
*Nancy Clark's Sports Nutrition Guidebook* by Nancy Clark, M.S., R.D. Cham-
    paign, IL: Human Kinetics, 1998.


SPORTS MEDICINE:

*The Complete Sports Medicine Book for Women* by Mona Shangold, M.D., and
    Gabe Mirkin, M.D. New York: Fireside Books, 1992.
*Sure Footing: A Sports Podiatrist's Perspective on Running- and Exercise-Related
    Injuries* by Peter H. Julien, D.P.M. Atlanta: 1998.


TRAINING:

*Better Training for Distance Runners* by David E. Martin, Ph.D., and Peter
    M. Coe. Champaign, IL: Human Kinetics, 1997.
*Bill Rodgers' Lifetime Running Plan* by Bill Rodgers, with Scott Douglas.
    New York: HarperCollins, 1996.
*The Competitive Runner's Handbook: The Bestselling Guide to Running 5Ks
    Through Marathons* by Bob Glover and Shelly-Lynn Florence Glover.
    New York: Penguin, 1999.
*Daniels' Running Formula* by Jack Daniels, Ph.D., Champaign, IL: Human
    Kinetics, 1998.
*The Essential Runner* by John Hanc. New York: Lyons & Burford, 1994.
*Galloway's Book on Running* by Jeff Galloway. Shelter Publications, 1984.

*The New York Road Runners Club Complete Book of Running* by Fred Lebow, Gloria Averbuch, and friends. New York: Random House, 1992.

*Road Racing for Serious Runners* by Pete Pfitzinger and Scott Douglas. Champaign, IL: Human Kinetics, 1999.

*Running 101* by Joe Henderson and Hal Higdon. Champaign, IL: Human Kinetics, 2000.

*Running for Dummies* by Florence Griffith Joyner and John Hanc. Foster City, CA: IDG Books, 1999.

*The* Running Times *Guide to Breakthrough Running,* edited by Gordon Bakoulis and Candace Karu. Champaign, IL: Human Kinetics, 2000.

*Runner's World Complete Book of Running,* edited by Amby Burfoot. Emmaus, PA: Rodale Press, 1997.

*The Total Runner's Log: The Essential Training Tool for the Runner* by Sharon Svensson. Trimarket, 2000.


WOMEN:

*The Bodywise Woman* by Judy Mahle Lutter and Lynn Jaffee. Champaign, IL: Human Kinetics, 1996.

*The Complete Book of Running for Women* by Claire Kowalchik. New York: Pocket Books, 1999.

*Exercising Through Your Pregnancy* by James F. Clapp III. Champaign, IL: Human Kinetics, 1998.

*Running and Walking for Women Over 40: The Road to Sanity and Vanity* by Kathrine Switzer. New York: St. Martin's Press, 1998.

Runner's World *Complete Book of Women's Running* by Dagny Scott and Amby Burfoot. Emmaus, PA: Rodale Press, 2000.

*Women Runners,* edited by Irene Reti and Bettianne Shoney Sein. New York: Breakaway Books, 2001.

▶▶▶▶▶▶▶▶▶▶▶▶▶▶▶▶▶▶▶▶▶▶▶▶▶▶▶▶▶▶▶▶

# Organizations, Publications, and Web Sites

## ORGANIZATIONS

*Charity:*

Joints in Motion
Arthritis Foundation
P.O. Box 7669
Atlanta, GA 30357-0669
(800) 283-7800
www.jointsinmotion.com

Team in Training
The Leukemia & Lymphoma Society Inc.
1311 Mamaroneck Avenue
White Plains, NY 10605
(914) 949-5213
www.teamintraining.org

*Federations:*

International Amateur Athletics Federation
17, Rue Princesse Florestine
Monaco, Monte Carlo 9800
(33) 9330-7070
www.iaaf.org

USA Track & Field
One RCA Dome, Suite 140
Indianapolis, IN 46225
(317) 261-0500
www.usatf.org
long-distance running division: www.usaldr.org

USA Triathlon
3595 E. Fountain Blvd., Suite F-1
Colorado Springs, CO 80910
(719) 597-9090

*Running-related information:*

American College of Sports Medicine
401 W. Michigan Street
Indianapolis, IN 46202-3233
(317) 637-9200
www.acsm.org

American Running Association
4405 East-West Highway, Suite 405
Bethesda, MD 20814
(301) 913-9517
(800) 776-2732
www.americanrunning.org

Fifty-Plus Fitness Association
P.O. Box 20230
Stanford, California 94309
(650) 323-6160
www.50plus.org

National Distance Running Hall of Fame
114 Genesee Street
Utica, NY 13502
(315) 724-4525

Road Runners Club of America
510 North Washington Street
Alexandria, VA 22314
(703) 836-0558
www.rrca.org

*Women:*

Melpomene Institute for Women's Health Research
1010 University Avenue
St. Paul, MN 55104
(651) 642-1951
www.melpomene.org

Women's Sports Foundation
Eisenhower Park
East Meadow, NY 11554
(800) 227-3988 (U.S. only)
(516) 542-4700

## PUBLICATIONS

*Marathon & Beyond*
206 North Randolph Street, Suite 502
Champaign, IL 61820
(217) 359-9345
www.marathonandbeyond.com

*National Masters News*
P.O. Box 50098
Eugene, OR 97405
(541) 343-7716
www.nationalmastersnews.com

*Runner's World*
135 North 6th Street
Emmaus, PA 18098
(610) 967-5171
www.runnersworld.com

*Running Research News*
P.O. Box 27041
Lansing, MI 48909
(517) 371-4897
www.rrnews.com

*Running Times*
213 Danbury Road
Wilton, CT 06897
(203) 761-1113
www.runningtimes.com

*Track & Field News*
2570 El Camino Real
Mountain View, CA 94040
(650) 948-8417

## WEB SITES

As with any subject, hundreds of Web sites are devoted to running and
related topics. This list includes some of the most comprehensive
and popular sites, as well as those related to specific topics covered
in this book. Happy browsing!

American Anorexia Bulimia Association: www.aabainc.org
A comprehensive site offering a wealth of information on eating
disorders.

American Dietetic Association: www.eatright.org
Information, advice, referrals, links relating to food, nutrition, and
eating.

Cool Running: www.coolrunning.com
This site's main draw is its links to a large number of races nationwide;
also includes news, training advice, race calendars, and more.

New York Road Runners: www.nyrrc.org
Comprehensive site of the world's largest running club and organizers
of the New York City Marathon. Coverage, news, events, information,
advice, and many links.

Run the Planet: www.runtheplanet.com
Information on running in locales around the world; useful if traveling
or relocating.

*Runner's World:* www.runnersworld.com
Training and nutrition information and advice; news; race calendars;
statistics; women's, children's, and masters running; running camps;
etc.—many links.

*Running Times:* www.runningtimes.com
Expert advice, race calendars, running camps, travel guide, shoe guides, rankings, pace charts, etc.; many links.

*Something Fishy:* www.something-fishy.org
A very helpful and comprehensive site for doctors, patients, friends, and families dealing with eating disorders.

*The Physician and Sportsmedicine:* www.physsportsmed.com
This useful site includes abstracts of hundreds of articles relating to sports medicine; links to related sites.

▶ ▶ ▶ ▶ ▶ ▶ ▶ ▶ ▶ ▶ ▶ ▶ ▶ ▶ ▶ ▶ ▶ ▶ ▶ ▶ ▶ ▶ ▶ ▶ ▶ ▶ ▶ ▶ ▶ ▶

# *Running Pace Chart*

## PACE CHART

| Mile | 5K | 5M | 10K | 15K | 10M | 20K | 13.1M | 15M | 25K | 30K | 20M | 26.2M |
|------|------|------|------|------|------|------|------|------|------|------|------|------|
| 4:40 | 0:14:30 | 0:23:20 | 0:29:00 | 0:43:30 | 0:46:40 | 0:58:00 | 1:01:11 | 1:10:00 | 1:12:30 | 1:27:00 | 1:33:20 | 2:02:21 |
| 4:50 | 0:15:01 | 0:24:10 | 0:30:02 | 0:45:03 | 0:48:20 | 1:00:04 | 1:03:22 | 1:12:30 | 1:15:05 | 1:30:06 | 1:36:40 | 2:06:43 |
| 5:00 | 0:15:32 | 0:25:00 | 0:31:04 | 0:46:36 | 0:50:00 | 1:02:08 | 1:05:33 | 1:15:00 | 1:17:40 | 1:33:12 | 1:40:00 | 2:11:05 |
| 5:10 | 0:16:03 | 0:25:50 | 0:32:06 | 0:48:09 | 0:51:40 | 1:04:12 | 1:07:44 | 1:17:30 | 1:20:15 | 1:36:18 | 1:43:20 | 2:15:27 |
| 5:20 | 0:16:34 | 0:26:40 | 0:33:08 | 0:49:42 | 0:53:20 | 1:06:16 | 1:09:55 | 1:20:00 | 1:22:50 | 1:39:24 | 1:46:40 | 2:19:49 |
| 5:30 | 0:17:05 | 0:27:30 | 0:34:10 | 0:51:15 | 0:55:00 | 1:08:20 | 1:12:06 | 1:22:30 | 1:25:25 | 1:42:30 | 1:50:00 | 2:24:11 |
| 5:40 | 0:17:36 | 0:28:20 | 0:35:12 | 0:52:48 | 0:56:40 | 1:10:24 | 1:14:17 | 1:25:00 | 1:28:00 | 1:45:36 | 1:53:20 | 2:28:33 |
| 5:50 | 0:18:07 | 0:29:10 | 0:36:14 | 0:54:21 | 0:58:20 | 1:12:28 | 1:16:28 | 1:27:30 | 1:30:35 | 1:48:42 | 1:56:40 | 2:32:55 |
| 6:00 | 0:18:38 | 0:30:00 | 0:37:17 | 0:55:54 | 1:00:00 | 1:14:32 | 1:18:39 | 1:30:00 | 1:33:10 | 1:51:48 | 2:00:00 | 2:37:17 |
| 6:10 | 0:19:09 | 0:30:50 | 0:38:18 | 0:57:27 | 1:01:40 | 1:16:36 | 1:20:50 | 1:32:30 | 1:35:45 | 1:54:54 | 2:03:20 | 2:41:39 |
| 6:20 | 0:19:40 | 0:31:40 | 0:39:22 | 0:59:00 | 1:03:20 | 1:18:40 | 1:23:01 | 1:35:00 | 1:38:20 | 1:58:00 | 2:06:40 | 2:46:01 |
| 6:30 | 0:20:11 | 0:32:30 | 0:40:24 | 1:00:33 | 1:05:00 | 1:20:44 | 1:25:12 | 1:37:30 | 1:40:55 | 2:01:06 | 2:10:00 | 2:50:23 |
| 6:40 | 0:20:42 | 0:33:20 | 0:41:26 | 1:02:06 | 1:06:40 | 1:22:48 | 1:27:23 | 1:40:00 | 1:43:30 | 2:04:12 | 2:13:20 | 2:54:45 |
| 6:50 | 0:21:13 | 0:34:10 | 0:42:28 | 1:03:39 | 1:08:20 | 1:24:52 | 1:29:34 | 1:42:30 | 1:46:05 | 2:07:18 | 2:16:40 | 2:59:07 |
| 7:00 | 0:21:44 | 0:35:00 | 0:43:30 | 1:05:12 | 1:10:00 | 1:26:56 | 1:31:45 | 1:45:00 | 1:48:40 | 2:10:24 | 2:20:00 | 3:03:29 |

| Mile | 5K | 5M | 10K | 15K | 10M | 20K | 13.1M | 15M | 25K | 30K | 20M | 26.2M |
|------|------|------|------|------|------|------|------|------|------|------|------|------|
| 7:10 | 0:22:15 | 0:35:50 | 0:44:32 | 1:06:45 | 1:11:40 | 1:29:00 | 1:33:56 | 1:47:30 | 1:51:15 | 2:13:30 | 2:23:20 | 3:07:51 |
| 7:20 | 0:22:46 | 0:36:40 | 0:45:34 | 1:08:18 | 1:13:20 | 1:31:04 | 1:36:07 | 1:50:00 | 1:53:50 | 2:16:36 | 2:26:40 | 3:12:13 |
| 7:30 | 0:23:17 | 0:37:30 | 0:46:36 | 1:09:51 | 1:15:00 | 1:33:08 | 1:38:18 | 1:52:30 | 1:56:25 | 2:19:42 | 2:30:00 | 3:16:35 |
| 7:40 | 0:23:48 | 0:38:20 | 0:47:38 | 1:11:24 | 1:16:40 | 1:35:12 | 1:40:29 | 1:55:00 | 1:59:00 | 2:22:48 | 2:33:20 | 3:20:57 |
| 7:50 | 0:24:19 | 0:39:10 | 0:48:40 | 1:12:57 | 1:18:20 | 1:37:16 | 1:42:40 | 1:57:30 | 2:01:35 | 2:25:54 | 2:36:40 | 3:25:19 |
| 8:00 | 0:24:50 | 0:40:00 | 0:49:42 | 1:14:30 | 1:20:00 | 1:39:20 | 1:44:51 | 2:00:00 | 2:04:10 | 2:29:00 | 2:40:00 | 3:29:41 |
| 8:10 | 0:25:21 | 0:40:50 | 0:50:44 | 1:16:03 | 1:21:40 | 1:41:24 | 1:47:02 | 2:02:30 | 2:06:45 | 2:32:06 | 2:43:20 | 3:34:03 |
| 8:20 | 0:25:52 | 0:41:40 | 0:51:46 | 1:17:36 | 1:23:20 | 1:43:28 | 1:49:13 | 2:05:00 | 2:09:20 | 2:35:12 | 2:46:40 | 3:38:25 |
| 8:30 | 0:26:23 | 0:42:30 | 0:52:48 | 1:19:09 | 1:25:00 | 1:45:32 | 1:51:24 | 2:07:30 | 2:11:55 | 2:38:18 | 2:50:00 | 3:42:47 |
| 8:40 | 0:26:54 | 0:43:20 | 0:53:50 | 1:20:42 | 1:26:40 | 1:47:36 | 1:53:35 | 2:10:00 | 2:14:30 | 2:41:24 | 2:53:20 | 3:47:09 |
| 8:50 | 0:27:25 | 0:44:10 | 0:54:52 | 1:22:15 | 1:28:20 | 1:49:40 | 1:55:46 | 2:12:30 | 2:17:05 | 2:44:30 | 2:56:40 | 3:51:31 |
| 9:00 | 0:27:56 | 0:45:00 | 0:55:54 | 1:23:48 | 1:30:00 | 1:51:44 | 1:57:57 | 2:15:00 | 2:19:40 | 2:47:36 | 3:00:00 | 3:55:53 |
| 9:10 | 0:28:27 | 0:45:50 | 0:56:56 | 1:25:21 | 1:31:40 | 1:53:48 | 2:00:08 | 2:17:30 | 2:22:15 | 2:50:42 | 3:03:20 | 4:00:15 |
| 9:20 | 0:28:58 | 0:46:40 | 0:57:58 | 1:26:54 | 1:33:20 | 1:55:52 | 2:02:19 | 2:20:00 | 2:24:50 | 2:53:48 | 3:06:40 | 4:04:37 |
| 9:30 | 0:29:29 | 0:47:30 | 0:59:00 | 1:28:27 | 1:35:00 | 1:57:56 | 2:04:30 | 2:22:30 | 2:27:25 | 2:56:54 | 3:10:00 | 4:08:59 |
| 9:40 | 0:30:00 | 0:48:20 | 1:00:02 | 1:30:00 | 1:36:40 | 2:00:00 | 2:06:41 | 2:25:00 | 2:30:00 | 3:00:00 | 3:13:20 | 4:13:21 |
| 9:50 | 0:30:31 | 0:49:10 | 1:01:04 | 1:31:33 | 1:38:20 | 2:02:04 | 2:08:52 | 2:27:30 | 2:32:35 | 3:03:06 | 3:16:40 | 4:17:43 |
| 10:00 | 0:31:02 | 0:50:00 | 1:02:06 | 1:33:06 | 1:40:00 | 2:04:08 | 2:11:03 | 2:30:00 | 2:35:10 | 3:06:12 | 3:20:00 | 4:22:05 |
| 10:10 | 0:31:33 | 0:50:50 | 1:03:08 | 1:34:39 | 1:41:40 | 2:06:12 | 2:13:14 | 2:32:30 | 2:37:45 | 3:09:18 | 3:23:20 | 4:26:27 |
| 10:20 | 0:32:04 | 0:51:40 | 1:04:10 | 1:36:12 | 1:43:20 | 2:08:16 | 2:15:25 | 2:35:00 | 2:40:20 | 3:12:24 | 3:26:40 | 4:30:49 |
| 10:30 | 0:32:35 | 0:52:30 | 1:05:12 | 1:37:45 | 1:45:00 | 2:10:20 | 2:17:36 | 2:37:30 | 2:42:55 | 3:15:30 | 3:30:00 | 4:35:11 |
| 10:40 | 0:33:06 | 0:53:20 | 1:06:14 | 1:39:18 | 1:46:40 | 2:12:24 | 2:19:47 | 2:40:00 | 2:45:30 | 3:18:36 | 3:33:20 | 4:39:33 |
| 10:50 | 0:33:37 | 0:54:10 | 1:07:16 | 1:40:51 | 1:48:20 | 2:14:28 | 2:21:58 | 2:42:30 | 2:48:05 | 3:21:42 | 3:36:40 | 4:43:55 |
| 11:00 | 0:34:08 | 0:55:00 | 1:08:18 | 1:42:24 | 1:50:00 | 2:16:32 | 2:24:09 | 2:45:00 | 2:50:40 | 3:24:48 | 3:40:00 | 4:48:17 |
| 11:10 | 0:34:39 | 0:55:50 | 1:09:20 | 1:43:57 | 1:51:40 | 2:18:36 | 2:26:20 | 2:47:30 | 2:53:15 | 3:27:54 | 3:43:20 | 4:52:39 |
| 11:20 | 0:35:10 | 0:56:40 | 1:10:22 | 1:45:30 | 1:53:20 | 2:20:40 | 2:28:31 | 2:50:00 | 2:55:50 | 3:31:00 | 3:46:40 | 4:57:01 |
| 11:30 | 0:35:41 | 0:57:30 | 1:11:24 | 1:47:03 | 1:55:00 | 2:22:44 | 2:30:42 | 2:52:30 | 2:58:25 | 3:34:06 | 3:50:00 | 5:01:23 |
| 11:40 | 0:36:12 | 0:58:20 | 1:12:26 | 1:48:36 | 1:56:40 | 2:24:48 | 2:32:53 | 2:55:00 | 3:01:00 | 3:37:12 | 3:53:20 | 5:05:45 |
| 11:50 | 0:36:43 | 0:59:10 | 1:13:28 | 1:50:09 | 1:58:20 | 2:26:52 | 2:35:04 | 2:57:30 | 3:03:35 | 3:40:18 | 3:56:40 | 5:10:07 |
| 12:00 | 0:37:14 | 1:00:00 | 1:14:30 | 1:51:42 | 2:00:00 | 2:28:56 | 2:37:15 | 3:00:00 | 3:06:10 | 3:43:24 | 4:00:00 | 5:14:29 |
| 12:10 | 0:37:45 | 1:00:50 | 1:15:32 | 1:53:15 | 2:01:40 | 2:31:00 | 2:39:26 | 3:02:30 | 3:08:45 | 3:46:30 | 4:03:20 | 5:18:51 |
| 12:20 | 0:38:16 | 1:01:40 | 1:16:34 | 1:54:48 | 2:03:20 | 2:33:04 | 2:41:37 | 3:05:00 | 3:11:20 | 3:49:36 | 4:06:40 | 5:23:13 |
| 12:30 | 0:38:47 | 1:02:30 | 1:17:36 | 1:56:21 | 2:05:00 | 2:35:08 | 2:43:48 | 3:07:30 | 3:13:55 | 3:52:42 | 4:10:00 | 5:27:35 |
| 12:40 | 0:39:18 | 1:03:20 | 1:18:38 | 1:57:54 | 2:06:40 | 2:37:12 | 2:45:59 | 3:10:00 | 3:16:30 | 3:55:48 | 4:13:20 | 5:31:57 |
| 12:50 | 0:39:49 | 1:04:10 | 1:19:40 | 1:59:27 | 2:08:20 | 2:39:16 | 2:48:10 | 3:12:30 | 3:19:05 | 3:58:54 | 4:16:40 | 5:36:19 |
| 13:00 | 0:40:20 | 1:05:00 | 1:20:42 | 2:01:00 | 2:10:00 | 2:41:20 | 2:50:21 | 3:15:00 | 3:21:40 | 4:02:00 | 4:20:00 | 5:40:41 |
| 13:10 | 0:40:51 | 1:05:50 | 1:21:44 | 2:02:33 | 2:11:40 | 2:43:24 | 2:52:32 | 3:17:30 | 3:24:15 | 4:05:06 | 4:23:20 | 5:45:03 |
| 13:20 | 0:41:22 | 1:06:40 | 1:22:46 | 2:04:06 | 2:13:20 | 2:45:28 | 2:54:43 | 3:20:00 | 3:26:50 | 4:08:12 | 4:26:40 | 5:49:25 |

| Mile | 5K | 5M | 10K | 15K | 10M | 20K | 13.1M | 15M | 25K | 30K | 20M | 26.2M |
|------|------|------|------|------|------|------|------|------|------|------|------|------|
| 13:30 | 0:41:53 | 1:07:30 | 1:23:48 | 2:05:39 | 2:15:00 | 2:47:32 | 2:56:54 | 3:22:30 | 3:29:25 | 4:11:18 | 4:30:00 | 5:53:47 |
| 13:40 | 0:42:24 | 1:08:20 | 1:24:50 | 2:07:12 | 2:16:40 | 2:49:36 | 2:59:05 | 3:25:00 | 3:32:00 | 4:14:24 | 4:33:20 | 5:58:09 |
| 13:50 | 0:42:55 | 1:09:10 | 1:25:52 | 2:08:45 | 2:18:20 | 2:51:40 | 3:01:16 | 3:27:30 | 3:34:35 | 4:17:30 | 4:36:40 | 6:02:31 |
| 14:00 | 0:43:26 | 1:10:00 | 1:26:54 | 2:10:18 | 2:20:00 | 2:53:44 | 3:03:27 | 3:30:00 | 3:37:10 | 4:20:36 | 4:40:00 | 6:06:53 |

# Index